Early Years Practice

This fully revised edition of *Early Years Practice: Getting It Right From the Start* integrates theory and practice and expands on the topics of early childhood practice as located within the context of international curriculum frameworks including Aistear, the Irish framework.

With two new chapters it introduces readers to the complexities and possibilities of a play-based pedagogy and the importance of pedagogical leadership. Drawing on recent international scholarship, the book pays particular attention to the role of outdoor play and learning and the impact of digital technologies. It considers how best to manage the competing demands, challenges and tensions that affect the daily experiences of educators and children in contemporary society. This new edition also revises the original text with expanded references on topics such as the ecology of early childhood settings, education for sustainability, developmental psychology, education and neuroscience. This timely text also reviews international literature from both research and practice, strengthens understandings of the key role of relationships to quality practice and the effects on the development and learning of young children. All the chapters provide specific examples of good practice with strategies and suggestions aimed at enhancing the overall experience of early childhood settings for both educators and children.

The information collected and explored in the book can be used by lecturers and educators alike to stimulate conversation, guide reflection and support the profession of early childhood educators to collectively work towards achieving, supporting and sustaining high-quality early years practice that adds constructively to the lives of babies and young children.

Nóirín Hayes is Visiting Professor at the School of Education, Trinity College Dublin and Professor Emerita, Technological University Dublin, Ireland.

Early Years Practice
Getting It Right From the Start

Nóirín Hayes

Routledge
Taylor & Francis Group

LONDON AND NEW YORK

Designed cover image: © Getty Images

First published 2024
by Routledge
4 Park Square, Milton Park, Abingdon, Oxon OX14 4RN

and by Routledge
605 Third Avenue, New York, NY 10158

Routledge is an imprint of the Taylor & Francis Group, an informa business

British Library Cataloguing-in-Publication Data
A catalogue record for this book is available from the British Library

Library of Congress Cataloging-in-Publication Data
Names: Hayes, Nóirín, author.
Title: Early years practice : getting it right from the start / Nóirín Hayes.
Description: Second edition. | Abingdon, Oxon ; New York, NY : Routledge, 2024. | Includes bibliographical references and index.
Identifiers: LCCN 2023032114 (print) | LCCN 2023032115 (ebook) | ISBN 9781032404547 (hardback) | ISBN 9781032405469 (paperback) | ISBN 9781003353164 (ebook)
Subjects: LCSH: Early childhood education—Ireland. | Child development—Ireland
Classification: LCC LB1139.3.I73 H38 2024 (print) | LCC LB1139.3.I73 (ebook) | DDC 372.2109417—dc23/eng/20230814
LC record available at https://lccn.loc.gov/2023032114
LC ebook record available at https://lccn.loc.gov/2023032115

ISBN: 978-1-032-40454-7 (hbk)
ISBN: 978-1-032-40546-9 (pbk)
ISBN: 978-1-003-35316-4 (ebk)

DOI: 10.4324/9781003353164

Typeset in Galliard Pro
by Apex CoVantage, LLC

Contents

About the author

Nóirín Hayes is Visiting Professor at the School of Education, Trinity College Dublin and Professor Emerita, Technological University Dublin, Ireland. Working within a bio-ecological framework of development and through a child rights lens, she teaches, researches and writes on early childhood education and care.

1 Considering practice in early years settings[1]

Introduction

This book is about early years practice in early childhood education and care settings. The term early childhood education and care is used throughout the book, reflecting the term agreed upon by participating countries in the OECD thematic review of policies and practices in early childhood known as Starting Strong. It covers all arrangements for children from birth to compulsory school age (Neuman, 2019). The term is intended to capture both the caring and educational role that informs quality practice in early childhood settings. Practice is a core component of quality settings, it is what makes the curriculum visible in what we do every day with young children. It is not a separate activity or a discretely defined part of our behaviour; rather it is a combination of the education and care we provide for young children and through which we exhibit our interest in and understanding of how we educate our youngest children.

This book is intended to be the starting point of a collective conversation about early childhood practice deriving from our knowledge and experiences. It is a conversation with many participants, a space where the ideas and arguments of the book form the basis of further conversations and discussions to maintain the flexible, responsive and flowing process which is early childhood education. It is intended to be a conversation, which can be returned to reflectively, either alone or with colleagues. This book is not a handbook or a manual. It is written on the assumption that the reader, student or early childhood educator[2] is inclined towards learning more about practice and the elements that go to make up the rich, nurturing and enhancing worlds of early childhood settings. To this end the book includes an Advanced Reading List where you can find more detailed reports and articles across a wide range of topics relevant to understanding early childhood education and care. This list is made up of those references with an asterisk in the regular reference list alongside some additional suggestions. This chapter outlines in broad strokes the topics which will be dealt with in greater detail by various chapters. Throughout there are links drawn to the Irish curriculum framework, *Aistear*,

DOI: 10.4324/9781003353164-1

and to contemporary understandings of how young children, including babies and toddlers, develop and learn.

As with any conversation it is important that participants know what values, beliefs and understandings inform different perspectives. We all carry beliefs about children, how they develop, what they need, how best to ensure the best for them, how to encourage good behaviour and so forth. In previous writing I have identified some basic core beliefs I have about early childhood (Hayes, 2010). I restate them here because I believe it is important that each reader understand what informs the points that I make about early years practice. They reflect my understanding of development and learning as holistic, interconnected and dynamic and my commitment to respecting the rights of all children, even the very youngest. In presenting them I hope that you can reflect on what they might mean to you, drawing on your own beliefs and your experiences of early years practice. If you have different priorities or beliefs it is useful to name them, discuss them and consider what any points of disagreement might mean.

In the first instance I hold the child as *central*. Each child is an individual born into a particular sociocultural context. It is within this context that the child develops and, in turn, influences context. In working with children and their families, we must take the time and interest to develop our own skills and knowledge to allow for the individuality of each child to flourish. Secondly, I believe that the child is basically *good*. No child is born bad, although many are born with considerable disadvantages. It is essential that early years educators understand and believe this. Underpinning more rigid and punitive practices is the belief that children need to be taught how to be good. Rather I believe they need to be supported and rewarded for behaving as we expect them to and assisted in understanding why certain behaviours are considered inappropriate. Thirdly I consider that the *interaction* between different aspects of development at different stages must not be lost sight of by our tendency to segment the child into dimensions of learning as we try to unravel the influences that shape her life. The holistic development of the whole child in context is what we must strive to achieve in our planning and practice. Fourthly I believe that the child is an *active agent* in her learning rather than a passive receiver of information. This belief has serious implications for practice and requires that adults allow children the freedom to make mistakes, to solve problems and to find solutions rather than interfering too soon in an activity or rushing to show children how, for instance, to 'draw the cat' or 'cut out the picture'. Fifthly I believe in the *importance* of the early years. I do not hold the extreme view that there is no hope for change after the child has reached, say, the age of seven. However, I do believe that the foundations for much future learning, behaviour and success depend on the quality of experiences children have in early childhood. It is, for example, unacceptable to say that a trauma will affect a young child less than an older one simply because they do not appear to understand it – it is this very fact of childhood understanding that makes early experiences so important and that places an important obligation on early childhood educators to be sensitive to children's experiences and how they might be affecting them. This sensitivity requires that you recognise that what something means to you may not, in fact, reflect what it means to the child. Finally, I believe in the powerful *role of the adult* in the young child's life. The quality of interactions and relationships is emerging from scientific research as a key factor in enhancing the learning and development of young children. Adults are significant in that they can expand the experiences and the horizons of the child during the early years by their attention, interests, listening skills, observations and the provision of opportunity. Adults must, of course, recognise their limitations. There are environmental influences and the influence of other adults, for example, that will prevail in certain circumstances (Hayes, 2010, pp. viii–ix).

Early childhood education and care

There has been a rapid growth in early childhood provision over the last decades in response to changes in society and this is reflected in the development of curriculum frameworks, enhanced qualifications and a strengthening professional identity. In turn, this has been supported and enhanced from within settings through professional development programmes. In Ireland these developments have been accompanied by two national practice frameworks, Síolta [the national framework for quality] and *Aistear* [the national curriculum framework], which have provided a common language and a common space within which to develop early education and care practice. While different in overall focus they both emerged from consultation with early childhood educators across the system and they share a common set of principles. This has provided a common framework system within which to commence curricular and pedagogical conversations, which have articulated and supported quality early childhood practice. The linking of both frameworks through the online resource of the *Aistear Síolta Practice Guide* [https://www.aistearsiolta.ie/en/introduction/] provides a rich array of materials and guidance to support educators.

Researchers tell us that the quality of a child's early experiences are crucial for overall learning and development and can have a profound impact on life success. The quality of experiences depends on a number of factors and one of the central influencing factors is the style and content of the day-to-day practice of the early childhood educator. We also know, however, that if practice is to be effective in supporting learning and development it must be informed by theory; that is, we must know not only *what we do* but *why we do it*. The most effective practices are those which are guided by clearly understood principles and informed by a solid understanding of learning and development. It is, therefore, important that educators feel confident in discussing and reflecting on the principles of their practice – that is their pedagogy. In early childhood education, pedagogy refers to the interactive processes between an educator and child within the learning environment (Siraj-Blatchford et al., 2002;

OECD, 2015) and both terms, practice and pedagogy, will be used throughout the book.

This book will discuss what constitutes good practice in early education and care and why exactly good practice is good; it will consider the research evidence on the impact of early experiences on learning and development and it will explore curricular and pedagogical literature to illustrate how curriculum and quality frameworks can be used to enhance the day-to-day practice of early educators and continue to support the learning and development of all children. From the very beginning of life babies are curious and socially competent and continue to be so as they grow and develop. They are active in their communication and engagement with people, places and objects that comprise their learning environments. This view of the child as an engaged, active participant in the world around them reflects the growing scientific understanding we have of the dynamic and interactive process that is child development and it also reflects a rights-based perspective to children, recognising them as individuals learning and developing in the social world. Central to their learning and development are the many relationships they participate in across all their learning environments. While the various social relationships children form with adults and other children are important, their interaction and relationship with materials, objects and ideas are also important. The role of the adult within all these relationships is most effective when the adult is 'present' with and attuned to the child in that moment and that space. Such a role can often mean standing back and observing, assessing the situations observed to inform future planning and provision. Children, from babyhood, in thoughtfully prepared environments are free to explore and play and learn aspects of self-control and self-discipline.

Right from the start a child's temperament contributes to the quality of interactions, which in turn impacts on other aspects of development such as attention. The adult has a central role in being attuned to such contributions, able to read the communications carefully and respond sensitively to children's behaviour. Wolfe and Bell (2007) found that there was a relationship between infant temperament, temperament in later early childhood and memory performance in early childhood. They argue that these associated and inter-linked characteristics of temperament and working memory highlight the importance of building on and supporting the early development of regulatory and attentional behaviours given the impact of these early skills on children's later development.

The early childhood educator works within a complex and dynamic context, whether in the home or early years setting. To develop and sustain quality early years practice, which is both personally satisfying and positive for young children, it is valuable to recognise that there is a rich theoretical and conceptual backdrop to good quality, effective practice. Recognising what high-quality early years practice looks and feels like in early years settings allows the educator to reflect on their own day-to-day practice and contribute to the virtuous circle of learning and developing. However, quality is a difficult concept to define and some authors suggest that trying to define it is like searching for 'fool's gold' (Penn, 2009). Nonetheless in practice we should be questioning the quality of our practice, challenging ourselves and others to consider what quality might mean for a particular setting or child at a particular time. To this end there are advantages in keeping up to date with contemporary research and pooling insights from developmental psychology, education, sociology and other disciplines to highlight the connectedness between the social, physical, linguistic, cognitive and emotional experience of young children and associated implications for practice and for optimal learning.

Practice is about the care and attention we give to the 'child in the now' when we think of the 'whole child in context'. This attention to the 'now' is most effective when it is practised by adults who know what their practice is and why it is as it is. It goes beyond naming the constructs of early education and care through into the translation of those constructs into the day-to-day relationship with and between adults and children. Knowing and understanding the science of development and learning and continually updating this knowledge through accessing various resources helps to make sense of why certain practices are worthwhile and others less so. The process of informed practice provides a language and a voice to articulate, discuss and explain what we do as educators because we have evidence to support us. This in turn allows us to consider our own practice in a more rigorous way, giving a confidence to explain that what we do is relevant and right and beyond the mere opinion that 'we know it works'. Knowing how children learn and develop allows us to explain to other professionals and parents why what we do is so important and why early childhood education is such a unique level of education.

Contemporary influences on early years practice

Young children learn and develop in the midst of society and are influenced not only by their immediate environments but also by the policies that support and assist families in raising children and the attitudes and values that societies have in respect to children and families. A number of international and national developments can be seen as directly and indirectly influencing the daily work of educators in early childhood settings. Internationally one of the defining moments in relation to our approach to children came in 1989 with the publication of the United Nations Convention on the Rights of the Child [UNCRC]. Ratified by Ireland in 1992, this document represents a profound commitment to children and young people and lays out a blueprint for how we, as adults, can respect and support children and young people. It has shaped the contemporary image of the child as an active participant in his or her own learning and development. Specifically, in relation to early education, which is not a named right in the Convention, the UN Committee on the Rights of the Child has issued a General Comment No. 7 on Implementing Child Rights in Early Childhood (2005). The general comment recognises early childhood as a critical period for realising children's rights and elaborates, in some detail, how early childhood services can provide for young children from within a rights-based framework. This and other General Comments are available at https://www.ohchr.org/en/treaty-bodies/crc/general-comments.

Internationally early childhood education has become recognised as a key and unique level of education in the lives of young children, central to their development and learning and crucial to combating inequalities at a global level. For instance, in the Sustainable Development Goals, Target 4.2 on education states that by 2030, globally we will 'ensure that all girls and boys have access to quality early childhood development, care and pre-primary education' (UN, 2015). Since 2001 the OECD [Organisation for Economic Cooperation and Development] has been comparing and reviewing early childhood education and care policies across countries through the Starting Strong project. Its many reports offer valuable guidance on factors that influence the quality of early years practice and can be accessed at: https://www.oecd.org/education/school/startingstrong.htm. At a European level the Commission agreed upon a recommendation on high-quality early childhood education and care systems. As an action a '*Quality Framework for Early Childhood Education and Care*' was published with the agreement of all EU States including Ireland (EC, 2018). This framework provides a blueprint for achieving accessible, affordable and inclusive early childhood services that support children's development.

Nationally the last twenty years have seen extensive policy attention and investment in early childhood education and care (Hayes & Walsh, 2022). Of significance to this book are three publications from 2021: the funding scheme for two years' free preschool for all children aged 3–5 years (DCEDIY, 2021a); the publication, and revision, of the curriculum framework, *Aistear* (NCCA, 2021); and the launch, by the Department of Children, Equality, Disability, Integration and Youth [DCEDIY], of a workforce development plan, '*Nurturing Skills*' (DCEDIY, 2021b). In addition the DCEDIY regulates and inspects settings and funds support structures and organisations such as Better Start, a quality development initiative and, at a local level the County/City Childcare Committees who develop policies and resources to support and enhance the quality of provision. These national and international policies, frameworks and commitments provide early childhood educators with significant supports which can be drawn on to guide high-quality and effective practice. They also offer support in the continuing struggle for the wider professional recognition of those working within early childhood education and care.

The active and competent nature of young children is widely recognised in curriculum documents internationally, including in *Aistear*, the curriculum framework which underpins practice in all early childhood settings in Ireland. Originally pubilshed in 2009 *Aistear* notes that:

> the modern day view of the child is one of him/her being a competent
> learner, capable of making choices and decisions; a young citizen and

participator in many contexts . . . actively learning in reciprocal relations with adults and other children.

(NCCA, 2009a, p. 19)

As active participants in society they have a right to expect that their early childhood settings, wherever they are and of whatever type, will challenge and excite them, provide safety and security and enhance their overall development and learning. Children are the social group most affected by the quality of early childhood services. While this may appear self-evident there may also be some complacency about what actually happens to children in their everyday experiences and a general assumption that just by attending an early years setting children will develop and progress positively. This is not the case and research evidence suggests that for positive outcomes in children attending early years settings they must be of high quality, particularly for children who may be identified as coming from more disdvantaged or challenging backgrounds. Indeed there is some evidence to suggest that poor-quality early years experiences are of little or no benefit to young children and their families (Sylva et al., 2011). In fact the quality of everyday experiences in early years environments, wherever children are, has a profound influence on them. Young children are not merely recipients or consumers of a service but are deeply influenced, individually and collectively, by their early years experiences. Children learn in context; the ordinary spaces, places and people they encounter make up that context. Adults who are attuned, who are 'watchfully attentive' and who are mindful in their day-to-day practices with children can make an important and positive contribution to their learning and development. There is no need to distance children from society in an effort to enhance their learning and development; indeed actively linking early years settings to other important environments in the lives of young children and carefully managing the various transitions they make is seen as an important dimension to quality early years practice (Fitzpatrick & Halpenny, 2022). Early years practice is a process that is happening in early years settings every day, it is the curriculum made visible, even where the curriculum may not be readily definable.

This book is intended as a contribution to explaining why good-quality early childhood practice is so critical and what it is about quality practice that has such a significant impact on young children's learning and development and why. Early years settings, including those within a home environment, are complex learning environments with many overlapping interactions between children, adults, objects, materials and ideas. In addition to being influenced by the learning environment and the people therein, children are also influenced by the values and beliefs that others have about how and what they should learn. Children learn in social and physical environments, developmental niches, the characteristics of which are, to a large extent, determined by adults but influenced by other elements also. Based on their beliefs about development and their expectations, adults select and provide experiences they believe are important for children and will prepare children for their future. These socialisation processes occur at different levels and so can be studied at different levels (Hayes et al., 2023).

The early childhood educator

Research is clear that the key element in quality practice is the early childhood educator. Effective early years practice and pedagogy integrate education and care with learning, development and experiences for children. We need to consider and understand what exactly the integration of education and care means in practice, what challenges it poses and what opportunities it can provide. As with many different professional areas there is a language (or jargon) specific to early childhood education. However, the language of early childhood can appear simplistic to those unfamiliar with its complexities and a real challenge is to reflect on our language, get behind the real meaning and elevate it in professional discourse. We talk of 'high-quality early education'; of our practice being 'child-centered'; we recognise the child as an 'active agent' in their learning; we work with the 'whole child' and recommend that we listen to the 'voice of the child'. But what does all this mean? If not used carefully and with thoughtful reflection these concepts can become meaningless. We need to know exactly what we mean when we say we work with the 'whole child'. We need to know why we believe this to be important. Unless we truly understand and explain what we mean when we use these important concepts to describe our practice we may in fact strip away the rich and unique features of early education and care.

Within our language we may carry the myths from our own past with us into our practice. But the knowledge base around child development and learning is expanding all the time and some of our understandings may be incorrect, incomplete or out of date. It is important to adopt a critical spirit in our approach to our practice, our use of language and our grasp of knowledge and take time to consider the assumptions we make. Unless we are willing to challenge and explore our own assumptions, we may never really provide our young children with the rich learning environments they need to experience in order to be able to adapt to the changing world.

Of course, the 'knowledge' we routinely use provides us with a familiar structure and it may be uncomfortable to reflect on or question it. However, without reflection we merely replicate what we have always done and do not afford a space within which to challenge ourselves and develop our professionalism. This taken-for-granted, or tacit, knowledge is rarely articulated, discussed or made visible; it is just the way things are. Educational research has shown that those working in education often come to their practice with informal theories about children's learning and development, informed by their training and their own experiences. As they derive from our own learning experiences, we may own them much more readily than we might accept the implications of theory and research from, so called, child development experts.

These implicit beliefs about child development and how children learn are termed 'folk pedagogy' by Bruner (1996) and, while they may enrich our practice, they do need to be challenged in the context of contemporary theory and understandings.

It is useful to review current understandings of how early years practices impact on children. Such a review can act as a stimulus for educators to reflect on their practice and the quality of provision for young children so that the experiences in early years settings will be a positive and affirming one for all those involved. The adult, and their style of engagement, has a profound impact on the learning experiences of babies and young children. The contemporary view of children as active agents in their learning requires educators to recognise and respond to the reality that even the very youngest children contribute to the context and content of their own development. This is not to underestimate the dependence of the child or the very powerful, protective role of the adult. It does, however, challenge adults to reconsider practice and to take account of the rich and diverse nature of each child when planning early care and education, designing learning environments and providing learning opportunities.

It is important for early childhood educators to interrogate the 'taken for granted' or 'folk' ideas that we may bring to practice, to unpack what they really mean and to share our understandings with colleagues so that a common understanding of practice emerges. In this regard, Fleer (2003) has identified four assumptions that may be thoughtlessly accepted in the language of early years practice rather than critically reflected on. They provide a useful starting point for discussions of beliefs and values we might hold about the way children learn and our role as educators in the process. The first assumption relates to how we position the child – do we see the child as part of the wider world or as part of the early years setting? This can affect the extent to which we broaden our own and children's experiences. For instance, a child-centred focus may distance the child from the reality of the world, from the world of adults and older children. A richer concept, one of 'child-embeddedness' (Fleer, 2003, p. 67), captures the idea of the child growing and developing in the midst of society as an active participant.

A second assumption relates to how we view children as learners – do children actively construct knowledge or do they learn from being told? Are they seen as active, participating meaning makers or as passive recipients of knowledge? The meaning of *active* needs careful consideration. It is not about physical activity alone – it includes being actively engaged in whatever is happening, active listening and careful, active observation; it is from careful looking that a child may expand what they are doing and their understanding. There is a key role for the adult here in acting as a model for learning, showing rather than telling. Understanding children's active engagement allows you to see where and how you might provide them with challenge and work with them in their Zone of Proximal Development, the construct developed by Vygotsky (1978) to capture the idea of learners striving towards the next step of learning, developing, understanding.

The third assumption refers to how we balance the individual child with the individual child in context. While it is important to understand each child as an individual it is also important to understand the child as part of their wider environment, familial and societal. Children can be both independent and also inter-dependent, they like to be with other children, to share knowledge and so extend their knowledge; they enjoy succeeding in groups and learn how to cope with failure too (Kernan & Singer, 2010). In practice we should plan for both the individual developing child and for the sociocultural, interconnected child.

The final 'taken for granted' assumption Fleer (2003) discusses is our approach to communication with children. In our practice do we see both child and adult as partners in learning together or as separate from each other with the adult in the more powerful position? Children are embedded in the social world and are active in their communication with it through various verbal and nonverbal processes. While there is of course an inequity between the child and the far more experienced adult this does not negate the value of considering children as partners. Carefully planned child-friendly environments provide learning opportunities that facilitate social and collaborative learning and rich communication. Communication is more than simply reading stories, asking questions and giving directions, which is insufficient and disrespectful to the capabilities of children; rather, it includes engaged and respectful conversations which are inclusive, considerate and democratic in practice and equip children with important developmental skills and proficiency.

While initial training provides a guided space for considering many of the issues raised previously, all early childhood educators benefit from the opportunity for ongoing professional development, whether through externally provided programmes or through an in-house environment which supports reflective, critical and informed practice at the individual and team level. Such opportunities contribute to creating a community of learning and a shared language of early childhood practice. In a seminal study considering professional development Mitchell and Cubey (2003) offer eight characteristics to assist in developing a critical learning approach to practice. In summary they challenge us to:

Incorporate our own aspirations, skills, knowledge and understanding into the learning context. To achieve this requires that there is a safe and open environment that encourages educators to look at their strengths and weaknesses in forming the basis of ongoing professional development. It suggests that shared learning can enhance an individual's learning while also enhancing the overall quality of the early years environment.

Gather theoretical and content knowledge and information about alternative practices. This challenges educators to continue to keep up with emerging research and knowledge about early years practice through reading, attending seminars, accessing resource materials and using them as the basis for personal reflection and group discussion.

Investigate pedagogy within their own early childhood settings. It is always easiest to start from where you are. Using honest examples or vignettes from your own early years settings and critically considering them in the context of, for instance, *Aistear* can give ideas on how to progress, enhance or provide the language that allows you describe your practice more clearly.

Draw on personal experience for data analysis. Here the authors are identifying the educator as an active researcher. Careful documenting of observations for later critical analysis allows this type of approach to considering practice and reviewing the effectiveness of certain approaches. It can pose new and unexpected questions and also provide insight into activities or relationships that might be easily overlooked if not recorded and considered.

Provide opportunities for critical reflection to challenge assumptions and extend thinking. While it may be simple to quickly review your practice, it is a great deal more difficult, but ultimately more valuable, to critically evaluate your practice and explore the values and beliefs that influence you. This requires planning and time and needs local pedagogical leadership in settings and a commitment from all educators.

Support educational practices that are inclusive of diversity. We are all different, all unique and so we all contribute to the diversity of settings, of society. With greater mobility, and as a function of increased migration, the extent of diversity in groups has grown and brought with it both riches and challenges. Explicitly discussing diversity in the context of practice provides us with the time and space to plan and develop inclusive early learning environments.

Help each other to change educational practices, beliefs, understanding and attitudes. Changing hearts and minds is not easy, even where people are willing to question themselves. It is important that due attention is paid to the needs and rights of others in discussion and to allow space for constructive argument and differing views. It is through discussion and argument that we can find new and often better ways to practice.

Help each other gain awareness of our own thinking, actions and influence. In order to grow in awareness, we need to have the desire to do so. Where we are collectively committed to achieving the best possible quality of practice there is an aim that can act as the driver for change.

Where the context for professional development is a safe one, where we trust and respect each other, it is most likely that everyone gains increased awareness of their thinking, their beliefs and how these can impact directly on practice through influencing our responses to behaviour, our expectations of different situations, our tolerance of change. Early childhood educators who recognise the importance of self-awareness and show a willingness to change and learn are certainly going to be more motivated in their daily work in early years settings than those who have become complacent. Essentially the points raised by Mitchell and Cubey highlight the importance of engaged, attuned and reflective educators and offer some suggestions on how to access those aspects of ourselves which we may not bring to mind in the routine day-to-day of early years practice, but which inform our actions and ultimately influence our interactions with the children in early years settings.

Early years settings

Adults set the scene for children's sense of engagement with the world and provide a context within which children can be seen and valued for their own sake and in the here and now.

Whilst the family is recognised as the first and central space for early education, learning and development, increasingly families share the early care and education of their children with different types of settings. These settings are part of the wider society and have links with other educational, social and cultural settings in the wider community. They provide an important bridge for children and parents alike, from the seclusion of the home through the early years setting into the local community and wider society. As a result early years settings provide a particularly important service for all families but particularly for minority or marginalised parents and their children. While the direct role of the educator is often characterised in terms of their work with the children attending settings it is important to recognise that they play an important indirect role in creating links across various sytems, particularly in relation to influencing and supporting the home learning environment.

Research shows that early childhood experiences are important to children in their daily life and into their future. Children are deeply influenced, individually and collectively, by their early childhood experiences. The quality of everyday experiences in the early years, wherever they happen, have a profound influence on them. Indeed, it is the day-to-day interactions and experiences children have that drive their development (Hayes et al., 2023). They are active participants in society and have a right to expect that early childhood settings will challenge and excite them, provide safety and security and enhance their overall development and learning. Viewing children as participants in the early childhood process allows adults to work *with* children as well as provide *for* them. In general children are motivated to learn, to seek meaning in their world and they expect that the adults they meet will assist them in this endeavour. It is in the immediate, day-to day experiences that children learn about the world around them, the ordinary things in their lives have the potential to be extraordinary, to act as the foundation for developing new skills, strengthening dispositions and learning new knowledge. The adult can contribute in making the experiences of the ordinary rich and meaningful learning experiences by careful observation and reflection to inform their practice. Through informed and attuned practice adults can expand children's language, thinking and understandings, they can fire children's curiousity, imagination and creativity and challenge and extend their skills through encouraging mastery and positive learning dispositions.

Children's curiosity and desire for knowledge is evident in their exploration, their play, their questions and their behaviour. In order to make the most of the early years children need adults who trust them, are excited, inspired and challenged by them. Where the child is seen as the centre of practice the day-to-day pedagogy and curriulum reflects this. In early years settings with good quality practices the adults actively include children in the regular experiences of the setting, engage with children and learn from them as well as enhancing the learning opportunities for them. This approach to practice is informed by a belief in the active, dynamic nature of child development and includes the child as a partner in development. Such an approach to practice reflects a shift away from a more traditional didactic educational practice to a more integrated, social and interactive approach.

The design, organisation and resourcing of the early years setting is central to practice and the early learning process. Settings, indoor and outdoor, should be both safe and challenging, providing rich and varied opportunities for exploration, play and risk-taking. However, while the planning and organisation of setting is important to early years practice it is insufficient. We know from research that settings which meet the static or checklist-type requirements of quality may not be effective in enhancing children's learning and development. Quality is deeply relational and is best considered as an ongoing process and, as such, it is what happens on a day-to-day basis that is at the heart of quality early years practice. Research suggests that the most effective practice is found in settings with well-trained, well-informed staff, familiar with child development and with subject or content knowledge, who recognise and respond to the dynamic and individual nature of development in the early years and who can work with an emerging curriculum which is driven by the interests and experiences of the children and the opportunities afforded by the environment (OECD, 2006; EC, 2020). A curriculum framework, such as *Aistear*, provides a rich base for such practice which, working with content derived from a combination of adult knowledge, environmental affordances and children's interests, is agile and responsive. Cultivating positive learning dispositions and feelings in young children leads to positive outcomes in emotional, social, linguistic and cognitive development and the skills necessary for later school success. It is a holistic, adaptive and, ultimately, more effective approach to early education. The process of quality practice is dynamic and interactive reflecting the dynamic and interactive nature of learning and development and it requires that educators are responsive and reflective throughout both their planning for and their engagement with children.

Implicit in the pratice outlined previously is a commitment to democratic principles that recognise the need to respect and engage meaningfully with children. This approach is reflective of an understanding of early childhood education and care settings as sites of democratic practice where children and adults can participate collectively in interpreting experiences and shaping decisions affecting themselves (Moss, 2019). Changing practice to meet the new vision of early years practice, one based on scientific understandings of development and contemporary approaches to children, is not an easy task. It requires ongoing practice, learning and reflection so that we continue getting it right from the start.

About this book

This book is intended as a contribution to widening our common understanding and language of why quality practice is so critical, recognising what it is about quality practice that has such a significant impact on young children's learning and development and understanding the role of the educator in contributing to quality of practice is so important. While there are examples given to illustrate different concepts and topics, this is not a book of examples of 'good' practice; rather it is intended to prompt discussion and reflection on the quality of practice in the average early years setting. Drawing attention to research and the experiences of the educator it provides opportunities for considering everyday practice in the context of current curricular and pedagogical knowledge. It provides readers with a research context that will help locate quality early years practice within a shared language, reflecting a shared understanding. It does so through illustrating points of practice by reference to examples drawn from the literature and curriculum frameworks and explores why practice is important and what aspects of practice matter most to positive child development and professional satisfaction. It is not a manual of exercises, rather it is intended to be the start of an ongoing conversation towards strengthening our understanding of the impact of early years experiences on children and their families and to provide a shared language with which to raise the awareness of others to the importance of this period of education and the critical role played by early childhood educators.

Rather than approach practice guidance by reference to curriculum frameworks such as *Aistear* through focusing on this particular theme or that particular principle this book suggests you look to your own practice examples and derive your use of information and guidance in the frameworks directly from there. You are already likely to be doing much of what is suggested in practice illustrations but perhaps not reflecting on it or theorising it sufficiently to fully understand, and evaluate, the potential impact on the learning and development of the young children in your setting. This is as true of the childminder with a small number of children in her own home as it is of students in practice or those working in more formal settings.

This chapter has set the scene and provided a lens through which to consider what high-quality early years practice looks like, what the role of the educator can be, and it raised a number of opportunities and challenges to achieving such practice. The next chapter considers the research that explains why this quality practice is important and how it impacts on children's development and learning. It draws attention to the integrated nature of practice, one that is inclusive by its very nature, that treats each child, irrespective of age, health and capabilities, with respect and compassion. In response to the persistent reference to and call for quality in curriculum and pedagogical documentation, Chapter 3 asks what quality actually looks like in early childhood settings. Drawing on the evidence from practice-based research, it identifies those factors considered central to achieving the best for children. Chapters 4 and 5 address the themes around which curriculum frameworks, including *Aistear* have been built. The chapters explore the research evidence supporting each theme and considers how to support each in practice. Chapter 6 takes a close look at the role of play and play-based pedagogy concluding with a section on the important role of pedagogical leadership. Chapter 7 reviews the previous chapters towards presenting an integrated reflection on early years practice to contribute to the conversation proposed so that we can all work towards achieving, supporting and sustaining high-quality early years practice that gets it right from the start.

Notes

1 This book draws on and extends my earlier publication of the same name (Hayes, 2013).
2 The naming of professionals in the field of early childhood education has proved complex. For the purpose of this book, I will be using the term educator to refer to those working with children from birth to six years of age. This captures childminders, preschool staff, teachers in early years classrooms and students in practice.

2 Understanding early years practice

Introduction

It is not enough to simply know that what we do is right; we need to be able to explain to ourselves and others *why* what we do is right. In order to be able to talk about early years practice at this deeper level it is necessary to recognise that practice is not simply a technology, doing what the book says. It is more complex than that, it is informed and guided by adult expertise and understandings of learning and development. It is for this reason that the term educator is preferred over the term practitioner to describe the professional working in early childhood education and care. The term 'educator' captures the unique professional expertise of those working with children in early years settings. This chapter explores early childhood practice and the features and factors that contribute to it. It makes the case that the pedagogy of early childhood is unique and introduces the idea of an integrating nurturing pedagogy, a practice which weaves early care and early education together, responsive to what we know about the way in which young children learn.

Practice happens all the time, it is bedded within the various levels of day-to-day activities from the beginning. It impacts on all children's developmental levels or dimensions. Holistic practice with children requires the attention of the adult *in context* to the whole child *in context* highlighting the importance of being present in the now and not thinking of what you will be doing once this activity is over. A reflective educator is one who is always checking up on their practice and asking why am I doing this? of what value is it to the child, the group, my colleagues, parents, community? It is a willingness to recognise that part of working professionally in the early years is to be willing to recognise that there is always something more to learn about child development, learning environments, practice in general. The word 'why' is key in quality early years practice, both literally and metaphorically. It challenges educators to evaluate the quality and relevance of early childhood education and care to children. It is through asking and answering the 'why' questions that educators begin to consolidate a shared understanding and language of early childhood pedagogy. Recognising the importance of linking what we know about child development and learning to the day-to-day practice of early education

DOI: 10.4324/9781003353164-2

brings the discussion of practice into the area of pedagogy – that is the theory of practice. Alexander (2004) highlights this link between practice and knowledge when he describes pedagogy as the 'act and discourse of teaching'. It can be seen as the art of translating agreed principles into responsive and flexible practice to meet the needs of children as individuals or as a group in the particular context of the day. However, while it may appear easy to 'do' practice it is not easy to describe the art of early years practice.

Most of us involved in working with young children have become involved because we value children, we enjoy their company, and we feel we can contribute to their overall development and well-being. Early childhood education and care has been slow to gain recognition in Ireland as a key educational provision for young children that is critical to their early learning, health and well-being. However, it has now matured to the point where we have national curriculum, quality and regulatory frameworks which have emerged from within the sector. These frameworks focus on the first level of education (birth–6 years) and have introduced a shared terminology which can break down barriers in the sector and bring together those who work across the different settings from childminders through various early years settings to primary teachers in infant classes. This emerging common terminology has derived from a common vision and a shared set of principles; it provides educators with the opportunity to consider their role, reflect on their practice, assess the needs of the field and participate in its growth and transformation. The pedagogy of Irish early education is reflected in the way we talk about our practice and translate the principles articulated within the frameworks into everyday practice.

International research suggests that educators in the early years are not confident in talking about their practice or about analysing and critically evaluating the impact of their practice on the young children they work with and there is no reason to expect things to be all that different in Ireland. In a study of pedagogical effectiveness in early learning Moyles et al. (2002) noted that respondents were reluctant to engage in pedagogical discussions and found it difficult to articulate or describe in any detail the specifics of their practice that were important to them or the values, beliefs and principles underpinning their practice. They also found that '[W]hilst principles [beliefs and values] underpinning practice were evident in . . . documentation . . . they appear to be the least well-developed area of practitioners' knowledge and understanding. Provision of materials tends to dominate activities' (p. 131). It seems that doing early years practice is often easier than describing or discussing practice. This is shortsighted for a number of reasons. In the first place it can lead to practice becoming mundane, routine and lacking in challenge. This can impact directly on children and learning opportunities can be lost. This, in turn can limit the satisfaction of the adult that derives from quality practice. While the Moyles study found that the ability to articulate and reflect on practice was related to the level of training it also found that this ability was linked to the 'ethos within settings, which positively promotes self-evaluation and reflection and adopts strategies for developing these' (p. 130). This suggests that pedagogical leadership and teamwork is important to sustaining and enhancing the quality of practice in early years settings. We know from research that purposeful or intentional teaching and learning occurs when educators' own understanding and knowledge informs their practice. This is most effective when coupled with the provision of rich and relevant learning experiences that assist young children, even the very youngest in making sense of their experiences in the world around them.

We recognise that children grow and develop within society and that, as such, they are impacted on by many factors, some more directly than others. The direct influences are those located close to children's experiences; the home and the variety of early years settings they may attend at different times. Older children would have an expanded set of settings to include such as schools, youth settings, sports clubs and so on. Recognising this is one thing but understanding how this actually influences child development and what implications it has for early childhood practice is more difficult. In an effort to consider the complexity of interactions influencing the development of an individual many people have found Bronfenbrenner's bio-ecological model of development a useful model within which to think about the dynamics of development and the implications for practice (Bronfenbrenner & Morris, 2006). The bio-ecological model reflects our current understanding of the integrated and dynamic nature of learning and development. This model recognises that individuals are embedded in, affect and are affected by different systems or contexts. These influences can be at both a distant, or distal, level referred to as the macrosystem or at an immediate, or proximal, level referred to as the microsystem. The model also draws attention to the need for educators to pay close attention to the complexity of interacting systems and the interactions between and within those systems (Hayes et al., 2023). To begin to understand this it may be useful to review the situation graphically (see Figure 2.1 below).

The systems identified in the model are called the microsystem, the mesosystem, the *exosystem* and the *macrosystem*. The child's most familiar *microsystem* is the family, but it also includes other settings such as early years settings and schools. The *mesosystem* is often the most difficult level to grasp as it refers to the communication and interaction between the various elements of the model; of most immediate relevance to the early childhood educator is the communication between the child's microsystems of the home and early years setting. The third level in the system is the *exosystem* and refers to factors external to the children and adults but impacting on them nonetheless such as early educational policy and frameworks like *Aistear*. The *macrosystem* represents the influence of such factors as societal values and the position of the child in general and the early years child in particular. This last system of influence can be seen to include the societal vision for children, in the Irish case this can be seen in the *First-5* strategy document (Government of Ireland, 2018) and the government commitment to making children more visible as citizens in the Irish constitution, Bunreacht na hEireann (Government of Ireland, 1937).[1]

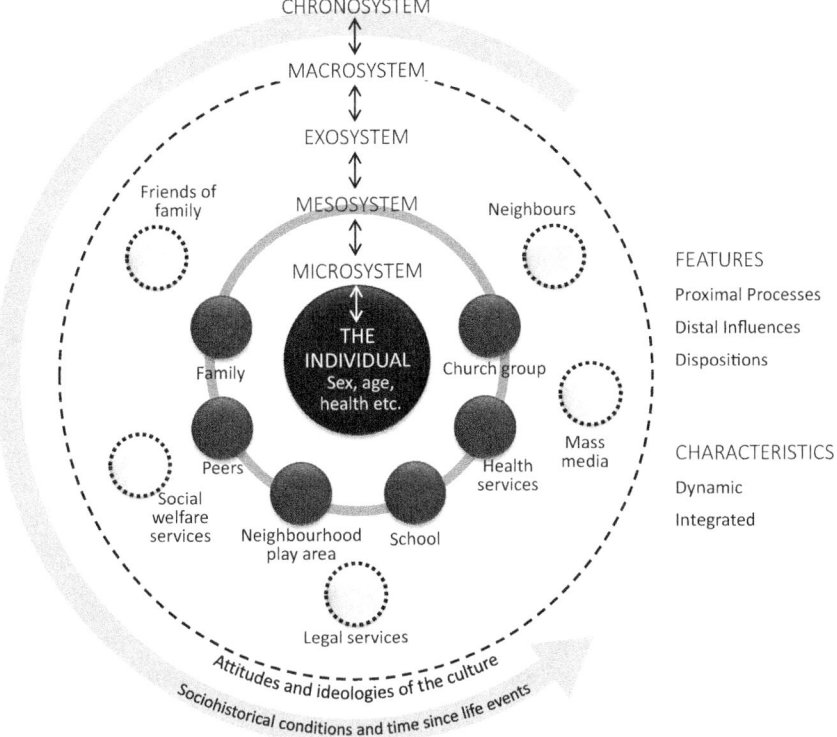

Figure 2.1 Bio-ecological model of development

Located within time, called the *chronosystem*, these systems, or levels, are organised from those closest, or *proximal*, to the child to those whose influence is distant and indirect or *distal*. The model, characterised as a set of nested levels with the child at the centre, has been used as a guide in early education, most notably by the New Zealand Ministry of Education in the development and implementation of their early years' curriculum *Te Whāriki* (New Zealand, 1996). There is also evidence of its influence in the *Aistear* (NCCA, 2009a) framework where, for instance there is a lot of attention to the importance of links (mesosystem) between early years settings and the home environment (microsystems).

Human development, especially in its early phases, takes place through processes of progressively more complex reciprocal interactions between an active and evolving person and the persons, objects, materials and symbols in the immediate external environment. We understand that to be effective, these interactions must be positive and occur on a fairly regular basis over extended periods of time. This in part accounts for why we have such extended childhoods compared to other species. Such enduring forms of interaction in the immediate environment are referred to as *proximal processes* and have been called the 'engines of development'. Examples of these important enduring patterns of proximal process are found in feeding or comforting a baby, playing with a young child, child–child activities, group or solitary play, storytelling, active listening, reading, learning new skills, athletic activities, problem solving, caring for others in distress, making plans, performing complex tasks and acquiring new knowledge and know-how (Bronfenbrenner & Morris, 2006).

To be developmentally effective these activities must occur on a regular basis over time and continue long enough to become increasingly more complex; mere repetition does not work. Secondly, developmentally effective proximal processes, or interactions, cannot be just one-way, there must be engaged interaction in both directions. In the case of interpersonal interactions, this means that there must a degree of active engagement between all those involved in the exchange. Finally, proximal processes are not limited to interactions with people, but also can involve interactions with objects, materials and symbols. In these latter circumstances, for reciprocal interactions to occur, the objects, materials and symbols in the immediate environment must be of interest, in a meaningful way and should invite and reward attention, exploration, manipulation, elaboration and imagination. It is clear that the adult, parent or early years educator, has a significant role in the quality of experiences influencing child development; a critical feature of this influence is the quality of the interactions facilitated and encouraged within the setting.

Considering the nature of child development

When reflecting on early years practice in terms of its effect on children's development it is useful to take some time to consider what is meant by the term development. The concept of development has two dimensions, the normative and the dynamic. In itself the idea of development has come to suggest a progression from one place or state to another along a reasonably predictable path. We learn about children's development in terms of different stages and we come to know what to expect of a child at particular ages. This understanding of a general developmental pattern has proved useful when considering how an individual child is doing in comparison to others of the same age. It is the basis of many standardised tests or assessments that are carried out to establish whether a child has achieved certain milestones such as walking, talking, reading and so on. We call this *normative development* – considering each individual child's development against a standard or norm that is normal for most children at the same age in the same cultural context. This normative approach to development has also given rise to the idea that there are activities and behaviours that are appropriate at certain ages and we can find many materials designed for use with children of specific ages. The description (or as some see it, prescription) of 'appropriate' here is closely tied to a normative view of development and is based on the notion of development as a continuous, predictable progression toward adulthood. However, while the normative approach to development can be useful in certain situations it has been found to be limiting in respect of early education. This is partly due to the fact that there is such a wide span of what constitutes normal behaviour, particularly in any group of very young children. For instance, it is quite common in practice to see a 1-year-old walking confidently while close by an 18-month-old is just toddling . . . what may appear appropriate for one child of a given age may not be appropriate for another of the same age. The reality of this variation in rate or pattern of development has been taken into account in the *Aistear* framework where the guidance on age ranges shows overlap: birth to 18 months, 12 to 36 months and 2.5 to 6 years.

From a practice perspective, it is important therefore to understand that there is a *dynamic* dimension to individual development. This dimension introduces the idea of development as an ongoing process unique to each individual child. It recognises that development is impacted by immediate and recent contexts and points to the complexity of development where there can be a developmental link between two dissimilar behaviours. A child's ability to engage in make-believe play at age 3 where, for instance, objects become symbols for different things, is related to word reading at age 5 where symbols, letters, are used to create words. In understanding this we see how important free pretend play is in any literacy strategy, even though pretend play rarely looks like reading! Dynamic development challenges us to consider what is best for the individual developing child at this moment, in this context. The essence of practising developmentally is rising to the challenge of valuing the moment for its immediate developmental contribution to a child whilst, at the same time acknowledging (but not overemphasising) its potential in respect to later development. While planning to achieve specific learning outcomes may be helpful in a general way providing learning opportunities is what day-to-day practice is about (Hayes & Filipović, 2017). This reality is one that early childhood educators need to understand and have confidence in as it provides a strong theoretical defence for the focus of quality practice in early childhood settings, practice which may not look 'educational' to those unfamiliar with the nature of early learning.

Viewing development as a dynamic and vital process, or as a 'to-ing and fro-ing' process allows us to view behaviour and development in early childhood as adaptive to the immediate demands of the child in context. Such an approach is not tied to the age or stage of development of the child but rather is linked to the sociocultural context of development for the child in the present. It is exemplified by the practices at Reggio Emilia in Italy and in the *Te Whariki* early years curriculum of New Zealand where pedagogy is directed by the connections, interactions and relationships between children and the wider world and by social, physical and emotional elements, rather than by any prescribed expectations of developmental outcome. It is also implicit in *Aistear,* which in both its design and content reflects this view of development as dynamic. Considering education and children's development as a dynamic process locates the child as an important contributor or agent in their own developmental and learning. The re-evaluation of 'children's agency and their contributions to society' can be traced back to the 1970s (Corsaro, 2020, p. 5). This shift in focus from the child as object to the child as agentic subject was reflected in the move from attention to the protection of children's rights to the promotion of their rights. The almost universally ratified UN Convention on the Rights of the Child (UN, 1989) was particularly influential and Article 12 on children's right to participate in matters affecting them provides a rationale for attending to and including the voice of the child as we try to better understand their lives and development (Horgan et al., 2016). Contemporary views of children characterise them as active participants in their own learning who, from their earliest days, construct models of their world, and their place in it, from their experiences and the opportunities available to them. They do this in the midst of a number of social contexts as illustrated by the bio-ecological model of development described previously. In their behaviour children exhibit and develop dispositions or habits of mind, which have a profound influence on them and direct the way in which they develop their skills and broaden and deepen their knowledge. Indeed, Bronfenbrenner writes that '[I]n order to develop – intellectually, emotionally, socially and morally – a human being, whether child or adult, requires the same thing: active participation in progressively more complex, reciprocal interaction with persons, objects and symbols in the individual's immediate environment' (Bronfenbrenner, 1989, p. 5). Research has found that the quality of interactions is closely related to the development and sustaining of behavioural dispositions, which can be either positive [generative] or negative [disruptive].

It is all very good to recognise that the quality of the interactions a child experiences, whether with people, objects, materials or symbols, is important to development but what exactly does that mean for practice? Why does the quality of interactions have important implications for development and for the effectiveness of early education? What is the power of interactions and the important role of the adult in planning for and facilitating them? In early education practice adults get the opportunity to guide and assist children in learning more positive, generative dispositions which contribute to their immediate well-being and later overall adjustment to school and society in general. Developmentally generative dispositions are important to positive learning and development and involve curiosity; the tendency to initiate and engage in activity, alone or with others; a responsiveness to initiatives by others; attention and perseverance; a readiness to defer immediate gratification in pursuit of long-term goals. On the other hand, developmentally disruptive dispositions can inhibit learning and development, and include impulsiveness; explosiveness; distractibility; inability to defer gratification and, in a more extreme form, a readiness to resort to aggression or violence; or at the opposite pole, apathy, inattentiveness, unresponsiveness, lack of interest in one's surroundings, feelings of insecurity, shyness, or a general tendency to withdraw from activity (Bronfenbrenner & Morris, 2006; Hayes et al., 2023). Through reflective observation of children and their interactions, where observation records and other documentation is revisited, reviewed and discussed, adults can come to understand the characteristics of the child and the environment, to inform their practice and facilitate the development of positive, generative dispositions for learning.

Effective early years practice, whether with infants or with children of 4 and 5 years of age, demands a great deal from the adult. Research tells us that early childhood educators resist talking enquiringly about their practice. Stephen (2010) makes the point that educators are often willing to talk about *what they plan* for children and *what they do* with them but are less likely to discuss *why*, they do things, what might be called their underlying pedagogical perspective. This inability to articulate a pedagogical perspective may reflect the absence of a common language of early education, one that captures the sophisticated understandings of child development and learning necessary to allow busy educators to plan for and respond effectively to children in the day-to-day messiness that is early years practice. Drawing on her research Stephen concludes that 'we have not yet developed a language for teaching that combines the 'language of technique' (what is effective) with the 'language of manner' (what is ethical, moral or caring)' (2010, p. 24).

We do have some elements of a common language of early education in Ireland deriving from the various policy documents, including the *Aistear* curriculum framework. Many of these materials were developed in close consultation with the sector and were informed by national and international research. To contribute to and strengthen the development of a common language and to make visible the underlying principles of effective and caring early childhood education there is a need to explicitly value the care element of early years practice (Hayes, 2007). At its simplest care can been seen as merely something that happens when adults, particularly women, are around children; those in early years practice know that it involves much more than simply being there. The caring practices in quality early childhood settings permeate everything and are informed by a fundamental understanding of and respect for children, as much caring *about* as caring *for* them. They are informed by kindness, compassion and ethical principles. To raise awareness about the crucial role of care in early childhood it is important to find a way of thinking and talking about care practice that recognises its central role in children's development and respects the role of the adult in providing a caring environment.

Nurturing pedagogy in early years practice

In my work I have argued that reconceptualising care as nurture can contribute to highlighting the educative nature of care practice in the early years and contribute to enhancing the status of the care concept within the field (Hayes, 2007). Despite many recommendations for the value of balancing the care and education elements of early education there remains a tendency to underestimate the developmental and educative role of caring. I have proposed that considering care as nurture gives it an active connotation, placing a responsibility on the adult to provide nurturance and to actively foster and encourage learning and development rather than to simply care for, mind or protect the child. To nurture requires an engaged, bidirectional level of interaction and confers on the early childhood educator an enhanced, educational role. Such a shift in emphasis should lead to a visible change in the language and discourse of early years practice providing a language with which to describe the day-to-day practices of caring for and educating young children, while also raising the expectations and status of this unique period of education. Rather than separate out the care and education dimensions of early childhood education and care, a nurturing pedagogy is one that recognises that the essence of quality early childhood practice is the interconnectedness and interdependence of education and care. The integrated nature of education and care in practice is illustrated in Figure 2.2.

Nurturing children's learning as part of a caring and compassionate educative process requires that adults develop skills of observation and reflection to allow for the nonintrusive planning and the provision of learning environments that support and extend children's own learning and quality interactive opportunities. Skills of observation and reflection are central to a nurturing pedagogy. They enhance practice and planning, are manifest in well-managed and yet responsive and flexible practice and assist in the provision of a learning environment that includes children and supports and extends children's

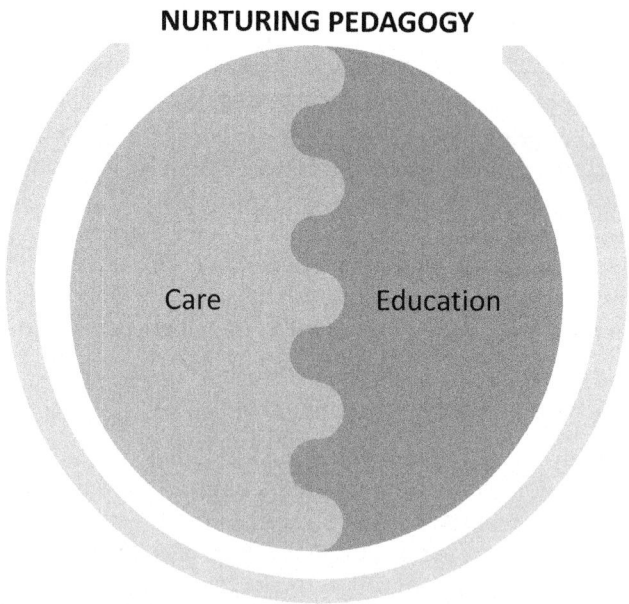

Figure 2.2 A nurturing pedagogy

learning. It is relational and allows for more careful attention to positive inter-actions between both child and adult and child and child. It also allows for planning by the adult for opportunities that might extend the child's own learning giving a key role to the adult which takes the child, rather than pre-scribed curricular content, as central. It encourages the movement away from the more traditional, organisational/management role of the educator and strengthens the focus on the educational, pedagogical role.

Linking the term nurture rather than care with pedagogy is intended to focus attention on the implications of this shift in focus for practice. The term 'pedagogy' captures the idea of a dynamic practice, the kind of practice we know is necessary to support children's holistic learning and development. The term 'pedagogy' is used to capture the integrated processes of caring, educating and learning alongside the principles, theory, values and approaches which underpin daily practice with young children in the range of early child-hood settings. Pedagogy is a more powerful, a richer word than practice alone as it suggests a theoretically informed practice that encompasses the many processes involved in children's learning and in the creation of learning oppor-tunities and environments that engage, challenge and interest young children. It acknowledges the sound theoretical base to day-to-day practice while also focusing attention on the everyday learning that adults themselves engage in, as they observe, reflect on and critically analyse the content of and approach to their work with young children, alone and with other adults. Combining the word pedagogy with the term nurture is intended to strengthen the early childhood professional space. The word nurture has quite a different tone to it than the word care. In comparing the meaning of the two words, 'nurture' appears more engaging and active than 'care'. The verb 'to care' is almost custodial in tone and requires a minimum of interaction; the adult merely provides for and looks after the child. To those outside early education the complexity involved in caring early years' practice is not immediately evident. To nurture, on the other hand conveys a more engaged level of interaction and requires the adult to actively nourish, rear, foster, train and educate the child through his/her practice.

Relationships and interactions are central to a nurturing pedagogy. There is a rich tapestry of relations between children themselves, between adults and young children, between adults and their colleagues and parents of the chil-dren they work with, and between learners and the environments where learn-ing takes place. Interactions are critical spaces for learning in the individual but also in groups. To create a significant shift in understanding the role of care as nurture in practice it is necessary to explicitly acknowledge the critical con-tribution of this interpersonal aspect of early education, to make it visible, to realise it in the practice of the everyday interactions, or *proximal processes*, that act as the engines of development. A nurturing pedagogy is a style of practice that may be new and different to that which many of us have experienced in our own education. It involves letting go of some of the older, more tradi-tional ideas about the relationship between the adult and the child, the teacher and the learner where the adult is the source of knowledge and children are there to receive this knowledge. Quality early childhood practice relies less on a content led curriculum and more on a framework of values and principles from within which a curriculum can emerge. It is explicit in engaging children, respecting them and integrating the learning opportunities provided across the care and education dimensions. It builds on the individual capabilities and dispositions of the child within the social context and derives from the belief that it is the close interactions, the proximal processes, between children and other children, adults and the environment that drive development and learning. Responding to our understanding of early childhood development requires that we prioritise relationships and interactions over direct instruction and teaching as the unique cornerstone of early educational practice. A nurturing pedagogy fosters these processes of interaction, dialogue and planning leading to the shared construction of knowledge, between children and adults, within the context of an emerging curriculum responsive to the child in the immediate now. Reflecting on practice in this way provides a collective context and opens up opportunities for discussing the central features that make early years practice unique and that are evident when observing skilled educators at work.

The role of interactions in development

Positive interactions, in language and content rich environments empower humans to move beyond their potential and have been proposed as the key drivers of development. This raises once again the question: why are interactions so important to development? Development is a process of continuous change that is self-maintaining, self-restoring and self-regulating. Early brain research indicates that the brain is only partially mature at birth and continues to develop over the first years of life. This makes it immediately susceptible to the ongoing influence of experiences of all types and thus the quality of interactions impacts on development (NSCDC, 2020). Studies indicate that the 'meaning-making' activity of babies and young children is enhanced by quality interactions. Results from observation of baby–educator interactions highlight the importance of touch and of joint attention to objects and events in assisting babies to come to attend to objects and recognise meaning-making and intention on the part of the other (Svinth, 2018). Such data suggests that the construction of knowledge does not simply involve a cumulative effect of multiple individual contributions, but rather it represents a stronger view of learning, which includes the baby as an active participant with the adult in the shared construction of meaning. It emphasises the importance of the actual act, the process of interacting itself, of shared meanings growing out of participation in shared activity. Current research from developmental psychology confirms that it is not simply the opportunity for interactions but the nature and quality of the interactive process itself that is important (French, 2019; Konrad et al., 2021). In particular research is highlighting the value of dynamic, bidirectional social interactions as crucial to early development. The importance of bidirectional, transformational interactions in stable and calm learning environments lies in their contribution to facilitating children to consider and explain their ideas to others, negotiate and argue a point and clarify their thinking thus refining their social, cognitive and metacognitive skills, the skills of thinking about thinking. Findings suggest that early years programmes which have a strong emphasis, both curricular [content] and pedagogical [practice], on the nurturing of emotional/affective development positively influence children's overall development, including their academic cognitive development. Social relationships seem to be central to the positive well-being of both the adults and children in early years settings. Positive learning environments are those which are warm and provide secure relationships to facilitate children's exploration, play and learning. This is as true for the child of 5 years of age as it is for the child of 5 months. Educators who provide for these learning opportunities, rather than focusing too closely on the development of academic skills, are supporting the development of fundamental aspects of learning consistent with young children's development. Positive and supportive adult/child interactions enhance children's security to explore and experience connectedness to peers and are important to well-being, flourishing and also to the development of early literacy and numeracy dispositions and skills (OECD, 2018). A number of studies have highlighted the danger of introducing academic training too soon in early childhood settings, in agreement with the point that 'there is no biological necessity to rush and put the start of teaching earlier and earlier. Rather, late starts might be reconsidered as perfectly in tune with findings from . . . brain research' (Blakemore & Frith, 2000, p. 4).

What is the evidence? What the research tells us

In reflecting on why early years experiences are so important to a child's development there are advantages to considering the research findings from a range of disciplines including developmental psychology, education and neuroscience which highlight the connectedness between various experience of young children in different developmental domains such as the physical, linguistic, cognitive, emotional and social. The cumulative knowledge of decades of research has contributed to a greater understanding of development in the early years. Research into early brain development clearly points to the importance of early life experiences and their impact on the basic architecture of the brain. Research suggests that direct physical and cognitive engagement with materials and experiences strengthen the brain connections (synapses) and neural pathways in babies, critical to their learning and development (Lally & Mangione, 2017). The quality of these very early experiences can determine how sturdy or fragile the foundations are for learning and behaviour over time. We now know that brains are built up over time beginning before birth and continuing into adulthood. A key ingredient in the process of brain development is the quality of early relationships between children and their parents and other significant adults. The 'turn-taking' or 'peek-a-boo' relationships, so commonly seen in the interaction between children and adults, seem to have a critical role in brain development. Researchers have coined the term 'serve and return' to describe those early responsive interactions between babies and adults that are fundamental to communicating. Serve and return is a relational activity, and its pace and content are informed by both the adult and the baby. It takes time and evolves as children develop. The back-and-forth nature of the process allows babies to both serve and return, recognising their agency in the process of communication. With a responsive adult responding the baby feels safe and comes to trust the process and this, in turn, gives confidence for further exploration and meaning making. These small acts of communication have a very powerful and positive effect on children's development

Young children benefit most from these relationships when they occur within stable, caring and interactive learning environments. From the start, even very young children, babies, are equipped with the skills necessary to initiate and maintain communication; they naturally seek out and attract attention through their vocalisations, their facial expressions and gestures. Responsive adults will reply in kind with vocalisations and gestures of their own and children in turn reward such adult attention by responding, smiling or mimicking behaviour such as sticking out the tongue. We have long known that children who grow up in restricted or depleted environments such as some institutional settings or chaotic and impoverished homes show signs of developmental delay from very early on. We now know that this is, in part because of the absence of close, stable relationships, the proximal processes described by Bronfenbrenner. The idea of the brain as a 'social brain' has been suggested as a way of strengthening our understanding of the importance of interactions and relationships to brain development; it may be a useful concept for those working directly with young children as it provides a clear verbal expression of the link between the environment [the space, materials, people and so forth] and the learning, developing child. We also know that the brain is most flexible in the early years and therefore more responsive to a range of environmental and interactional influences. As the child grows older this flexibility diminishes and it is more difficult to change existing brain circuitry. Take language development for instance: in the first months of life the baby will respond to a wide range of sounds but quickly begins to differentiate and specialise in those sounds she is exposed to and loses those less heard sounds.

There is amazing development occurring in the first 6 years of a child's life. They move from the tiny babe in arms at birth through physical development from inability to move from one place to the next through crawling, toddling and so on to the competent physical child we see at 6 years of age. Language development is also visible as we watch a child change from a being who has a limited range of sounds (the cry, the laugh, the coo) through to a 2-year-old making sentences on to a 6-year-old with an expressive vocabulary of some 1,500–2,500 words and who can understand over 20,000. We see the influence of good food, of exercise, of language opportunities in the children we know and those we work with. What is less visible and even more amazing is the development of the brain; research has found extensive evidence of the degree to which the interplay between genetics and early experience can create either a sturdy or weak foundation for learning and development.

In summarising some of the central findings derived from research into early brain development five central points have been identified:

> *Brains are built over time from the bottom up*: early experiences have a strong influence on how a child's brain architecture develops and this, in turn, can influence the strength or weakness of the foundation for future learning, development and behaviour.
>
> *The interactive influences of genes and experience shape the developing brain*: interactions are central to this developing architecture. The key process in the influence is the turn taking, the 'serve and return' nature of the interactive relationships. It is important therefore that the adult is attuned and responsive to the early signals from children. Young children need positive relationships, rich learning opportunities and safe environments in all their early years settings.
>
> *The brain's capacity for change decreases with age*: research suggests that the brain is most responsive to change during the early years and so this is highlighted as a crucial and sensitive period. However, we still have a great deal more to learn about the brain, how it develops and what role the environment plays.
>
> *Cognitive, emotional and social capacities are inextricably intertwined throughout the life course*: as research grows so too does our understanding of the complex, interrelated and dynamic nature of development. From a practice point of view we need to be aware that everything we do with and for children may have an impact and so we need to be alert and present in our practice so that we can come to understand more fully how our practices are influencing children's development and learning across a range of dimensions.
>
> *Toxic stress damages effective brain architecture,* which can lead to lifelong problems in learning, behaviour and physical and mental health: we know that children who grow up in poverty or in chaotic households need a great deal of support directly and indirectly to overcome the stresses they are living with. However, we must also recognise that while early years settings can provide a nurturing, safe and secure space for young children, and can provide a protective context within which they can develop and learn, such settings are only one of a number of supports that may be needed for such children (see: https://developingchild.harvard.edu).

Babies and young children require stable, caring, interactive relationships with adults for healthy brain development. Supportive relationships and positive learning experiences begin at home and are also provided in high quality early years environments. For those babies and young children experiencing severe poverty, abuse or stress, additional specialised and supportive interventions are needed to address, insofar as possible, the cause of the stress and protect the child from its consequences. It is clear that the brain is a complex and interconnected organ and it should come as no surprise that social, emotional and cognitive capacities are intertwined. Positive early experiences contribute to personal health and well-being and the development of social skills necessary to function in society. Both well-being and social competence contribute to a child's sense of self-confidence, which in turn contributes to their learning and their cognitive development. As one might expect the evidence also indicates that stress associated with poverty, neglect, abuse or poor parenting can compromise the positive brain development so essential to later achievement and success. High-quality early childhood experiences in cases such as these can counteract, to some extent, the impact of negative stressors and set the child on a more positive developmental path. This happens not only as a result of direct impact on children but also indirectly through influences on parents and the home learning environment.

From this evidence it is clear that the early years of a child's life are crucial to brain development which, in turn, influences the path and trajectory of a child's overall development and learning. Supportive relationships and positive learning experiences are key to this and so the role of early childhood educators cannot be overstated. Through their quality practice, early educators can provide learning environments which stimulate and challenge children and give them a secure sense of well-being and belonging, within which they can explore, play, learn, develop and strive to reach their full potential. As Lally and Mangione note, 'the "tender loving care" advocated by early childhood educators for many decades is not only the kind way to treat children but a crucial part of early brain development' (2017, p. 19).

With developments in technology, we can describe what is happening in the brain under different circumstances and this informs our understandings of brain development and its possible impact on development and behaviour. However, we still lack a full understanding of how the brain actually works. With all the attention to brain research it is important to understand that there is a distinction between the brain and the mind. While the terms are often used interchangeably there is a difference; the brain is a physical organ and we can see images of brain activity in response to external stimuli. The mind, on the other hand, is an abstract, philosophical concept. The mind manifests itself in our thoughts and words and is unlocked within the social world. Brooks (2011) makes the point that we are born into relationships and are created through relationships. Our physical brain develops within our own individual skull but '[A] mind only exists within a network. It is the result of interactions between brains, and it is important not to confuse brains with minds' (p. 43).

Developing and learning to learn

But what is it about positive brain development that influences an individual's learning and development and why is it important to early years practice? The skills necessary to control and coordinate information, so critical to success in life in general and school success for children in particular, are developed in the early years and provide the foundation for all later learning and development. These skills are often referred to as the *Executive Functions* as they are the functions that we use to manage our behaviour, our emotions and our attention. The term executive function is used to describe this set of mental processes that are central in helping us organise and order our actions and behaviours. Executive function involves both concrete behaviours and abstract, thought-based concepts and research indicates that children who have good executive functioning and self-regulation do better in both the academic areas such as literacy and numeracy and in general social adjustment. The level of development of executive function skills depends on the biological maturity of the child and the process is heavily influenced by environmental experiences. It is through the quality of their early learning experiences that children have the opportunity to develop these functions and the adults in their lives are of critical importance in facilitating this.

The elements of executive function are characterised in different ways but include (i) working memory and recall, (ii) activation, arousal and effort, (iii) mental flexibility and (iv) self-control. A *working memory and recall* are key components of executive function and involve problem solving, reasoning and planning. It is through our working memory that we make sense of things over time. It requires that we hold in mind what has happened and relate it to what is happening now. It assists recall. Those of you familiar with the HighScope (https://highscope.org) model of early education will know that this is foregrounded through the *plan/do/review* process. To be effective this process requires the full attention of the educator and sufficient time for the child to work through all three components of the process. Adults are expected to respond to children, give them the time to talk about their ideas and their plans, allow them the space to actively explore their environment, create opportunities and time for them to review their plans and encourage their thinking and recall. Working memory is also necessary to connect ideas, to link what you have done, heard or read with what you are doing, hearing or reading right now and to remember instructions and carry them out in the correct order. In addition, it is our working memory that helps us to understand cause and effect, central to understanding science and to the scientific method.

Activation, arousal and effort refer to the child's willingness and ability to get started at something, to pay attention to the activity and to put in the effort necessary to complete it. Such skills will only develop where the child is comfortable, feels secure and has a sense of belonging. Providing children with the opportunities, materials, time and space to make choices and decisions in their play and activities while facilitating them in thinking about what they are doing is a key role that the early childhood educator fulfils – it is the essence of quality early childhood education and care.

Mental flexibility includes being able to switch perspectives, to see things in a new light. It is being able to see opportunities and take advantage of them and being able and willing to change course if what you are doing seems wrong or is not working. It is this flexibility of mind that fuels imagination, allows people think outside the box and to be creative. It also has important behavioural dimensions in that it helps us understand another person's point of view, contributing to the development of empathy.

Self-control is crucial to successful learning and development. It allows us to stay focused, avoid distraction, stay on task and helps to limit and manage impulsive behaviour. Where children are impulsive, they are less likely to persist at an activity and are also less likely to pay attention. From longitudinal research we know that this can lead to later difficulties in school and less success in adulthood. In a study that tracked a population of children from birth into adulthood, Moffitt et al. (2011) found that self-control, as measured by parents, teachers and self-report ratings during the first ten years of life predicted physical and mental health, employment, financial security, substance use and criminal conviction (and lack thereof). Self-controlled children are less likely drop out of school, smoke or become teenage parents. Other studies have found the early years settings that encourage the development of self-regulation and effortful control are most effective in supporting other skills important to academic attitudes and success (Sezgin & Ulus, 2020). Apart at all from these later impacts children who have well developed self-control are more likely to have enjoyable and satisfying everyday experiences; their childhoods are more likely to be happy and content than fractious and stressful.

While understanding how our behaviour impacts so profoundly on children and at such a crucial and deep level is important, it is also a huge responsibility, and this can be daunting and paralysing. The thing is that even without understanding the impact of our practice it has an impact on the children! Knowledge helps us to consider our practice a little more carefully, it challenges us to consider the implications of such knowledge on our practices, it allows us to appreciate that feedback and the form that it takes has an influence on young children's confidence, mental flexibility and self-control. Through the provision of opportunities, materials, times and space to explore, play, take risks and rise to social and physical challenges in a setting that is secure and comfortable children develop a sense of belonging, they feel that they are trusted participants in the learning environment and this in turn facilitates healthy development and learning.

Through observation adults can see executive function at work in children's play when, for instance, they talk themselves through an activity as they move objects around or place things in a particular order. The example below is an illustration of a young child at play. If you follow closely you will be able to see the different elements of executive function in action and the educator's role in extending the opportunities presented.

At planning time, Gabrielle says, "I'm going to play with the doggies and Magnatiles in the toy area.

I'm making a tall elevator." At work time, Gabrielle builds with the magnetic tiles while playing with the small toy dogs, as she planned. She stacks the tiles on top of one another in a tower-like form – her "elevator" – then places some dogs in it. The elevator then falls over. She repeats this several times, but the elevator continues to fall over. Gabrielle then arranges the magnetic tiles into squares, connecting them to form a row. Gabrielle says to Shannon, her teacher, "I'm making doghouses because the elevator keeps falling down." Shannon says, "I was wondering what you were building, because you planned to make a tall elevator going up vertically, and now you are using them to make doghouses in a long horizontal row. You solved the problem by changing the way you were building." Gabrielle uses pretend talk while moving the dogs around. At one point she says, "Mommy, Mommy, we are hungry" and opens one of the doghouses and moves the dog inside where a bigger dog is placed. Gabrielle says, "Mommy says the food's not ready, so go play."

While moving the dogs around, Gabrielle says to herself out loud, "We have to find something to do until the food is ready." Gabrielle says to Shannon, "Let's pretend we are going to the park." Shannon agrees and says, "I'm going to slide down the slide three times and then jump off the climber." As Shannon pretends to do this with one of the dogs, Gabrielle watches then copies her and says, "My dog jumped higher than yours." She then says, "Mommy says we have to go home now. We need to move our dogs over there so they can eat." The pretend play continues.

At recall time, Gabrielle is using a scarf to hide some objects she played with. When it is her turn to recall, she gives clues about what is under the scarf. She shows the group a couple of magnetic tiles and dogs. Shannon asks her what she did with these materials during work time. Gabrielle talks about the problem with the falling "elevator" and then recounts the story about the doggies. [From: Lockhart (2010)]

In this example you will have noticed how, with the careful intervention of the early childhood educator, Gabrielle was made aware of the fact that through her own actions, her behaviour, she had solved a problem. Later in her play she was given the opportunity to see planning in action when Shannon, the early educator, talked through her plans for sliding on the slide. Finally, we see Gabrielle given the opportunity to recall and share her activity with others. Where playful everyday experiences are available in well-designed and interactive early years settings children have the time, encouragement and the context within which to develop the dispositions and skills necessary to function competently and effectively at their own level. The presence of observant, attuned and engaged educators enriches their experiences and expands and strengthens their learning and development.

Enhancing practice to guide learning

The importance of relationships and interactions in the process of development has been supported by research, which has shown the powerful role that the social context plays, even in the lives of very young children. Studies into collaborative learning have informed a move towards a respectful, nurturing pedagogy which sees the child as an active participant in the learning process and the adult as an informed, compassionate guide. Collaborative learning is considered particularly important in early childhood where the collaborative opportunities in a safe environment enhance children's opportunities to refine their cognitive and metacognitive skills. The importance of bidirectional, transformational interactions has been defended in terms of its contribution to facilitating children to explain their ideas to others, negotiate, argue a point and clarify their thinking. It is as children describe, explain or justify their thinking in conversation or discussion that they are developing their cognitive and meta-cognitive skills – that is their ability to think about thinking – to abstract.

A most effective practice in encouraging and supporting the development of cognitive processes in children is where educators engage in the activity of 'sustained shared thinking'. Sustained shared thinking, or SST, is a term used to describe an interaction, which 'involves an adult being aware of the child's interests and understandings and involves the adult and the child interacting together to develop an idea or skill' (Siraj-Blatchford et al., 2008, p. 29). It has been linked to improved cognitive outcomes for children and is recognised as one of the key elements of quality early years practice. Implicit in the concept of SST is the power of conversation to enrich and extend children's learning and thinking. Building on the literature French (2014) introduces the idea of explicitly facilitating SST through engaging in what she calls, extended purposive conversations, a way to realise SST in early years practice. Early childhood professionals who are sensitive and responsive to children's cues are better able to engage in SST and are able to assess what type of assistance children need, if any, and as a consequence, ensure their responses are accordingly child centered. SST underpins a range of techniques used in education of young children, such as facilitating the construction of understanding, encouraging problem solving, supporting philosophising, and scaffolding children's learning. Such a view recognises the young social child as capable of reasoning, by and while making sense of the world and presents the child as capable of higher order functions such as thinking about thinking, connecting ideas through reflection or 'going meta' (Bruner, 1996, p. 57).

While individual children need opportunities to explore, play and learn in an uninterrupted way, collaboration with peers and adults, as opposed to individual work, is also valuable because it results, in practice, in explaining one's thought processes and seeing things from another's viewpoint, learning opportunities that are important in encouraging the development of higher order cognitive functions such as metacognition. One of the benefits of developing meta-cognitive skills, the skills of thinking about thinking, is that it assists in the development of self-regulation. Meta-cognitive capability facilitates children's understanding of their thinking process and that of their peers which in turn contributes to their understanding of the social rules around sharing and turn-taking. This growing understanding of and attention to the shared or social nature of learning corresponds with the idea of the individual as a social learner even when interacting with objects or concepts.

One of the central tasks of childhood is the ability to regulate cognitive functioning, to exercise conscious control over, for instance, attention and memory. Such self-regulation has an affective or emotional dimension. Many studies have found that later school success is more dependent on emotional and social capabilities consolidated in early childhood than on a child's fund of facts or ability to read. It is more important, in the long, run for children to be interested; to know what kind of behaviour is expected and how to rein in the impulse to misbehave (self-regulation); to be able to wait, to follow directions, and to turn to adults and peers for help. This view is similar to that proposed by Maslow (1987) when he characterised the 'self-actualised' child as one capable of tolerating uncertainty, of being problem-centred rather than self-centred and with a concern for the welfare of the wider world, an outside-looking rather than an inside-looking child who enjoys satisfying interpersonal relationships. Behaviours and dispositions that can be nurtured to assist children in achieving self-actualisation, or facilitate them on their journey, include their ability to become absorbed, to concentrate; a willingness to try the new; a facility to listen to themselves as well as others; an honesty that allows them to be individual; a readiness to assume responsibility; the ability to work hard and persevere. Also important to this process is a sense of belonging, the connectedness that assists in the development of well-being. The evidence from scientific research indicates that prioritising emotional and social development, particularly in early education, can assist children in their overall development in the present and into the future.

This review of the research findings informing our understandings of effective early years practice suggests that high-quality settings are those in which educators interact with children in a compassionate and responsive and informed way, encourage verbal interaction and are not harsh with children. Development is enhanced if group sizes are small, settings are child-focused and well organised, with adults playing a facilitative role rather than a didactic one. Organisation and structure are important and are provided by adults who carefully plan and prepare the learning environment and who have high expectations of children in terms of social and linguistic development. The evidence confirms that settings facilitating more involvement with and attention to activities by children themselves result in them learning more skills and concepts, including the kind of knowledge that gets tested on achievement measures. In addition, children from such learning environments show more cognitive advance and have more verbal and social skills. It seems that allowing children the time and space to make decisions and take some responsibility for their own learning and actions may help them internalise control and cultivate the dispositions that enable them to succeed and flourish.

The importance of dispositions

The development in children of an identity as learner is seen as an important outcome from early education. It facilitates flexible, responsive learning to changing contexts and situations and rests comfortably with the contemporary emphasis on lifelong learning and learning how to learn. Katz (1995) urges early childhood educators to consider developing the emotional/affective dimension of cognitive development by assisting the child to become a 'good learner' rather than focusing on their being a 'good person'. She is concerned that too much attention to becoming a 'good person' may encourage performance for praise rather than learning for personal satisfaction. The two identities of 'good person' and 'good learner' may become blurred unless educators are very clear about their role and thus in their communication with children in relation to their behaviour.

An individual's learning power, or cognitive functioning, can be considered as having two dimensions: *capabilities* – that is the skills and strategies – and *dispositions*, the tendencies to learn and learn from learning. This latter dimension relates to less measurable, but no less important, sides of cognitive behaviour such as the motivational and affective dimensions. Understanding where motivation or inclination comes from, how the inclination to apply skills or knowledge develops and how this might be cultivated in early education is an important challenge as it can set the stage for future success. The term affective is derived from the Latin *affectus* meaning 'disposition' and refers to emotion or desire, especially in influencing behaviour. We have noted earlier that, in considering children's developmental trajectories Bronfenbrenner identified two dispositional types: *Generative* and *Disruptive*. Generative, or positive dispositions include curiosity, engagement, perseverance and problem solving, while disruptive, or negative dispositions include impulsivity, inattention, apathy and a tendency to withdraw (Bronfenbrenner, 2005). Dispositions are not merely the result of biological inheritance but reflect the interaction between individual traits and the various contexts in which development occurs. The individual, acting upon the environment in turn 'embodies the micro and macro environment around them so that experiences and *context* become part of the *person*' (Hayes et al., 2023, p. 50). In practice this places an important responsibility on the adult to facilitate the development of positive dispositions and redirect, as far as possible the more disruptive ones.

The affective dimension of a child's development influences a child's disposition and motivation to learn and it also shapes the sense of self as learner. The dimension of development, which predisposes the learner to apply the knowledge and the skills acquired with some understanding of their role in the process, has been characterised as 'mastery' oriented learning (Dweck, 2016). Dispositions have been defined in a variety of ways depending on the focus of the author and often reflect how the role of contexts and interactions in the acquisition of dispositions is understood. In a comprehensive review of the definitional difficulties surrounding the concept of disposition Katz (1993) highlights the ambiguous and inconsistent use of the term in educational and developmental studies. Arising from her review of the literature she proposed that dispositions were patterns of behaviour exhibited frequently and in the absence of coercion, constituting a 'habit of mind' under some conscious and voluntary control that is intentional and oriented to broad goals.

Katz has suggested a number of reasons for including the development of dispositions as a goal in early education:

1. The acquisition of knowledge and skills alone does not guarantee that they will be used and applied; one must also have the disposition to use or apply.
2. Explicitly attending to and encouraging learner dispositions is important because the didactic, instructional process through which some knowledge and skills are acquired may damage or undermine the disposition to use them.
3. When children's experiences are supported to manifest dispositions, they become robust; without such supports they are likely to weaken or disappear.
4. The process of selecting content and practice strategies should include consideration of how desirable dispositions can be strengthened and undesirable dispositions can be weakened.
5. On the basis of evidence accumulated from research on mastery versus performance motivation, it seems that there is an optimum amount of positive feedback for young children above which they may become preoccupied with their performance and the judgement of others rather than their involvement in the task.
6. Dispositions must be included in the evaluation and assessment of early years programmes.
7. Dispositions are not likely to be acquired through didactic processes but are more likely develop in young children as they experience being around people who exhibit positive dispositions. Therefore, practitioners and parents should become aware of what dispositions can be seen in them by the children for whom they are responsible (1993, pp. 11, 12).

Informed and intelligent early years practice enhances the development of dispositions or 'habits of mind' as an explicit aspect of education alongside knowledge and skill. The importance of developing learning dispositions; encouraging a mastery, or learning, orientation; promoting meta-cognitive skills; developing cognitive and social self-regulation and fostering engaged involvement and emotional well-being are generally considered important aims of early years practice.

A general disposition to learn, or mastery orientation may be present in some form at birth. Its manifestation is likely to change with development, to be related to the child's experience, and to be increasingly varied and differentiated across children with increasing age and experience. Dispositions are an integral part of the individual child and can be identified through observing children's choices, decisions and actions. To develop and function they require a balance between the inclination of the learner and the goals of knowledge, skills and abilities to be learned. This suggests an active role for the early childhood educator and the learning environment itself in the development of learning dispositions as well as in the encouragement of other skills and knowledge. This developmental view of dispositional learning is in keeping with our current understanding of the complexity and dynamic nature of learning and is the reason that consideration must be explicitly given to nurturing learning dispositions in early education particularly as they appear to facilitate the later application of the literacy and numeracy skills and competencies valued by primary education. It helps explain why early years practice is specialised and focuses on developing and nurturing the less definable skills, such as motivation, organisation, inclination and attitude to learning. In attending to dispositional aspects of learning it is important to provide a context which is meaningful and relevant to the child through interactions and relationships aimed at nurturing the affective dimension of learning within a content rich context. In this way it will impact on those 'basic skills' identified by policy makers as so important to later life success.

Learning, or mastery-oriented children tend to exhibit positive learning dispositions and maintain persistence in the face of difficulty, locating any difficulty or problem in the context rather than within themselves. Quality early years settings provide extensive opportunities for learning and the educators are instrumental in shaping the dispositions through careful observation of children as they explore, play, interact with others and the environment or sit quietly alone. Through such careful observation they identify the emerging dispositions particular to individual children at particular times and in particular contexts. Where feedback to children, either praise or correction, is clear, explicitly articulating the features of the context, the task, the process and their role in it, it is most beneficial. It is important however to note that by the age of 5 years, young children exhibit a vulnerability to adult criticism and this has been associated with the development of a negative, 'helpless' learning orientation in older children. It is also worth noting that negative feedback can impact up to three times more powerfully than positive feedback. Thus, educators must consider carefully how best to give feedback, particularly if the feedback can be perceived as negative in nature. Feedback should be focused on behaviour rather than on the child. It is not simply about correcting children, it is about being respectful and sensitive when correcting them and pointing out clearly and calmly whatever difficulty there may be with their behaviour.

We know that early childhood education is one of the most important influencing factors for the development of the 'soft' and difficult to measure aspects of development such as aspirations, dispositions, social skills, motivation and learner confidence – those aspects influenced by the developing executive functions. Research confirms that an emphasis on the emotional/

affective dimension of learning in early childhood positively influences children's later academic cognitive development. This approach yields foundational short-term benefits and sustainable long-term benefits across social and educational dimensions (UN, 2015). Rather than attempting to provide a balanced approach to guiding academic skills and affective skills development in young children, it appears that it is more productive to foreground the affective, over the academic, dimension of development in early education. This approach is evident in New Zealand early years curriculum, *Te Whariki*, it underpins the practices found in Reggio Emilia early years settings and can also be seen in the *Aistear* framework.

In summary we can conclude that quality early years settings provide rich learning opportunities for children. The review of research highlights how important it is for early childhood educators to facilitate the development of learning dispositions; encourage a mastery, or learning, orientation; promote metacognitive skills; assist the development of cognitive and social self-regulation and foster engaged involvement and emotional well-being. The picture emerging is one of quality early years settings as dynamic learning environments rich in interactions and communication where learning and development occurs in a complex, dynamic and shared context and not simply as a result of individual differences in ability or inclination.

While contemporary education policy emphasises the importance of children learning to learn and to develop an identity as learner in their early education, policy also identifies specific outcomes for education, such as school-readiness, that may compete with what we understand about the focus of effective early childhood practice. This tension can influence practice and the learning environment and may in fact be encouraging early years environments that facilitate a performance rather than a learning orientation. To be able to counteract this trend and resolve the tension early childhood educators require a shared understanding of their role in the education of young children and a common language of professional early years practice. This can be supported by reference to the principles in curriculum frameworks and other policy guidance which share a common view of early childhood and early years practice. This is considered in greater detail in the following chapters.

Note

1 On 10th November 2012 the *Thirty-First Amendment of the Constitution (Children)* was passed by referendum.

3 Enhancing quality practice

Introduction

Research tells us that to be effective for young children early years experiences need to be of a high quality. To recognise and enhance quality our understandings must be informed by the most up-to-date data in respect of the role the environment plays in how young children develop and learn. This chapter explores what is meant when we talk about *high quality*, noting that defining the quality of early childhood experiences is difficult. Historically, quality has been considered across two domains, distinguishing between the more static and measurable aspects of quality, known as structural quality and the more fluid aspects of quality, known as process quality. Structural quality refers to the visible and measurable elements including the adult/child ratio and the environmental, health and safety aspects of a setting. Process quality, on the other hand, is more difficult to capture and measure. It refers to unique features of a particular setting and includes such things as the general quality of relationships and interactions, the ethos, the responsiveness to individuality within the group, the realisation of curriculum and the atmosphere of a setting. The early childhood educator and the quality of their practice is central to process quality. The chapter also examines the role of curriculum frameworks in guiding practice and how the values and principles can direct how educators conceptualise their role in early childhood education and care.

Identifying quality indicators for structural and process quality in early years settings is a complex undertaking and is a task that must evolve with due regard to the context of early education and care. For different interested parties or participants, quality means different things. One way or the other, educators and policymakers are faced with the challenge of providing effective early education based on their current understanding of quality and in light of existing standards (Duignan & McDonnell, 2022). In some countries, such as Ireland, there are two inspection systems evaluating the quality of settings – one focusing mainly on the 'care' dimensions of health and safety/structural issues and the other looking into the educational/pedagogical dimensions of quality. This approach to quality regulation perpetuates the distinction between care and education we mentioned in Chapter 2 and constrains the move towards

DOI: 10.4324/9781003353164-3

recognising and valuing the intertwined and intricate nature of the relationship between care and education which make early childhood education and care a unique period in the educational lives of children.

In spite of the debate in the field about the definition and measurement of quality, there is general consensus among early childhood professionals regarding the types of quality indicators that are useful and desirable. The environment should be well organised, stimulating and attractive to the child; it should be uncluttered and pleasing to the eye; it should have responsive and well-trained staff working within a flexible and balanced curricular framework and be conducive to effective practice. It should provide opportunities for individual and small group activities and have generous adult/child ratios. Research on quality early education (EC, 2020) locate the responsibility for quality firmly with the adults. Adults are the key people in the lives of children and are the most important tools of practice. Adults who are attuned, who are 'watchfully attentive' and mindful in their day-to-day practice really make a difference. Additionally, effective educators demonstrate a high level of relevant and meaningful training; give specific attention to individual children; work with small groups of children and use strategies which are responsive to the child's interests and normal developmental needs. To be successful in their work they also need to be confident in their knowledge and skills and value the work they do. In valuing their work educators are strengthening their professional identity and locating it within the unique field of early childhood education and care, one where play and wonder, curiosity and imagination, risk and exploration are the norm. Rosenow (2012) observes that those working with or for children should nurture themselves as tenderly as they nurture the children in their care, and they should delight in the wonders of the world and be eager to share them with children.

We also know from research that high-quality early learning environments should provide opportunities for children to carry out learning activities without undue interference from the adult but with guidance and assistance when necessary. Enabling environments, both indoor and outdoor, are those which provide opportunities that are exciting, interesting and challenging for children and that encourage them to engage in activities that stimulate them, that build on their existing skills, knowledge and competencies, encouraging the expansion of these skills to new and more complex tasks and be supporting of them in a view of themselves as competent learners. When we talk of high-quality early years practice, we are referring to the quality of what is happening in early childhood settings every day. The importance of the day-to-day, the ordinary rests on the fact that it is from within the ordinary that the early childhood curriculum emerges. It is through the ordinary experiences of the early years that children create the foundation on which the development [positive or negative] of emotional well-being, sound physical and mental health, social competence and cognitive skills are based. To unlock the full potential of this, young children require well trained and informed adults who, in their direct work with children, and their indirect work with them through support and guidance of parents and other professionals, can be as effective as possible. Practically, at the day-to-day level this means the provision of enriching and challenging learning environments, which recognise the developmental trajectories and different paths of development in children. It also means creating an atmosphere of secure relationships where children feel that they belong and are valued members within the learning space. The gain from such practice and provision can be seen in the general run-of-the-mill contentedness, playfulness and satisfactions of both children and adults, and the foundational impact of such experiences on later learning, caring and solid citizenship. Swedish research (Sheridan, 2011) reports that high-quality early years settings are characterised by learning environments rich in challenge and learning opportunities where children actively participate, communication between adults and children share a similar focus and the adults interact with the children in the 'here and now' by being physically and emotionally present for the children. The adults focus on the interests, knowledge and experiences of the children within an agreed vision for the outcomes of their own work. By contrast, poorer-quality settings can be identified as characterised by limitations of space and materials, poor interactions, communication and reciprocal encounters between the adults and children with few opportunities for child participation. Although physically present, the adults in poor-quality early years settings appear to be more focused on keeping control and maintaining order than on engaging with the children or providing challenging and interesting learning opportunities for them.

In a wide-ranging keynote address to the European Early Childhood Education Research Association annual conference (2012), Margaret Carr called on educators to consider the importance of 'democracy, dreaming and doubt' on the learning journeys we all take. Stressing the importance of clear observations that are open to all that is to be 'seen' she gave many wonderful examples of how practice can respect, for instance, children's democratic participation in practice. In the following example, Carr (2012) introduced us to a creative young artist whose work was on display in the early years setting and who was explaining it to an adult.

> As he was explaining a younger child from the setting came over and, unexpectedly, reached over to the paintings, tore them off the display stand and scrunched them up. As one might expect the young artist was upset. How to react? In this case the early childhood educator acknowledged the upset of the young artist and agreed it was reasonable. However, there followed some discussion about why the younger child behaved as he did and how he simply did not realise that he was 'destroying' the work of the older child. While the older child could understand this, he was still sad and thought something needed to be done. The adult agreed and asked for his ideas on what could be done. His suggestion on how to stop this happening again was to have the 'museum

line' in the art display area of the setting. On further investigation by the adult, it transpired that this was a reference to the line in museums and art galleries over which patrons are asked not to step, it keeps the art at a bit of a distance whilst still allowing viewing and discussing. With this as the suggested solution it was introduced into the setting.

In this example we see that the adult was respectful of both children, recognising the impulsiveness of the younger child while at the same time recognising the upset of the older child. Furthermore, the educator took the time to tease out how best to respond to the situation and both listen to and act on the suggestion of the older child. Overall, there was specific respect for the views of the children, which created a true sense of belonging for both children. This is a lovely example of democratic practice in action. This example also gives us further insight into the type of practice in the setting. The conversation between the educator and the child in advance of the disruption suggests that the educator and the child were engaged in discussions and conversations over time and what the children had done and learned were noted and recorded. Finally, we can infer from the availability of the story that the information on this event was documented by the adult for sharing and future reference.

One way to identify opportunities for this level of engagement with children is through ongoing observation of their activity and play. Play is recognised as a key process through which children extend their learning and development during early childhood in particular. The UN Convention on the Rights of the Child has a specific article, Art. 31, on the right of children to play, recreation and leisure. To elaborate specifically on the right to play the UN published a General Comment (UN, 2013) in which they note that play takes place when children are alone, together with their peers or with adults. The Comment emphasises the role of loving and caring adults supporting children's development in their relationships with children through play. It is through play that children provide adults with unique insights and understanding into the worlds that 'builds respect between generations, contributes to effective understanding and communication between children and adults and affords opportunities to provide guidance and stimulus', pointing out that 'the benefits are diminished . . . if control by adults is so pervasive that it undermines the child's own efforts to organize and conduct his or her play activities'(p. 2). Lester and Russell (2010) have argued in their writings on children's right to play that, in play, children create worlds where they are in control

and can seek out uncertainty in order to triumph over it – it is primarily behaviour for its own sake, for the pleasure and joy of being able to do it. Yet play is more than mere indulgence; it is essential to children's health and wellbeing.

(2010, p. x)

However, recognising the right to play is an insufficient reason to explain the importance of play within early childhood curriculum and pedagogy. It is important to provide evidence to explain why play is important to children's development across a variety of different developmental domains. While children are biologically equipped to play from birth, they need sensitive adults to guide them through their frustrations and share in their fulfilments. Effective play is promoted and nurtured by adults who provide quality learning environments [indoors and outdoors], objects, activities, time, opportunities and encouragement. It is through their play that young children explore, create, imagine, experiment, manipulate, negotiate, problem-solve and consolidate their understanding of the world. Play provides a safe 'magic circle' (Huizinga, 1938/2016) within which they can struggle and strive and succeed; it is the space that allows them to explore feeling and to test their fears; it is through play that they come to experience the nature of materials such as water and sand and begin to explore the foundations of science and mathematics. In the main children are curious and interested in understanding the world around them and through their play they become competent and confident learners who are prepared to take risks and challenge themselves to learn more about that world.

While adults prepare environments to support and encourage play there are times when it may be appropriate for them to participate in play. Participating in play with children can provide valuable opportunities for educators to extend or elaborate a particular theme through guidance, the introduction of new vocabulary or new materials. We saw an example of this in Chapter 2 with Shannon and Gabrielle. Care needs to be taken, however, when considering participation in children's play and it is most successful where educators are invited into a play situation as a participant and respect the direction of the children so as to avoid intruding, interrupting or disrupting the flow. Observant and sensitive early childhood educators use play as a window into children's worlds, into their interests, their skills and knowledge, their friendships and their level of development in different areas; they build on this knowledge to extend children's learning. Records of play observations can inform curriculum planning and development and allow educators to determine how best to meet the individual needs of children and what particular interests can be built on. Observations of group play can also highlight the quality of social interactions and identify those social skills which may need supporting, strengthening or redirection.

Gathering records and other documentation of learning, whether for learning, assessment or planning, is most effective when approached collaboratively rather than through isolated individual activity. While individual observations of individual children have a key role to play in certain aspects of early years practice [such as gathering specific developmental or social information] the more general day-to-day documentation in practice is a social activity and its value rests in that fact. When we talk about collaboration in this context it often includes, as in Carr's example noted previously, the active participation of the children themselves. Apart from the value of such collaborative engagement in relation to learning and to practice this reflects the ambitions outlined in many contemporary policy documents which commit to hearing children's voices. Realising the commitment of accessing the voices of children, and of hearing them, in a democratic and respectful manner, particularly with very young children can be a challenge (French, 2022; O'Toole et al., 2023) but there are a growing number of methods and resources to assist. For instance, in her writings on the value of Learning Stories, Carr has written extensively on how the visual, in terms of drawings, photos and video clips, can be more powerful than the traditional written documentation (Carr & Lee, 2019). There is a democracy in ethically sharing photos of children with other children, their families and visitors to the setting; it is a really inclusive practice where all children can participate at some level. Through such visual displays, which are shared and discussed, they see themselves as belonging to the place and recognise the past as part of their present.

Adjusting practice to encourage the active involvement of children with adults and other children can be unsettling as it may alter the power balance in a setting. However, this does not shift the balance from adult to child, nor does it lead to a situation of chaos or unwelcome, undirected behaviour in the children; rather it facilitates a context where learning is collaborative and becomes more reciprocal, where children learn in an engaged way with adults and other children who respect each other and where adults are also open to learning. Such reciprocal practice makes visible for children their place in the setting and enhances their sense of belonging and self-worth; it also reflects a culture of democratic practice. While observations of individual children are useful in focusing on specific issues there is a danger that some observations of individual children may inadvertently omit or remove the context of the observation and compromise the quality of the interpretation and analysis. Too individual a focus can limit our true understanding of the real meaning behind the observation. This may be problematic when seeking the meaning of an action or behaviour as learning is, in many instances, located within a broader social context. We should appreciate that children bring to settings cultural and personal experiences and knowledge which inform their actions. Being alert to these 'funds of knowledge' (Hedges et al., 2011) enhances educator understanding of individual children in context and enriches practice. Educators can develop strategies and skills to capture social context through small-group observations and documentation that captures the critical social/relational dimension of learning that we now know is so critical for young children.

Considering the early years curriculum

Views and conceptions about early learning are often captured in the values and principles that are provided in curricular or practice frameworks. Traditional early childhood curricula may include the assumption that learning in early childhood is a preparation for future learning. The term preschool reinforces the idea that early learning environments are sites of preparation and this is reflected in policy commitments to ensure that children become 'school ready'. Such assumptions consolidate the unhelpful view of the young learner as a lone individual involved in learning a given set of skills or knowledge. Many authors are critical of this focus on what has been called 'schoolification', centred on the development of future academic skills necessary for primary school success, at the expense of a curriculum and pedagogy respecting the unique nature of early childhood in and of itself. New conceptions about the curriculum recognise that it is in early childhood that children get their first messages about themselves, about what it is to be a learner, about where they fit within a social context and about the expectations and constraints that an environment can place on this. It is also the period where they develop dispositions, consolidate the essential skills and learn the new knowledge that guides them in their learning journey.

Looking at the early childhood curriculum from the point of view of the development of the child raises the question, what should be 'learned'? There are different views on what the purpose of early education is and on what it should emphasise in terms of the learning and development of young children. Many researcher and educators agree that the primary outcome for early education is adaptive learners who are curious, flexible and open to learning opportunities. Research suggests that there are two opposing learning orientations, styles or learning dispositions, that can be found in children as young as 4 or 5 years of age: a learning orientation and a performance orientation (Smiley & Dweck, 1994). *Learning orientation* children strive to increase their competence, to understand or master something, to attempt 'hard' tasks, solve 'difficult' problems and persist despite failure or setback. This has been characterised as a *growth mindset* by Dweck in her later writing (2016). *Performance orientation* children, on the other hand, are less likely to attend to tasks as they strive to gain favourable judgements from others, try to avoid failure and negative judgement of their competence. They are anxious to appear competent to the extent that they avoid harder tasks and difficult problems where the outcome is uncertain. This uncertainty in their own mastery can inhibit their facility, and enjoyment, of learning. Quality early years settings provide sufficient challenge and risk in an enabling environment to encourage young children to develop a learning orientation or disposition rather than the more limiting performance orientation. Realising an enabling curriculum in early years practice requires deliberate, intentional and thoughtful consideration by adults in order to establish a learning climate in which stereotypes are questioned, new challenges are tackled and it is standard practice to risk being wrong.

We have seen in Chapter 2 that it is important to consider fostering dispositions as well as capabilities when seeking to understand the complex process of cognition and adjust curricular aims and pedagogical practice in early education to facilitate the transfer of such learning to new learning contexts. Early education and care can develop and nurture those less definable, soft skills, such as motivation, organisation, inclination and attitude to learning, which appear to facilitate the later emergence of the literacy and numeracy skills and competencies valued by primary education. In attending to these dispositional aspects of learning it is important to provide a context which is meaningful and relevant to the child as learner through interactions and relationships aimed at nurturing the affective dimension of learning within a content-rich context. Research has found this practice approach to be constructive in the present and have a later impact on those skills identified by policy makers as so important to later school success.

Defining what exactly an early year's curriculum is has proven to be quite difficult (Edwards, 2021). It can vary from the highly prescriptive and detailed through to the more general definition given in the influential New Zealand, *Te Whariki* curriculum (New Zealand, 1996/2017) where curriculum is interpreted as 'all the experiences, activities and events, both direct or indirect that occur within the early childhood education setting' (2017, p. 7). In some cases, an approach to early years practice can quickly become characterised as a curriculum. Such is the case with the fluid and emergent curriculum evident in the Reggio Emilia approach (Edwards et al., 2012) where no specific curriculum framework exists. Different curricular approaches to early years provision can reflect polarised views on the aim of such provision with a strong focus on either an academic or a play-based curriculum. As the name suggests, an academic programme is guided by the content of the curriculum and academic learning outcomes. On the other hand, a play-based programme functions in the belief that learning occurs as the result of children's own activity, their play and playful behaviour. The evidence suggests that introducing formal academic or direct instruction in the early years may jeopardise the development of desirable dispositions and there is no compelling evidence that early introduction to academic work guarantees success in school in the long term. On the contrary, there is reason to believe that, because of the dynamic nature of development, the cumulative effects of early introduction to academic work may act against development of desirable learning and thinking dispositions, resulting in performance rather than learning. For instance, while the early introduction of academic work may result in young children developing literacy and numeracy skills it may also inhibit the development of the dispositions to become readers, scientists and utilise mathematics. There is a significant and important difference between being able to read and being disposed to read, being able to listen and having a disposition to listen. Both are interdependent; learning a skill or developing an ability may tend to make one more inclined to engage that skill or ability and, conversely, the disposition to learn about something tends to lead to greater engagement and associated success. There is a concern that early childhood educators who encourage the development of literacy and numeracy skills may, in fact, underestimate the general cognitive abilities of young children and may focus on skills rather than extending and building on children's existing knowledge and willingness to learn. It may be that the expectations such educators have for young children's learning are, in fact, set too low. As we have seen in the previous chapter research supports the fact that young children are capable of developing higher order thinking skills, metacognition and the dispositions to apply this higher order thinking. Cultivating the disposition to apply higher order thinking challenges early educators to consider how best to create learning environments which provide experiences that nurture the affective or emotional dimension of learning and support the development and application of learning dispositions.

The primary problem resulting from the ongoing arguments over curriculum focus, goals and methods is that both sides in the struggle may overlook curriculum and practice that has moved beyond this traditional dichotomy of academic versus play-based. The results of many studies suggest that both sides underemphasise and undervalue a third option, namely, considering an early childhood curriculum and pedagogy that guides learning, is dispositional, affective and academic through addressing and building on children's current interests and the progress of their development. This more integrated approach is distinct from both the direct instruction emphasis on academic learning and future outcomes and the child-centred learning emphasis on children's play and self-initiated learning in the immediate present. This 'third' approach can be called the process approach and its essence is that the curriculum is located within a firm set of pedagogical principles rather than guided by a set prescribed objectives or goals. These pedagogical principles can guide the early childhood educator to respond to children's interests and activities and meet the immediate learning needs of the child. This informed, responsive approach to practice allows the educator to plan for future development and learning in line with an individual child's own interest, experience and developmental level. In addition, it responds to play as the primary activity of early childhood, which can best be understood as a continuum which ranges from free play through to more guided play and beyond (Zosh et al., 2018). In responding to children's play educators direct involvement will vary depending on the circumstances and the context. At the free play end involvement is primarily concerned with creating and maintaining a pleasant, calm, inviting and challenging learning environment. At the guided-play end, however, the educator is more directly involved in the child's play, a subject to which we will return in Chapter 6. Research has found that a 'balanced' early childhood curriculum is found in settings ranked highest in process quality, where a balanced curriculum is one with roughly equal emphasis on play, self-regulation and emerging academic activities (Slot et al., 2017).

Emphasising the dynamic nature of early education, the role of play and the multilayered effect the interactive processes on both the educator and the child has led to a move away from drafting curriculum in the more traditional, prescribed manner of primary and secondary school curricula towards issuing curricular guidance through frameworks. This trend reflects a shift from the more formal, didactic modes of instruction and a loosening up of centrally determined curriculum content. The result is greater attention to a pedagogical style that is child and context sensitive, emphasising the social, experiential and active nature of early learning. This approach is less content bound, a unique feature of early education when compared to later stages of education. While such curricula are less content bound, to be effective and enriching in terms of development and learning, early childhood practice must be content rich. Rather than prescribed content however, the content emerges through the process of relationships and interactions within and around the learning environment. This dynamic, entangled early learning process can present a difficulty when seeking to separate out early childhood pedagogy from curriculum content. They are both central elements of a continuous process where the one depends on the other and it is this that makes early childhood education and care such a unique period of education.

We know, from current evidence, the importance of interactions and reciprocal, respectful relationships to learning and development. The dynamic process approach to early education offers more for children's positive development than either the academic or play focused alone. Research consistently shows that successful early education facilitates the child in active learning in learning environments that are well planned, where staff are well trained, confident and supported in their work. Interpretation has become central to both children and adults as they participate in the process of early education: children interpreting and making sense of the world and adults observing, reflecting on and interpreting children's behaviour to plan on how best to guide their practice. From the pedagogical perspective, quality models of early education are characterised by underpinning principles which present a view of the child as a competent, active partner in the integrated and ongoing process of learning reflecting a strong commitment to developing the social and affective dimensions of learning, as well as the more traditional emphasis on cognitive development. It is important that within this nurturing pedagogy early childhood educators do not ignore skills development or knowledge acquisition. Practice aimed at encouraging the development of learning dispositions and meta-cognitive skills cannot be content free; indeed, it is essential that children's interactions with their environments are challenging and rich in both language and content. This can occur either directly, in terms of the content of social interactions with an adult or advanced peer, or indirectly through the carefully considered provision of materials, objects, activities and opportunities.

Discussions on content, particularly in relation to the older children in early years settings, often come around to a discussion on the importance to children of developing sound literacy and numeracy skills and how to balance this against the value of a play-based early years approach. Research suggests that children, even very young babies, bring a broad prior knowledge to new experiences and learning but educators may underestimate this or be unaware of it. Such prior knowledge can provide a valuable basis from which to extend early language, social and physical development and, later, extend learning in subject areas such as science, technology, maths and literacy. However, to do so effectively educators require confidence that they have a sufficient breadth and depth of personal knowledge and understanding in different knowledge domains. Hedges and Cullen (2005) have argued that there are four themes to consider in high quality early years practice:

knowledge of pedagogy and philosophy,
knowledge of learners,
knowledge of context
subject-content knowledge.

Where educators have confidence in the depth of their knowledge, they are more aware of their own content gaps. In such cases educators are also more confident in acknowledging these gaps and admitting that there are things they too have to learn. In such learning environments, educators are also more likely to welcome children's ideas, contributions and questions. Research is clear that practice which encourages positive dispositions and soft skills provides a more solid foundation for later learning than progammes that overemphasise the development of academic skills. Developing the skills of adaptive learning and learning to learn have positive immediate and long-term benefits when provided in high quality early learning environments with well-informed educators. Too strong an academic emphasis in early childhood practice, even with the older children, has been criticised as being inappropriate for young children with too much emphasis on future outcomes and insufficient attention to the importance of day-to-day experiences, or the natural curriculum, on their actual development. Focusing on principles and the learning opportunities provided by the children and the environment, rather than focusing on externally determined learning outcomes or goals, allows for greater flexibility and responsiveness to the immediate learning context for the child. This makes particular demands on the pedagogical skills and knowledge of the educators to unlock the opportunities for all young children to learn effectively during the early years (Hayes & Filipović, 2017).

Curriculum approaches

In a review of different early childhood education and care curriculum policies the OECD (2001) noted that

when Early Childhood Education and Care focuses primarily on familiarising children with early schooling, there is a risk of downward pressure from a school-based agenda to teach specific skills and knowledge in the early years, especially with regard to literacy and numeracy.

(p. 41)

They go on to point out that it seems that

> if countries choose to adopt a view of the child as full of potential and capable of learning from birth, and a view of childhood as an important stage in its own right, then Early Childhood Education and Care provision can be concerned with both the present and the future.
>
> (p. 43)

Different systems of education are driven by different beliefs and values about early childhood and their early years practices vary accordingly. Variations in curricula reflect the different values and understandings societies have concerning how and what young children learn. These values and beliefs inform the design of curricula, the location and support of services, the role of the educators and the degree of involvement of children in the process. In addition to values and beliefs, theories of child development also inform curriculum development and design and impact on practice. There is an international trend towards reconsidering early years curriculum and practice to ensure that it takes account of child development, cultural and contextual variables and the dynamic interactions that are the essence of early education. This is evidenced by the emergence of national curricular guidelines or frameworks to support early childhood educators.

For instance, the New Zealand curriculum framework, *Te Whariki* (New Zealand, 1996/2017), directs early years practice towards children's well-being, belonging, contribution, communication and exploration. Within defined learning areas the Te Whariki curriculum, for children from birth to 6 years of age, offers guidance in terms of principles and aims. It provides an integrated curriculum characterised by a tapestry, or weave, of increasing complexity and richness. Such an integrated approach also emphasises the importance of considering assessment as pedagogy. This highly regarded curriculum framework was published following a period of extensive collaboration across the widely diverse cultural groups within the early education sector. The principles underpinning the New Zealand curriculum are presented as part of a complex weave of interacting elements, reflecting the diverse cultures and practices found within New Zealand and captured in the title of the curriculum, Te Whariki, which means a weave. The New Zealand principles are brief and state that an early years' curriculum should:

> Empower children with the tools to capitalise on and extend their learning
> Take a holistic approach to learning and development
> Create systematic links to parents and the community and
> Encourage and provide responsive relationships.

These principles are then linked to aims addressing four interacting strands, each with identified goals. The aims are to facilitate (i) the well-being of the children (nurture and protect); (ii) belonging for children and their families; (iii) communication through reciprocal relationships at all levels; and (iv) exploration that recognises active learning as the means for learning, constructing meaning.

While there are a wide variety of programmes run throughout the US the HighScope programme has become internationally recognised as particularly effective. The original HighScope curriculum emerged from one of the earliest intervention programmes, known as the Perry Preschool Project, which was developed to provide quality early education services to children aged 2.5 to 5 years coming from backgrounds of disadvantage. This project forms the basis of an influential longitudinal study, which is still reporting and has found long-lasting social and educational effects sustained over its lifetime. The history of the development and evaluations of the HighScope curriculum can be found at: https://highscope.org/our-practice/preschool-curriculum/. Drawing explicitly on the work of Piaget, Vygotsky and Dewey the following principles guide educators in the HighScope curriculum:

(i) Active learning – through which children construct knowledge that helps them make sense of their world
(ii) Positive adult–child interactions – central to facilitating active learning
(iii) A child-friendly learning environment – organised into specific interest areas containing a wide range of well-labelled materials to support children's interests
(iv) A consistent daily routine, carefully managed and includes the 'Plan-Do-Review' process which enables children to express their intentions, carry them out and reflect on what they have done and
(v) Team-based daily assessment to allow for individualised curricular planning (Hohman & Weikart, 2002).

Within this approach learning is conceptualised as developmental change and is characterised as a complex physical and mental process. The role of the adult is to support children in their learning through observation and interaction. The *'plan-do-review'* method, mentioned in Chapter 2 and developed by the HighScope team, is central to their model of practice and was developed with the intention of facilitating the development of meta-cognitive and cognitive skills.

An influential early educational programme to emerge from Europe is that developed by the Reggio Emilia municipality of Northern Italy (Edwards et al., 2012). It is a publicly supported programme for children from birth to 6 years of age and has become known as the Reggio approach. Developed within the region of Reggio Emilia by Loris Malaguzzi, it acts as a proxy for the type of early education provided throughout Northern Italy and, to some extent, throughout Italy as a whole (Cagliari et al., 2016). Services offer full provision to young children in specially designed settings and are staffed by multidisciplinary teams. Children are grouped in mixed age groups with a key teacher for the entire period they are in the setting and there is close liaison between the early education, families, the primary school system and the wider community.

In keeping with the dynamic, integrated and interactionist approach to young children learning evident in the Reggio Emilia approach it is not easy to find a list of principles underpinning their 'emergent curriculum'. However, in talking about the way in which the curriculum for early education emerges within the social constructivist tradition of development Rinaldi (2012) makes the point that the primary principle guiding the work of Reggio Emilia is the image of the child:

> The cornerstone of our experience, based on practice, theory and research, is the image of the children as rich, strong and powerful. The emphasis is placed on seeing the children as unique subjects with rights rather than simply needs. They have potential, plasticity, the desire to grow, curiosity, the ability to be amazed and the desire to relate to other people and to communicate.
>
> (p. 102)

In addition, the Reggio approach explicitly include the environment as the third teacher in the pedagogical system alongside the educator and the child. For details see: https://www.reggiochildren.it/en/reggio-emilia-approach/.

Content and the early years curriculum

It is difficult to isolate the content of the *Te Whariki* curriculum framework as it is holistic, integrated and embedded within the principles and outlined in terms of short term, empowering learning outcomes. The learning outcomes describe various skills, knowledge and attitudes recommended for children as they develop through the early childhood period. The framework offers guidance on how the outcomes link into essential skills and essential learning areas. Given the holistic nature of the underpinning philosophy guiding the curriculum, the weave is crafted as a whole rather than being unravelled into specific aims, objectives and outcomes (New Zealand, 1996/2017). The early years educator is challenged to draw together the various strands of talents and dispositions of the young child with the agreed areas of learning within a context that reflects the principles identified as central to a culturally authentic curriculum. The four guiding principles reflect a view that early years practice should respond to the culturally complex and context-sensitive nature of development and the interactive nature of learning within and across contexts. The curriculum is designed to be empowering, holistic, transactional and ecological. In practice the learning and assessment of learning are integrated into the overall pedagogy with teachers documenting development, assessing its meaning and deriving curricular guidance from reflecting on their engagement with the children and their evaluation of the considerable and varied documentation maintained.

It is in New Zealand that the concept of learning dispositions in early education has been most extensively elaborated and researched. Certain learning dispositions have been linked directly to elements of the *Te Whariki* curricular framework. These include the dispositions of:

courage and curiosity to find something of interest here in the learning community
(Curriculum Strand – Belonging)

trust that this is a safe place to be involved, focusing ones attention, and encouraging the playfulness that often follows from deep involvement over a period of time
(Curriculum Strand – Well-being)

perseverance to persist with difficulty or uncertainty
(Curriculum Strand – Exploration)

confidence to express an idea or a point of view
(Curriculum Strand – Communication)

responsibility for justice and fairness and the disposition to take on another point of view (Curriculum Strand – Contribution)
(Carr, 1998, p. 4)

In contrast to the weave described above the content of the *HighScope* curriculum is presented in the form of fifty 'key experiences' or statements describing the social, cognitive and physical development of children. There are two distinct curriculum manuals – one for infant and toddlers and one for preschool children between the ages of 2.5 and 5 years. The 'key experiences' are modified to meet the developmental level of each age group and are grouped under topic headings which reflect their Piagetian origin: creative representation; language and literacy; initiative and social relations; movement; music; classification; seriation; number; space and time. The programme emphasises the importance of interactions and the task of the adult is to provide a safe and attractive environment in which these key experiences can occur, to recognise and support them and then to build on them with the child. The learning environment is an important part of the *HighScope* programme and is designed to elicit independent activity from the children. In rooms for the infant–toddler group the space is organised into play and care areas which, reflecting the Piagetian influence, contain a variety of sensorimotor materials to encourage the babies to explore and play. The programme for older children also pays close attention to the environment which is organised into different play areas and labelled to encourage independent learning. The daily routine is seen as an important part of *HighScope* curriculum planning. It provides a balance of experiences and learning opportunities and involves both individual and group activities. The most important part of the daily routine is the '*plan-do-review*' activity where each child plans what they will do, has the opportunity to carry out their plan and, later, has the opportunity to discuss their plan and the outcome of the activity/play with the educator. The intention behind this daily routine is to encourage and strengthen the higher order thinking necessary to the development of the executive function, fundamental to later school success.

There is no written curriculum for early education in Reggio Emilia. Rather the focus of attention is on projects and activities, which act as the content around which early experiences are designed and extended. In the early years settings of Reggio Emilia where children are educated together from birth to age 6, they refer to the 'hundred languages of children' meaning all the different ways in which children can communicate and through which they can express themselves (Edwards et al., 2012). Children do not spend time in formal classes developing literacy or numeracy skills. Rather, the interest and curiosity of the children are used by the educators as a key to their learning and from which skills and knowledge arise. The processes of exploration, experimentation, discovery, representation, transformation, interpretation, creation and evaluation are foregrounded for attention and expression by the educators, mostly through the use of project work through the arts. In order for educators to be able to respond helpfully to the children they build in opportunities for reflection and maintain rigorous quantities of documentation that they use as a basis for their reflection, a form of continuing professional development. Practice decisions are made, not on the basis of a prescribed curriculum, but on the basis of evidence and experiences drawn from careful analysis of the learning environment and children's actions.

The important content of the Reggio Emilia approach is not the content of the curriculum but the content of the relationship. The content is not focused on routine and management but on the work in hand. Shared activities are considered something that is valuable to both children and adults. The benefits of this approach are the active engagement of children in the learning process and the active, collaborative engagement of the adult in teaching for learning. The content, to all intents and purposes, is the 'proximal processes' that are crucial to the development of generative dispositions in the child. The educator's role is key as there is no prescribed content but rather that which emerges from the task which becomes a shared curriculum where, for instance a problem has to be identified and then solved. This approach allows for rich developments in skills and knowledge in a dispositional milieu which is encouraging learning dispositions meeting the values of the community.

In reflecting on the pedagogy of the Reggio approach Katz notes the importance of creating a sense of belonging, of relationship, in young children and points to the rich content that such relationships can have. For relationships to be effective they must be about something, to allow for engagement by the child and the adult and to allow for feedback and for guidance. Katz suggests six lessons for practice to be learnt from Reggio:

1. Children and educators together examine topics of mutual interest in depth and detail and using a variety of media and approaches
2. When children are engaged in this way they attend to their work with great care. The work is a form of documentation of the process of their learning which they evaluate as well as the adults
3. Early introduction of observational and representational skills does not deter their creativity
4. The work in the projects provides rich content for the educator–child interactions
5. Many features of the adult's behaviour convey to the children that all aspects of their work are taken seriously
6. The driving force behind the principles for the programme is community/ family rather than corporate (1995, pp. 36, 37).

One of the most striking features of the Reggio approach is the willingness of the educators to learn, not just from each other, but from the children as well. Reggio practice is not based on the notion of teaching as applied child development; it demands of educators a clear understanding of the interests that children have, what children are doing, what is being offered as their learning environment, materials, interactions and context. Practice is not the application of a curriculum within a particular pedagogical formula; it is responsive and fluid and acts as the basis for unlocking the emergent curriculum. While there has been a lot of international interest in the Reggio approach, with many authors writing extensively about the principles and practice, it cannot simply be transposed to another country without adapting it appropriately to that culture.

Early years quality and curriculum in Ireland

Historically in Ireland early childhood settings evolved in an *ad hoc* manner and varied greatly in curriculum approaches. With the expansion of the field and growing attention to early childhood as a key period of learning and development attention has been drawn to the needs and rights of young children and to what constitutes effective high-quality early years practice. Arising from this, two practice frameworks were developed and used together, they have enhanced practice in early years settings. The quality framework, *Síolta* (CECDE, 2006) and the curriculum framework *Aistear* (NCCA, 2009a) were originally published as separate documents. However, in combination the frameworks act as a basis from which to review setting practice, enhance knowledge and skills, maintain and sustain quality and monitor and evaluate progress. The NCCA published a short report on the similarities and differences between *Aistear* and *Síolta* concluding that the frameworks were 'important milestones in early childhood care and education' which if used together 'present significant potential to support the development of practice for all adults who care for and educate children from birth to six in Ireland' (NCCA, 2009b, p. 15). The report goes on to point out that *Aistear* can be used to support all the *Síolta* standards but 'it gives particular support in the case of standards related to the rights of the child, environments, parents and families, interactions, play, curriculum and identity and belonging' (2009b, p. 11)

While the frameworks focus on two different aspects of practice, quality and curriculum, together they can inform and expand our understanding of how to enrich and sustain quality early years practice. Both frameworks are underpinned by key principles or core beliefs about early childhood and young children derived from consultation with early childhood educators and wider interested parties. They present the vision or philosophy for guiding quality curriculum and pedagogical planning and development. They are *complementary* in that both were striving, through their different focus, to guide early childhood educators in providing high-quality learning experiences for children. Both frameworks were developed for children from birth to age 6 and sufficiently broad to be applied in any early learning setting from the home through to the infant classes of the primary school. In addition, this age range is subdivided into the same bands within both frameworks: babies of birth–18 months; toddlers of 12–36 months and young children of 2.5–6 years. It is an important aspect of *Aistear* that the age bands used to frame the curriculum are overlapping. It reflects a move away from the more traditional 'ages and stages' approach of the primary school curriculum towards explicitly recognising and responding to the dynamic nature of development present in each individual child. Realising the potential of both frameworks in early years settings is best approached if the frameworks are considered together in the context of the day-to-day early years practice. They have now been merged online as the *Aistear Siolta Practice Guide* [https://www.aistearsiolta.ie/en/introduction/] and this integrated guide is regularly updated with interviews on current issues of relevance to quality practice, videos of best practice and many resources for use in both indoor and outdoor early learning environment and it provides useful resources whether you are working with babies, toddlers or older children. The frameworks can be used as part of the daily routine, as the basis for planning the learning environments, creating content- and language-rich spaces, providing a safe, risk-rich environment and as the context for posing questions to the children, yourself, those you work with and those you come in contact with.

At the time of writing the National Council for Curriculum and Assessment [NCCA] is in the process of reviewing the *Aistear* framework. Building on existing *Aistear* material the review also refers to the *Síolta* frameworks recognising that 'many of *Síolta's* standards relate to curriculum and the frameworks are interconnected' (NCCA, 2021, p. 5). The rationale for the review is to reflect on and respond to the considerable policy, curriculum and pedagogical changes in the early childhood education and care that have occurred over the years since the original publication in 2009. However, the review is not intended to be a major revision but rather 'an opportunity to re-vitalise and re-invigorate interest in, appreciation for and use of the framework to enhance children's experiences in early childhood' (NCCA, 2021, p. 3).

Both national and international research underpin the integrated *Aistear Síolta Practice Guide*. In developing the original iteration of *Aistear*, the NCCA commissioned four background research papers to inform the development of the framework. In addition to considering national and international research, the frameworks also reflect the detailed consultation with the sector that was undertaken. This process of reviewing national and international research and consultation continues in the current review of the *Aistear* curriculum framework. In addition, a background paper has been prepared, which presents current evidence and thinking on issues of curriculum and pedagogy (French & McKenna, 2022). The research and consultation reports can be accessed through the NCCA website at www.ncca.ie.

Aistear is informed by an understanding of early childhood which considers children to be competent and confident learners and through four interconnected themes it provided a 'a key resource in ensuring children in early

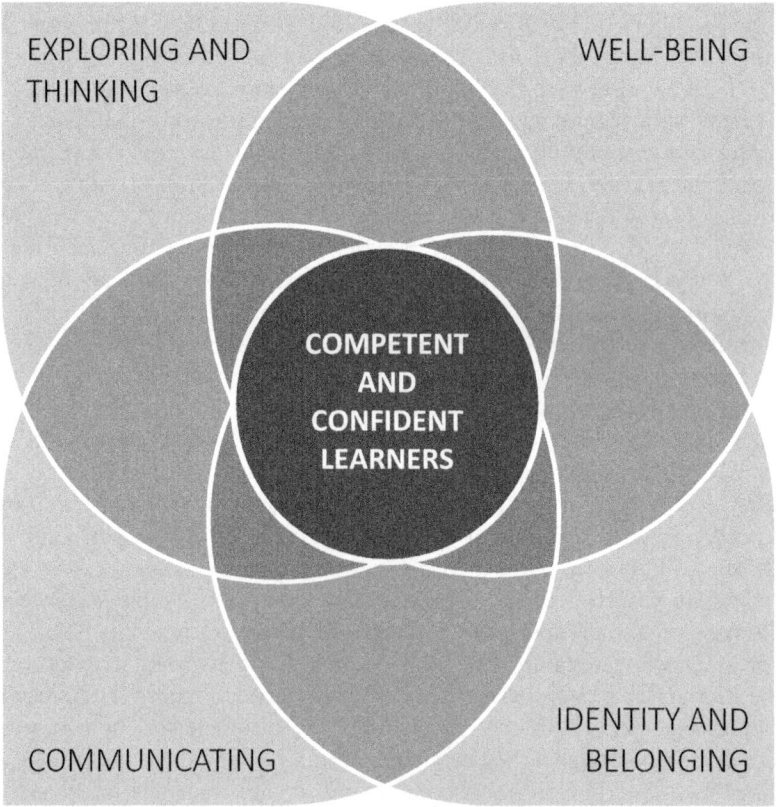

Figure 3.1 Aistear curriculum themes

childhood settings are given rich and varied experiences to support and progress their learning and development' (Daly & Forster, 2012, p. 103). The original framework described children's early learning and development in terms of these four themes and clearly influenced by the original *Te Whariki* curriculum. The revised document will maintain this focus (NCCA, 2021) and the graphic above outlines the way in which the themes relate to the overall development of the child

The first theme, *well-being*, considers how children develop to be happy, healthy and confident; *identity and belonging* is the second theme and this explores how children form a positive identity of themselves in the world and how they evolve a strong and healthy sense of belonging to that world; the third theme is that of *communicating*. This theme is concerned with understanding how children share their experiences, feeling, fears, ideas and thoughts to others and how this extends and expands over time. The final theme is *exploring and thinking* and considers how children make sense of their world and the objects and people in it. It is concerned with how children play, interact, investigate, question and test out their ideas.

Translate themes into quality practice requires educators to explore and come to understand the importance of these themes to children's development and learning and to contextualise them within their working context. To facilitate this the original *Aistear* material identified four headings to guide practice. While these guidelines are likely to be updated in line with contemporary knowledge and understandings, they remain valuable guidance points for an informed nurturing pedagogy. They capture the overarching elements of the context within which to address the four main themes and they are considered in more detail.

Building partnerships between parents and educators
Learning and developing through interactions
Learning and developing through play
Supporting learning and development through assessment.

Building partnerships between parents and educators: At its most ordinary this is about the way we work together, with our adult colleagues, the children and their families. It involves recognising and respecting differences of culture, opinion and values. It requires us to be responsible and respectful in our dealings with others. For quality practice it is important to balance professional understandings with sensitivity to individual situations and to other professional roles. As Ireland becomes more diverse there are opportunities to actively include parents and family members from different cultural and linguistic background into setting practice and enrich cross cultural connections. Increasingly diverse early childhood settings provide opportunities for extending children's knowledge and understanding of the world and their place in it. With new cultures come new languages and language may be perceived as a barrier. While it may be a challenge for early childhood practice there are many ways in which educators can be assisted, not least through involving parents with different linguistic experiences at different levels in the setting. In addition, there are excellent resources to assist educators in making connections across linguistic barriers developed by Mother Tongues, an organisation established in Ireland in response to our increasingly diverse and multicultural society. Materials and information can be access at: https://mothertongues.ie.

We also know from research that one of the most important influences on children's early learning and development is the quality of the home learning environment [HLE] (Toth et al., 2020). Early educators have a particularly rich opportunity to influence the quality of the HLE through talking with parents about the interests of their children, through modelling practices and providing ideas about how to meet these interests in the home. Many parents of young children, particularly new parents, welcome suggestions about books, examples of simple activities, inclusion in events in the early years setting and links to information, seminars or talks on child development, learning or health and anything that may be of relevance to them and their children. This places quite a responsibility on those working in the field in a trusted position that needs to be cultivated in the best interests of the child. Early childhood educators play a pivotal role in the developmental trajectory of children and are often the first to notice changes in circumstances and may often be in a position to identify and intervene early in a difficulty to the benefit of all. Research suggests that parents are comfortable talking with and listening to early educators in a way they may not be with other professionals. They recognise their shared interest in the child, and they are, in the main, willing to hear about how their child is developing and learning. For this reason, educators need to be thoughtful and careful in how they approach sensitive issues around a child's development. Linking in with other, related professionals is also important when addressing specific needs of a child. However, not all professionals recognise the uniquely powerful role of the early childhood educator and for this reason, among others, it is valuable to cultivate and sustain working relationships with other professionals and community leaders.

Learning and developing through interactions: One point of common agreement among those researching and working in the early years is the critical role of meaningful relationships and interactions, not only for influencing the development of young children but also for the professional satisfaction of early childhood educators themselves. From a theoretical perspective we have seen that Bronfenbrenner has, in his bio-ecological model of human development, identified these interactions, which he called *proximal processes*, as the engines of development (Hayes et al., 2023). The daily activities of an early years setting, whatever it might be, form the context within which development and learning is occurring. The nature of the interactions depends on a number of features associated with the people and the environments they come from and those they share. To be effective interactions need attention and reflection and they must occur on a fairly regular basis over an extended period of time. Time can be seen in terms of its extension over an extended period and this allows for forward planning for individual children but also for the early childhood setting itself. However, of perhaps more relevance to early childhood practice is the power of thinking of time in terms of the moment, the immediate now. This view of time of the present nature of time can give meaning and importance to interactions, conversation or activities as they happen, in the process. Time is something that the educator can factor in when planning their practice or responding to an activity: it is with time that young children find the space to really explore their environment, express their concerns, show their delight and solve the exciting problems that the world and those in it present. For the early childhood educators, it is enriching to recognise the treasure that time is to young children, to be prepared to allow for time in the daily routine in such a way that all children gain benefit. The importance of relationship and of time are often captured in the literature by reference to slow, relational pedagogy with babies and toddlers (French, 2021) and the wider concept of nurturing pedagogy which underpins *Aistear* (Hayes, 2007).

Learning and developing through play: Irrespective of how one chooses to define play or seek to find its meaning there is general agreement that the developing child needs the opportunities, both indoors and outdoors, to be active and playful. Play comes in many shapes, which include play that is adventurous, risky, communicative, solitary, enjoyable, involved, meaningful, sociable, interactive, physical, symbolic, therapeutic and voluntary. It is through play that children create meaning and develop their understanding of the world and their place in it. It is also through play that they acquire and strengthen, among other things, their ability to share, to negotiate, to take turns, to self-regulate, to direct their curiosity, to handle emotions, to manage their behaviour and to behave according to the requirements of a situation or a particular context. Play is also a process through which educators can gain insight into the development and learning of individual children as individuals but also as group members. The unique role of play in early childhood curriculum and pedagogy is addressed in more detail in Chapter 6.

Supporting learning and development through assessment: We make judgements or assess all the time, about all sorts of things even when we may not recognise it. For the early childhood educators, it is the mechanism we use to make decisions that inform our practice, planning and responses. In *Aistear* assessment is defined as 'the on-going process of collecting, documenting, reflecting on and using information to develop rich portraits of children as learners in order to support and enhance their . . . learning' (NCCA, 2009c, p. 72). It is difficult to assess development. Assessment is a way of doing things. In keeping with quality reflective practice, it is useful to stop yourself from time to time to see what judgement motivated a particular action or planning decision. When considering assessment, it is useful to approach it as either 'assessment for learning' or 'assessment of learning'. The former, assessment for learning, is more common in practice with younger children. It informs the style of practice that nurtures and supports learning, it enhances planning for individual children but also for the group. Assessment of learning

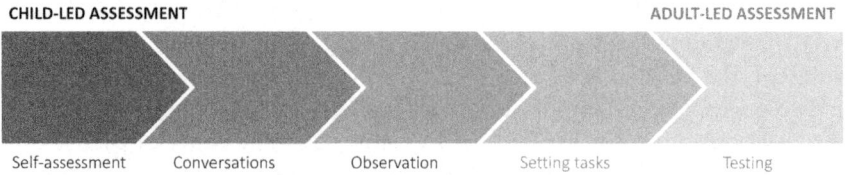

CHILD-LED ASSESSMENT   ADULT-LED ASSESSMENT

Self-assessment   Conversations   Observation   Setting tasks   Testing

Figure 3.2 Forms of assessment

is the process we use for measuring what children know. In the early years this aspect of assessment may have limited value although it can be helpful if there is a particular cause for concern and you want to develop an understanding of the child's normative development to inform planning for practice or intervention. Early childhood literature on assessment recommends a continuum of assessment methods to assist educators in reviewing and considering their practice. The methods range from child-led self-assessment through observation on to more adult led assessment as illustrated in Figure 3.2. In keeping with our understanding of early learning as a dynamic process which provides rich insights into learning within the day-to-day and the ordinary, most assessment occurs to the left side of the figure with observation having a central role. It is only in very rare situations that one would use either task based assessment or testing in an early childhood setting.

One of the most influential assessment systems to emerge in early childhood is the Learning Story Approach, developed in New Zealand in response to the demands of the *Te Whāriki* curriculum framework. In an effort to respect the process nature of early childhood education and care, for both educators and children, Learning Stories were devised as a way in which educators can document children's learning over time in collaboration with children and their families (Carr & Lee, 2019). Episodes from day-to-day activities and events are recorded in writing and interpreted to identify the learning opportunities and the pedagogical implications. Learning Stories are often accompanied by photographs or drawings which make visible children's learning dispositions and styles over time, they show the connection between new learning and earlier examples of learning and provide a context and guidance for further child learning and educator support. They also have a role in giving visibility to the children who collaborate in the documentation, they see that they are valued and this contributes to their sense of belonging.

The value and effectiveness of Learning Stories in assessment depends on the expertise, skills and knowledge of the educator and some studies suggests that, without full appreciation of the approach, their potential my only be partially achieved. To gain the maximum benefit from using Learning Stories as a form of pedagogical documentation Carr and Lee (2019) characterise the educator contribution as a journey in practice and suggest that information that may contribute to a Learning Story is, in fact gathered by educators across

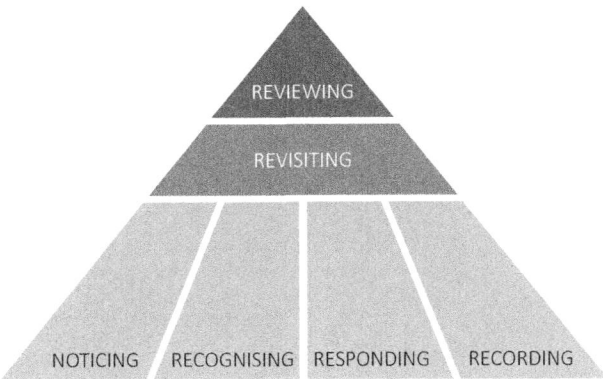

Figure 3.3 Analysising pedagogical documentation

a period of time. Carr and Lee (2019, p. 157) suggest that educators, through what they call 'a progressive filter', are data gathering as part of daily practice. It is through this practice that material for documentation is identified and, where relevant, used in Learning Stories. The process involves the following steps and is illustrated in Figure 3.3:

Noticing a particular behaviour, activity in passing
Recognising that it is something of note for that particular child
Responding to it with a smile, a nod of recognition
Recording some of these remembered events in a child's Learning Story
Revisiting the story with the child, their parents or alone
Reviewing the Learning Story as part of an assessment for or of learning.

Gathering materials for reflection and consideration assists the quality of the assessment and judgement you make of the children you work with. It is in this thoughtful and informed way of attuned practice, collaborative recording and measured revision that the pedagogical value of the Learning Story and other pedagogical materials can be unlocked. This is further enhanced if these reflections occur in the context of a critical friend or the team you work with. Procedures can be put in place to allow for collecting data, documenting processes or progress, reflecting on materials and using the findings from reflection and discussion to inform further practices.

This chapter has reflected on way in which we can enhance quality practice. Drawing on different curriculum frameworks and programmes it has highlighted the way in which the values and principles can inform the direction of curriculum guidance and, in turn impact on the practice style and focus of the early childhood educator. Drawing specifically on the *Aistear* framework the chapter ends with some specific practice guidance to give a broad overview of the key issues to consider when reflecting on early childhood practice. The next two chapters take six themes that can be seen explicitly or implicitly in many curriculum frameworks across early childhood education and care. Chapter 4 examines the themes of Well-being, Identity and Belonging and Chapter 5 looks into the themes of Communicating, Exploring and Thinking.

4 Well-being, identity and belonging

Introduction

In this chapter we consider the concepts of well-being, identity and belonging, three themes included in the *Aistear* curriculum framework. In bringing together these three themes we foreground their interconnectivity and influence on children, particularly on the socio-emotional aspects of development. Research has shown that 'the experiences of belonging are important for children's agency, development, evolving identities, and their overall well-being' (Johansson & Puroila, 2021, p. 1). Within the chapter we look in detail at each of the individual themes and their particular contribution to children's learning and development. We review the various different practice approaches that can support and enhance children's well-being, including the role of nature and a calm learning environment, strengthen their sense of belonging in inclusive early childhood settings and secure connectivity with the home learning environment and, in this multilingual, multicultural society how we can respectfully make visible children's individual and cultural identity.

Well-being

The concept of well-being and children's well-being in particular has emerged as an important policy item nationally and internationally and is an accepted ambition in many early childhood curriculum frameworks. Kickbusch (2012) argues that 'children's well-being must be introduced as a central building block . . . not only as an investment in future adults but as a pledge to the children of today' (p. 13) and considers children's well-being 'a key dimension of sustainable development and social resilience; it is about our present and our future' (p. 9). This latter point has particular relevance and resonance as we emerge from a global pandemic and leaders internationally are addressing issues of sustainability and the health of populations and the planet. While seeking the global improvement of children's well-being requires a significant shift in political priorities there is potential at a local level for early years settings to play an important and immediate role in respect to the well-being of children from the earliest age. In a review of the literature on well-being and

DOI: 10.4324/9781003353164-4

early childhood Lewis (2019) points out that while there are many different ways to think about well-being in the early years there are certain factors that are acknowledged as part of well-being including general happiness, contentment and flourishing.

Kickbusch identifies three reasons for action on children's well-being:

- *Children's well-being* is about supporting a happy, secure and flourishing childhood, a value in its own right
- *Children's well-being* is about the moral imperative of social justice and equitable life chances, it contributes to a better and more just society and to well-being for all
- *Children's well-being* is about our present and our future, as individuals and as societies. It supports long term social and economic development. It promotes life-long physical, emotional, mental and spiritual health, what some define as the development of the whole child (2012, p. 13).

Relating well-being to the whole child perspective reflects an important Irish policy commitment, first outlined in the National Strategy for Children (Government of Ireland, 2000) but carried through much of contemporary child policy, which places 'the "whole child" . . . at the centre of policy development and service delivery' (p. 10). The 'whole child' perspective recognises the complexity of children's development, the critical role of context and culture and the reality that children actively shape the world around them, contributing to it through their and engagement with the people, objects and ideas that contribute to their ongoing development. We know from research and practice that the process of learning and the contexts within which it is facilitated enhance a child's sense of mastery and capabilities thus strengthening the child's sense of well-being. One of the key components to providing for well-being in the early years is the quality of early years practice. In a review of quality early childhood provision for children under two years of age Dalli et al. (2011) noted that research 'at the interface of neurobiological and developmental psychology, suggests that responsive attuned caregiving within stable relationships is the type of caregiving that facilitates both emotional and cognitive well-being, and thus learning' (p. 51).

Settings can support children's well-being through providing safe and secure environments of learning where the four pillars of education as defined by UNESCO (Delors, 1996) – *learning to know, learning to do, learning to live together and learning to be* – can be provided for in a responsive and reflective way. This provides the basis for a democratic early years practice which respects children's rights and facilitates meaningful participation in the early learning environment. To achieve such practice Zanatta and Long (2021) argue that educators must move away from merely protecting children's rights in practice and take on the role of advocates for children's rights also. Such rights-based practices lay the foundation for a pedagogy that encourages an atmosphere of caring, empathy and respect, fundamental to social justice and democracy.

UNICEF has identified well-being as a key to the realisation of children's rights (2007) and most discussions of well-being emphasise that the quality of relationships is a central component of well-being, particularly so in relation to children. However, it is difficult to define well-being; it is a concept that has a plurality of understandings reflecting different perspectives at different times and in different contexts. In considering well-being in general the Department of Education and Skills (2019) proposes the following definition: 'Wellbeing is present when a person realises their potential, is resilient in dealing with the normal stresses of their life, takes care of their physical wellbeing and has a sense of purpose, connection and belonging to a wider community' (p. 10). It is a fluid way of being and needs nurturing throughout life. Broadly speaking well-being is characterised objectively by the absence of distress and the presence of a sense of happiness, of content. Well-being also has a strong subjective dimension, how we feel about ourselves and/or our lives contributes to our overall well-being.

Well-being is not a fixed trait but derives as a result of the dynamic interaction between the characteristics and capabilities of the individual and multiple contextual factors. This ecological understanding of children's developing well-being is best realised in practice that facilitates opportunities for children to actively engage with people, objects, materials and symbols, enables them to exercise their democratic rights through being heard and allows them participate, insofar as they can, in planning and reviewing decisions that impact on them and their experiences. Such a connected whole child-in-context approach to children's well-being requires attention to the careful inclusion of children's views. The extent to which practice can include children's views will vary with babies of 6 months requiring a different approach to that of a 3- or 6-year-old. Nonetheless, awareness of the need to think about this and discuss with colleagues how this might be achieved will increase the likelihood that children's voices will be heard more widely and meaningfully in early years settings. Based on the understanding that all children are competent and that they co-construct meaning through their play and other activities Clark (2017) has developed an extensive literature on the application of the Mosaic Approach to engaging with young children. She describes it as a multi-method approach involving talking, child-led tours of the early childhood settings, interviews, drawing and photography by children, with children reviewing their images and listening through multiple means of communication, including verbal communication, body language, drawings and photography by children. This approach unlocks the possibilities of using arts to enhance the development of self-worth and strengthen well-being. Through the arts children experience wonder and delight and through exploring with different media they fuel their imagination and their play (Hayes et al., 2017; McCabe & Flannery, 2022).

In the introduction to the theme of well-being in the original *Aistear* framework (NCCA, 2009a) the distinction is drawn between psychological well-being (feeling and thinking) and physical well-being (health and mental health). 'Children . . . become positive about themselves and their learning when adults value them for who they are when they promote warm and supportive relationships with them' (p. 16). Well-being fosters a positive outlook and is important for overall development and learning precisely because it gives children a sense of their own importance and helps them appreciate that they have control over their own lives, development and learning. A central point in this approach is the recognition that one's sense of well-being is critically influenced by the context within which it develops and the feedback received. For instance, in environments that are critical, unsupportive or impatient with children it is difficult for them to attain either psychological or physical well-being; indeed, children in such environments may come to feel stressed, anxious and unloved. From such a perspective it is difficult for children to become excited by possibilities, or curious to explore the environment and learn more about the world and their place in it. Adults play a key role in providing a truly rich, stimulating and secure environment guiding children towards 'being flexible and having a positive outlook on learning and on life . . . [and] . . . to become resilient and resourceful and to learn to cope with change and situations in which things go wrong' (p. 16). Positive well-being is the basis of mastery, of that sense one has of a certain degree of control over things, a willingness to try without an unrealistic fear of failure. Such a sense of well-being provides a good place within which to grow and learn.

We know from research with schoolchildren that a majority of Irish children and young people consider themselves to be happy and healthy (UNICEF, 2021). This finding echoes a national study on children's observations of well-being which suggests that, despite discrete differences across age and gender, there is a common understanding of well-being (Nic Gabhainn & Sixsmith, 2005). The study showed that children understood the complexity of well-being and the various factors impacting on it. Not unexpectedly, interpersonal relationships were found to be central to children's understanding and sense of well-being along with the value they place on actively doing things. At all different phases of the study the participating children discussed 'how relationships (with people and animals) and the activities within or context of those relationships gave them a sense of belonging, being safe, loved, valued and being cared for' (2005, p. 64). This reflects an explanation of well-being that captures feeling good: being happy and able to live life to the full. The focus of responses on animals and places as well as people illustrates the extent to which children interact with the natural world around them as well as the interpersonal. It also broadens our understanding of the impact of interactions to include interactions with objects and materials as well as animals and people.

We know less about the understandings very young children have of well-being because it is difficult to access their views on such an abstract concept. Taking a lead from the voice of children reported previously we can, however, identify what makes young children happy and content and able to live life to the full. This can guide us in creating situations to allow them to illustrate this in their own way. In an effort to access the views of very young children on this abstract topic a study was carried out for the organisation Start Strong in

2011. Called 'If I had a Magic Wand' the project worked with a number of early years settings to unlock the wishes of young children. They recorded the findings through compiling a selection of the drawings made to illustrate the wishes and recording the words of a sample of the children which captured the main themes. The book derived from the project can be accessed in e-book form at https://issuu.com/startstrongireland/docs/if_i_had_a_magic_wand

Not surprisingly this study found that it is the simple things that children wish for, that make them happy. It also found that children enjoyed being in early years settings. Some of the key themes to emerge from children's ideas and images included:

> *The value children place on being able to shape their own daily activities*
> *The centrality of play in young children's lives*
> *The importance of opportunities for children's creativity and imagination*
> *Young children's wish to be outdoors and engage in physical activities*
> *The pleasure and interest for young children in being with animals*
> *The importance to children of having their families around them*
>
> (2011, pp. 6, 7)

These findings offer us advice on how best to support children and create environments that are conducive to happiness and positive development. They highlight the value that children place on their own active role in making their wishes come true, their attention to play, the importance of the outdoors and of relationships. And we know from research that all these factors contribute to the well-being of children and can be linked to a basic human flourishing. It is interesting to observe how closely children's wishes and dreams reflect the four necessary elements to flourishing that Gaffney (2011) has identified. In the first instance we need *challenge*; some call or demand on us to do something, to get over an obstacle, to engage with some life task, to make something happen. We also need c*onnectivity* – that is being attuned or connected to what is happening inside us but also outside of us. Connectivity orients us to the challenges and opportunities and prepares us to deal with them. *Autonomy*, where we feel free to move and to act in pursuit of a particular challenge, is the third element. This gives us the energy to get going and sets the direction of our task. Finally, we need to *use our valued competencies*; we need the experience of using our talents, especially the strengths we most value in ourselves.

In order to nurture and support children and their well-being we need to assist to develop flexibility, self-control and self-regulation while also encouraging their curiosity, exploration and creativity. We know from research that this happens best in high quality environments where educators are confident and knowledgeable, where practices are well informed and relaxed and children are supported, safe and healthy. This research knowledge has guided a curricular vision in which all young children are afforded equity of access to early education opportunities that enrich their lives and contribute positively to their optimal well-being, learning and development. This vision can be seen in *Aistear* which points out that children 'need to feel valued, respected, empowered, cared for and included' (NCCA, 2009a, p. 6). The importance of relationships and interactions to children's well-being cannot be overstated. Children can develop well if they are in close relationships with adults and other children who love, value, respect and care for them, even in the absence of much of the materials we associate with early years practice. The socio-personal context is empowering and inclusive and assists children in strengthening their sense of self-worth and giving them a sense of mastery – so critical to later skills and success.

For the educator to be an effective support and model for children it is important to be actively present in all engagements with them, as individuals and as part of a group. A relational nurturing pedagogy with babies is exemplified in educators who are emotionally connected to the baby and develop consistent, and thus trusting relationships. Being present with babies includes being available to touch them and sooth them with song and conversation. Touch has been found to have a calming effect on babies and contributes to lowering stress and enhancing development and many settings use baby massage as a standard practice (Svinth, 2018; French, 2019). Babies flourish where educators care in a calm manner that allows them to explore with all their senses to smell, taste, hear, see, touch and grasp the world they are exploring. Good quality settings commit time to encouraging babies to do things for themselves, strengthening their initiative and positive dispositions to learning.

Being present with children does not mean always doing things with them or organising activities for them but neither is it sufficient to simply 'be there'! Rather being present means being alert, attuned, vigilant, aware and engaged in the process of early years practice. It means that while engaged in early years practice, we should attend to the 'now', recognise that this moment is the present moment, the moment in which we should be present rather than planning what we are going to do at future moments. It is in their presence that educators support children's emotional well-being. Quality early childhood practice exhibits adaptability and flexibility and a readiness to catch the learning moments as they come along. Educators should also model in practice those characteristics they want to see developing in young children such as compassion, kindness, resilience, resourcefulness, coping strategies for change, resolutions when things go wrong. We all develop and sustain our own self-image through our understanding of how others see us and value us and to children the adults in their world are the key models from whom to learn and the primary source of influential feedback.

In addition to relationships and the particularly powerful influence of the adult on emotional well-being one must consider children's physical well-being. In this regard the environment itself, both indoor and outdoor, becomes a crucial element to examine. The environment plays an important role as children need and want the opportunities to experience challenge and risk in an unobtrusively safe environment (Start Strong, 2011). Enabling environments can take many different forms and will depend on the age of the child, the type of setting and the particularities of any given day. In addition, they must also be healthy and safe for all those present and balancing environments that meet the safety and health requirements of babies as well as the toddlers and young children, who delight in walking, running around and taking risks, requires careful thought.

Aistear points out that '[P]hysical well-being is important for learning and development as this enables children to explore, to investigate, and to challenge themselves in the environment' (NCCA, 2009a, p. 16). In a study of children's physical activities in early childhood setting Tonge et al. (2020) found that children were more likely to be physically active in settings that allowed free access to both indoor and outdoor environments and where movement, physical activity and exploration were encouraged. With growing concerns about children's lack of access to outdoor play facilities, their disconnect to nature and the risks associated with physical play Kernan (2014) advises on the need to design outdoor learning environments to maximise the affordances, the opportunities provided to children in their play spaces. Not only does outdoor play facilitate the development of physical skills it also acts as an 'enabling environment for language development and creativity, particularly for boys, where the vocabulary used outdoors was seen as more expressive and wider ranging than that used in indoor and static learning contexts' (Pascal et al., 2019, p. 45). The importance of opportunities to access the outdoors and nature was particularly evident during the COVID-19 pandemic and its value in many aspects of development, including children's sense of well-being, has been widely reported. However, realising that contact with nature impacts on children's development and well-being is not new. Indeed, it has been supported by education scholars as far back as Froebel who conceived of the Kindergarten [children's garden] as a specially designed space where young children could play. A contemporary response to improving children's access to nature and the benefits from being in the outdoors can be seen in the rise of interest in Forest Schools. Originally established in Scandinavia in the 1980s they began to spread so that there are now Forest Schools in many countries including Ireland, where there are over 35 such settings (Egan et al., 2022).

This increased attention to the importance and value of nature in early childhood education also brings attention to the associated topics of climate change, biodiversity and the sustainability of the planet. This latter has led to quite an extensive literature on the role of early childhood education in education for sustainable development [ESD], particularly in the context of the Sustainable Development Goals [SDGs]. The SDGs were formulated in 2015 by the UN and were adopted as a call to action to end poverty, protect the planet, and ensure people enjoy peace and prosperity into the future. There are 17 Sustainable Development Goals [SDGs] which are integrated, where an action in one area affects the outcomes in others and development is understood as a balance between social, economic and environmental sustainability. The fourth sustainable development goal focuses on education and Target 4.2 is specifically about early childhood education and care noting that it is multidimensional, encompassing several aspects of a child's well-being: physical, social, emotional and mental and that, in general, development takes place in a predictable pattern. The SDG Target 4.2 acknowledges that children have an inherent right to develop to their fullest potential pointing to the Convention on the Rights of the Child, which clearly highlights the importance of early child development, stating that a child has a right to develop to 'the maximum extent possible' (article 6). In line with many other international documents the SDGs called for investment into quality holistic early childhood development, care and education as an essential strategy to support improved learning and tackle equity.

Children have been identified as a significant social group in all dimensions of sustainable development. The argument is that they have a right to thrive and develop in a sustainable world and so investment in supporting their development is crucial to the wider aims for a sustainable world. The argument made has been that in order to contribute meaningfully to society children's early lives need to be given priority with enhanced services to their families and directly to them in early childhood settings that are of the highest quality. In situation where children are at risk, for whatever reason, the SDGs support the need to provide additional intervention support. Thulin (2008) makes the point that sustainable development can be seen 'in terms of children's learning, and the development of an identity, a sense of belonging to a specific discourse' (p. 128).

Pramling Samuelsson and Kaga (2008) have observed that the traditions of early childhood pedagogies align with education for sustainability in the interdisciplinary nature of practice, holistic practices, use of the outdoors for learning, integration of care, development and education, learning through concrete experiences and real-life projects, and involvement of parents and communities. They argue that it is not necessary to invent entirely 'new' pedagogies in order to 'do' education for sustainability in the early years, rather early childhood educators can build on existing pedagogical traditions. In considering education for sustainable development, they call for practice that moves beyond simply taking children outdoors to explore and describe the beauty of nature but must also include opportunities for children to engage in conversation regarding sustainability; it should also include learning to be compassionate and respect differences, equality and fairness. In terms of concrete actions Pramling Samuelsson and Kaga suggest that educators, instead of talking about the 3Rs (reading, writing and arithmetic) should refer to the 7Rs for education for sustainable development (reduce, reuse, recycle, respect, repair, reflect and refuse) (2008, p. 12).

In response to calls for education in general to respond to the SDGs the National Council for Curriculum and Assessment (2018) has drawn attention to a relevant principle in the *Aistear* framework which views young children as citizens. It reads:

> Children are citizens with rights and responsibilities. They have opinions that are worth listening to and have a right to be involved in decisions about matters that affect them. In this way, they have a right to experience democracy. From this experience they learn that, as well as having rights, they also have responsibilities to respect and help others and to care for the environment.
>
> (p. 16)

The report goes on to provide illustrations of ways in which the *Aistear* framework provides opportunities for educating young children on issues related to sustainability including providing 'opportunities for babies, toddlers and children to gain all the key competencies for sustainability, albeit in age appropriate ways . . . the competency of self-awareness, followed by collaboration . . . followed jointly by the critical thinking and anticipatory competencies' (NCCA, 2018, p. 18).

A review of research into how settings approach the topic of sustainability found that early childhood educators have differing degrees of understanding of what ESD means in practice (Hedefalk et al., 2015). At the first level early childhood educators see it as educating children about the environment and involves activities around nature such as learning about animals and plants and storytelling to raise some issue such as pollution. A more advanced understanding however, sees educators focusing on trying to affect children's behaviours and fostering in them a concern for caring for and protecting the environment. The most advanced level of understanding found was in educators whose aim was to educate children to think critically about sustainability and their role in it, to create linkage between practices within the early childhood setting and the environment to enhance their understanding of their role and responsibilities in protecting the environment. In their research review Hedefalk et al. (2015) found that practices evolved from teaching children facts about the environment and sustainability issues to educating children to act for change. This more advanced approach focused on fostering children's environmental awareness in order to encourage them to develop environmentally friendly approaches, so that they will protect the environment, both now and in the future.

Identity and belonging

In considering the implications for early years practice it has been noted that

> promoting positive identities and a strong sense of belonging requires clearly defined policies, procedures and practice that empower every child

and adult to develop a confident self- and group identity and to have a positive understanding and regard for the identity and rights of others.

(CECDE, 2006, p. 95)

Children come to early years settings with their identity already in development. They come with personalities, capabilities, behavioural patterns, likes and dislikes which have been shaped by their early life experiences. They also come with the influences of family, significant others, their community and wider society. They have an emerging sense of belonging to their immediate environments. The process of identity formation is strengthened through relationships and connections in their lives. Identity is a personal attribute, a sense of uniqueness and of individuality; belonging, on the other hand, refers to a social attribute, a sense of being part of a community. In considering the interconnectedness of identity and belonging the NCCA (2004) noted that identity comprises characteristics, behaviours and understandings that children may have either as individuals *[I am Alex]* or shared with others *[I am a girl]*. 'Shared identities enable children to develop a sense of belonging or a close relationship with or affinity to a particular group' (NCCA, 2004, p. 2). Achieving a balance between the two so that children feel part of a shared, social environment, or community while at the same time having a strong sense of themselves is part of the process of development. Early years settings have a valuable role to play in this dynamic process and can, through inclusive practice and an informed sensitive approach, create welcoming environments from children from diverse backgrounds. Through showing awareness, interest and respect for individual children, their families and different cultures, languages and abilities early years educators support an atmosphere of belonging where children consolidate their personal identity as part of a wider shared identity. This is best supported where clear and agreed policies and procedures have been developed which support children and adults alike to develop confident self- and group identity and to respect the identity and rights of others (CECDE, 2006). It is also helpful for educators, individually and as part of the setting team, to explore their own attitudes and values as these will affect practice and influence children as surely as their behaviour does. Developing self-awareness and personal insights into our own value system will enhance the overall inclusiveness of an early years setting, something of increasing relevance in multicultural and multilingual societies.

Children have a right to an identity under Article 8 of the UN Convention on the Rights of the Child [UNCRC], which reads:

1. States Parties undertake to respect the right of the child to preserve his or her identity, including nationality, name and family relations as recognized by law without unlawful interference.
2. Where a child is illegally deprived of some or all of the elements of his or her identity, States Parties shall provide appropriate assistance and protection, with a view to re-establishing speedily his or her identity (UNCRC, 1989).

This is endorsed throughout the convention, particularly strongly in Articles 29 and 30 which speak to the rights of children to education. These articles explicitly mention the rights to cultural and linguistic identity.

Positive identity is realised through strong and trusting early relationships. It is through interactions and the quality of relationships that educators can make visible and respond to the child's right to an identity. How you relate to children, name them, label their belongings and talk about them will send messages to them about how they are considered by you and the extent to which their identity is respected. This feedback is very powerful and children, even very young children, are quick to pick up these signals. Educators need to be attentive and attuned to picking up on any evidence of misunderstandings or missteps so that messaging is clear. Where most children come from the same background there is less difficulty but with increased mobility across the world, for whatever reason, we have children coming to early years settings with, for example, names that may be unusual or difficult to pronounce. Names are central to personal identity and it is important that early years educators make the effort to pronounce and spell names correctly and help others in the setting to do the same. It is perfectly okay to explain to children and their families that you may need to practice a name to get the pronunciation right and getting advice on spelling can help this also. Children feel they belong and are valued in their early childhood settings where they are recognised and see themselves and their families reflected in the environment.

Belonging is at the core of quality early childhood practice. While belonging is different to identity they are interconnected, and a sense of belonging helps to strengthen a child's personal identity. In their report *'Enhancing a sense of belonging in the early years'* Woodhead and Brooker (2008) note that:

> while there is no explicit right to belonging named in the UNCRC it is a concept that is implicit to realising many of the key rights articulated within the convention. If a child is not helped to feel part of a community or group then she/he will feel insecure or an outsider, and it is difficult for them to develop positively.
>
> (p. 3)

They draw our attention to the fact that children's well-being and happiness in day-to-day life depends to a large extent on their sense of belonging. It is difficult to realise the right of identity if you do not feel part of the early years setting you attend. Healthy belonging is characterised by reciprocity, it is two-way. Where children, even very young babies, experience strong, positive relationships and feel respected for their views and feelings they do realise their sense of belonging. Woodhead and Brooker further note that

> belonging is the relational dimension to personal identity, the fundamental psycho-social 'glue' that locates every individual (babies, children and

adults) at a particular position in space, time and human society and – most important, connects people with each other.

(2008, p. 3)

While the idea of belonging is one that most of us recognise it is difficult to pin down exactly what achieving belonging in an early years setting actually looks like. Despite its presence as a goal in many early childhood curriculum frameworks, including *Aistear*, the concept of belonging itself has been found to be poorly defined and vague (Tillet & Wong, 2018). Such vagueness makes it difficult for educators to judge the extent to which their practice is successful in achieving a sense of belonging for children and their families. Addressing the challenges of understanding what the term belonging actually means in early childhood curriculum and practice, Sumsion and Wong (2011), following an extensive review of the literature, mapped the concept and identified ten overlapping dimensions of belonging. The dimensions illustrate the complexity of exploring the concept of belonging and suggests that belonging takes different shapes depending on the context. The dimensions identified were 'emotional, social, cultural, spatial, temporal, physical, spiritual, moral/ethical, political and legal' (p. 33). While difficult to untangle, this mapping provides an important context for investigating the interconnecting and dynamic aspects associated with belonging during the early years. A more recent study by Johansson and Puroila (2021) suggests that there are four interconnected aspects of belonging: belonging as a universal and basic human need, a sense of being connected, an acknowledgement of belonging to specific groups and a political frame from both societal and individual levels. Erwin et al. (2022), reflecting on the limited research into belonging in early childhood scholarship, suggest that researchers should access children's perspectives on what belonging means arguing that studies through an adult-lens alone are insufficient. They conclude that '[B]y learning directly from and with young learners about belonging, a more inclusive articulation is achieved, which ultimately impacts on their lives and informs larger social action and research agendas' (p. 11). In reflecting on practice, educators can consider these features to assist them explore the extent to which their practice is actually achieving them in practice. Research indicates that those settings that successfully create a sense of community are sensitive to the importance of relationships and alert to the diversity of children's interests and nurture feelings of belonging, self-worth and powerfulness in even the very youngest child. Belonging is a sense that grows out of secure and dependable relationships and strong connections with parents, siblings and others. In the normal course of events children develop a sense of pride in being part of their family, part of their early childhood communities. This emerges through being treated as a valued and participating group member and receiving respectful and genuine attention and praise for effort and ideas as well as achievements. This all builds into the positive development of children's dispositions, skills and knowledge as they develop and grow, which assist them develop a pleasure and satisfaction in their own persistence, exploration and learning which, in turn, supports their sense of mastery and control of themselves and the world in which they live. We all thrive and flourish in environments where we recognise that we are valued and feeling valued comes from being valued as a member of the different groups of which we are a part.

Your role as an early childhood educator is to build on the child's sense of identity and belonging and to strengthen both. Under the heading of identity and belonging we have an opportunity to consider the question of our own values and views of young children in practice. It is a particular challenge to the early educator who may work with babies, toddlers and young children from diverse background and with different experiences of advantage or disadvantage. In working to achieve and maintain quality practice it is really important that all educators have a clear understanding of the implications that their views and their values have for their practices. If working in an early childhood setting rather than in a home environment it is helpful if the team discuss this among themselves and come to an agreement on the values underpinning their practice and see how this is realised in the daily practices with children, families and with colleagues. The attitudes and values that we bring to a setting will influence our behaviour and the way we relate to children and their families. It will also affect the way we work with other adults in the setting. We can view children from different perspectives, and this will influence how we plan for, interact with and assess children. Some will see children as dependent on adults whilst others will see them as competent and independent learners. Children's experiences of a positive sense of identity and belonging is supported in environments where they experience respect, approval, encouragement; where they feel and believe that they matter, that they are important, that their views and opinions are heard and appreciated. The role of the early educator in creating such an environment is critical and often involves very careful analysis and consideration of individual children and the other environments in which they live and develop. Where there is too big a gap between home experiences and experiences in an early years' setting it is difficult for children to feel comfortable, to feel part of the new community. Indeed, it is just as important to a child's developing sense of identity that their families, their culture and beliefs, their way of living, their language are seen to be valued as much as they are. Positive messages give confidence to children, which, in turn assists them in their growing sense of belonging.

Early years educators are among the first new people outside of their family that children meet and, as such, carry a particular responsibility in helping children settle into the new cultural milieu, to develop a sense of belonging in the felt knowledge that they are valued in and of themselves and that, in turn, their own background and family life is respected and valued. I use the term 'felt knowledge' as it is rare that children actually talk or reason about their sense of belonging, but they certainly feel it and attuned and sensitive educators can pick this up. Where the culture of the early years setting is in harmony with the culture of the home and shares similar interests and approaches to children, the child is more likely to feel a sense of belonging. For this reason, it is important that educators actively work to create a sense of harmony between the two environments where young children spend so much of their time.

Our current understanding of child development is moving towards the view that adults can actively assist children in becoming aware of their own understanding of how they think and how they organise knowledge and information. Through informed practice they can assist children in learning how to learn, in recognising themselves as competent and masterful learners who can explore and problem-solve and are sufficiently self-aware to seek assistance when necessary. The affective and cognitive abilities described can be developed through attending to the quality of interactions, communication and relations between individuals and their social environment. This, in turn, can reinforce the development of a sense of personal identity and belonging, connectedness and community identity, critical foundations for later educational and social success. In practice we can assist and strengthen the development of a child's sense of identity by really getting to know each individual child, their likes and dislikes, their fears and their dreams. This can be done through a willingness in the setting to exchange experiences, discover similarities and difference and to be willing to explore more thoroughly the differences and use them as an instrument for creating an inclusive and caring early years environment for all those participating. In our increasingly diverse society, it is insufficient to simply focus on the similarities between children – 'sure we're all the same really' – particularly where there are manifest differences. Far better to acknowledge and celebrate diversity and recognise that we too are part of the diversity and for young children from a minority culture you may actually represent what is different or diverse to them!

Diversity is a space that includes us all and recognising what you don't know about cultures and languages shows a willingness to learn. Giving positive messages with a respectful and balanced use of the knowledge helps consolidate an inclusive setting. Embracing the wide range of individual differences that you come across, showing awareness of your own views, allowing yourself to be discomfited and then reflecting on it alone or with others also informs more inclusive settings. Don't wait until you find yourself in a difficult position, rather try to imagine different scenarios and be prepared. Working within a group or a team can be very productive as it helps us identify our own attitudes and biases and, collectively develop procedures and practices that encourage respect for difference. Whether you have a range of cultures and languages in your early years setting or not it is valuable to broaden children's horizons and exposure to difference and there are many resources books, pictures and digital materials that can be used.

Individual and shared identity formation is dynamic and is constantly evolving; it is influenced by how we interpret how others view us, even from a very young age. Research has found that children note differences and their response to difference is influenced by the reactions of others to difference. As part of this process humans use categories to make sense of the world around them. We can see this when children move from calling all four-legged animals sheep to being able to clearly identify sheep, cows and horses as separate groups. The tendency to categorise emerges early on, even in their first year, babies can differentiate people and we can see it when they begin to 'make strange' when meeting new people. Young children are also interested in differences and it is important to understand that developing and acting on their preferences is not the same things a being prejudiced (Thomson et al., 2021). Three to 6-year-olds show in-group preferences as they begin to see themselves as both individuals and group members. Derman-Sparks and Olson Edwards (2019) point out that: 'Differences do not create bias. Children learn prejudice from prejudice, not from learning about human diversity. It is how people respond to difference that teaches bias and fear' (p. 9).

The anti-bias curricular approach (Derman-Sparks & Olson Edwards, 2019) is a popular guide to practise suggestions on how to address issues of equity and diversity. It introduces four pillars of practice and associated outcomes which educators should consider when planning for equity and diversity:

Identity:

(i) Nurture each child's construction of a knowledgeable, confident self-concept and group identity
(ii) Children will demonstrate self-awareness, confidence, family pride and positive social identities

Diversity:

(i) Promote each child's comfortable, empathic interactions with people from diverse backgrounds
(ii) Children will express comfort and joy with human diversity, use accurate language for human differences and form deep, caring connections to all dimensions of human diversity

Justice:

(i) Foster each child's capacity to critically identify bias and will nurture each child's empathy for hurt bias causes
(ii) Children will increasingly recognise unfairness (injustice), have language to describe unfairness and understand that unfairness hurts

Activism

(i) Cultivate each child's ability and confidence to stand up for oneself and for others in the face of bias
(ii) Children will demonstrate a sense of empowerment and the skills to act, with others or alone, against prejudice and/or discriminatory actions

---

The application of these four pillars should permeate the practice both in your setting and in your interactions with families and the wider community. The pillars offer a valuable lens through which to reflect on the extent to which you are including and valuing all the children in your setting and assisting children respond respectfully to differences.

In keeping with the historical traditions of early childhood education and care all settings should be inclusive in their design and practice. However, as society and early childhood settings become more diverse it is important for practice to take account of guidance and advice from specialists to ensure this inclusive approach is maintained. In Ireland the *Diversity, Equality, and Inclusion Charter and Guidelines* (Department of Children and Youth Affairs [DCYA], 2016) recognise that early childhood settings can offer significant support to families and children new to a community, often with limited English and to those who, for whatever reason, feel marginalised or disadvantaged. The document, informed by, among other resources, the anti-bias curriculum, was developed to empower those working in the early childhood education and care to explore, understand and develop inclusive practices for the benefit of children, their families and wider society. Within the document the charter sets out to promote the values of diversity, equality and inclusion for all children attending early childhood services supported by the guidelines which are intended as a reference and working document which early childhood educators can utilise on an ongoing basis (2016, p. 1). To assist settings in providing inclusive environments for young children with disabilities an Access and Inclusion Model (AIM) was developed. Launched by the Department of Children and Youth Affairs in 2016 it promotes access and participation in early childhood education and care for children with additional needs or disabilities and provides graded resources across seven dimensions to support children's access to and inclusion in settings. Details can be found at: https://aim.gov.ie.

Research has suggested that settings vary in the degree to which they understand the complexity of working to address issues of diversity and equity (Murray, 2017) but there are examples of good practice. In their research with multicultural and multilingual settings Garrity et al. (2017) found that in the early childhood settings they studied the staff roles extended beyond working directly with the children to working with the families. They often acted as go-between liaising with other services on behalf of families and clarifying what services are available and how best to interact with them. The findings from the study identified a number of key characteristics for best practice in settings with diverse populations including:

> *a clearly articulated philosophy*, valuing diversity, respecting all families and children; this philosophy is "lived" within the settings, underpinning the approach to practice of staff and management
>
> *continuing relevant professional development* and a professional approach to practice is promoted

a well-developed and thoughtful pedagogy, privileging care and creating
community, adapts to the needs of the children attending
a strengths-based approach to working in partnership with families is
cultivated.

(2017, p. 318)

As reflective and professional educators it is important to discuss with peers
and colleagues what exactly it means to respect children as individuals and
competent learners and how does it impact on practice in early years settings?
What does it look like? Respect for children as learners who are curious and
anxious to explore and understand their world is a key attribute for effective
practice. Where adults believe that children are dependent or weak and need
to be taught how to behave the children themselves will recognise this and
may behave and perform in response. However, where adults have a faith in
children's competence and willing and have high and realistic expectations
children rise to the opportunities provided to extend their learning.

Central to the success of practice is the quality of your relationships and
interactions with children and the extent to which you facilitate and encourage positive interactions between children. Educator engagement must be
genuine and authentic, it is an essential characteristic of the early childhood
professional. There are two dimensions to engagement with children. On the
one hand there is engagement at an emotional level where we genuinely feel
for and care about the children we work with, where we sympathise, empa-
thise and are joyful with them. Such an engaged, inclusive practice nurtures a
secure sense of belonging and group identity in children and also give comfort
to their families. On the other hand, there is the intellectual dimension to
engagement which involves respect for their efforts and their views, it is not
about being amused by their cute little mistakes or their unrealistic efforts
to achieve something. Rather, it demands that you take them seriously and
respect their efforts, try to understand their mistakes and guide them in their
attempt to achieve their ambitions through drawing on your understanding
of their development. Taking time to listen to children and giving them time
to talk, modeling patience and respect in your interactions all contribute to
an environment where children feel safe and, within this space children learn
to cope with challenges and overcome difficulties, they develop a sense of
mastery, a positive personal identity and learning dispositions. Give them a
sense of importance, with responsibilities that are real and authentic, and they
will take on those roles and responsibilities with pride. Create risky but safe
opportunities for them so that they are really challenged and can overcome a
real difficulty, barrier or problem. Such opportunities are rich in possibilities
and can be used by educators to achieve a range of learning goals in the short,
medium and long-term.

In your practice, when thinking about identity and belonging, try to encourage interactions and assist children in managing their behaviour and their
responses to difference, whether it is a cultural difference, a new experience, a

challenging view or an unexpected behaviour. Where there is a diverse group of children with a variety of cultures and linguistic backgrounds the strength of parental involvement in the setting becomes crucial to enhancing children's sense of community and belonging whilst at the same time recognising and respecting their individual identities. Families may feel nervous about sharing the care of their young children and may even feel alienated within early years settings, even where you feel you may be very welcoming. Not only is it helpful to involve parents in the daily life of the setting it has also been found that assisting the development of parental/family networks can add the cohesion of a community and consolidate the sense of belonging within diversity. While family networks may arise spontaneously it is in fact rare and educators in early years setting can certainly facilitate it by providing opportunities for families to meet each other, share ideas or solve problems.

What does belonging look like in an early childhood setting? To take an example: most settings have a greeting procedure, which can depend on the size of the setting and the number of children arriving at particular times. What is central to good practice is that the adults in the setting recognise the importance of this transition link to other adults in the lives of the children and are vigilant in their efforts to maintain contact with them. This should be done in a way that includes the child and takes account of the particular characteristics of the family. Some settings nominate a key worker who pays particular attention to a small group of children and takes responsibility for engagement with their families, among other things.

The Family Wall, a suggestion suggested in the anti-bias curriculum, is a powerful way to welcome and include families from diverse background. The Wall can be a daily point of conversation with photos and contributions to generate discussion about each child and their family. The photographs used are selected and brought in by the parents and child and displayed in a part of the setting easily accessible to all. The Wall shows that all children have families and that they differ in many ways. The wall provides a point of discussion between children and also information for educators. A key to the success of the Family Wall is to build it into routine practice and to keep it looking fresh and interesting. Educators should be sensitive to any unintended consequences of their requests for material given that different families value things differently and may be less willing to share certain information. Another way to integrate children into settings and make them feel welcome is called 'name stories' where parents are asked to explain the story behind the name they chose for their child, what the name meant. When asked, the parents felt the exercise was so good and informative that they wanted to keep a record of it and so they each agreed to write down the story of their child's name in letter form and place it in an envelope. The envelopes containing the letters were then presented in the form of a multilingual poster, where parents and visitors could choose ones to read. 'The name stories send a message that every child is important and that every family has a story to tell and a contribution to make to our community' (Wagner, 2008, p. 22). There are many examples of inclusive practices emerging from the literature and what we know about how other countries adapt to the arrival of children from different cultural and ethnic backgrounds. In response to the diversity of families in the settings studied by Garrity et al. (2017) they found that the pedagogical focus adopted by educators acknowledge and welcomed difference as part of their day-to-day routine. For instance, rather than focusing on holidays or religious festivals the educators ensured that the diversity was reflected in the environment in the books representing different family types and different cultures, the wall displays and the materials they provided and activities available. Helpful guidance on creating welcoming environments can be found in the *Aistear Siolta Practice Guide*.

In settings with children from diverse cultural background responding to the different languages in the setting can be a challenge for educators. Because the increased presence of multilingual groups in early childhood is a relatively new phenomenon there is limited research into how best to support children's belonging and identity in a way that assists their integration into their early childhood group while at the same time respecting their linguistic and cultural heritage. Research does indicate that linguistically diverse children face unique challenges which, when understood, can assist educators, informing those practices that offer children the best opportunity for development and learning. We know that many children from linguistically diverse backgrounds have less well-developed vocabulary knowledge and emergent literacy skills in the language of the early years' setting and, as a result, may struggle with fluency and literacy in their later educational settings. This is not a surprise given the close connection between a child's skill in English and their later achievement. In working with a multilingual group of young children it is important to welcome all children equally into settings and strive to support everyone in their communicating. It is also essential to create an environment that is welcoming and where children [and their families] feel they belong. From the research we know that welcoming environments actively ensure the inclusion of home languages in the day-to-day curriculum and facilitate family involvement; it is not recommended that settings reject the home languages in favour of English. While it is easy to agree with these suggestions we know from research that it is challenging in practice. Some studies have found that a successful way of bedding home languages into the curriculum is through encouraging children to use all their available language skills in whatever language across all situations. This sends a message of welcome to children and indicates that their sociocultural experiences and knowledge are respected. With young children in particular, but less so their parents, relaxed and calm exposure to the dominant [in this case English] language can facilitate their fluency. The last decade has seen a growth in available guidance and resources for educators working with children and families where English is a second language. There are simple and thoughtful actions that can be very effective such as knowing each child's name, its spelling and pronunciation. The group Mother Tongues [https://mothertongues.ie], mentioned in Chapter 3, has many resources and some key message for parents and early educators. In particular they note that the child's home language should be respected and recognised as a core part of their identity, it should not be rejected or suppressed.

All children need to develop good language and communication skills in the early years, regardless of their linguistic background. In early childhood settings there has always been a diversity of linguistic competence, albeit usually within a single language, and early childhood educators are well placed to interpret the many different ways that children communicate. There is extensive evidence of the cognitive benefits to be derived from bilingual or multilingual competence and so supporting all children in the development of their oral language skills is to be encouraged. Such an integrated approach to language learning allows for children's implicit knowledge of language to become explicit in their conversations and their oral responses to storytelling and to questioning (Kirwan, 2017). Within linguistic studies this integrated approach has been called 'translanguaging'. The idea of translanguaging was first suggested in 1994 as an approach to developing expertise in both English and Welsh simultaneously and to a high standard. Languages are not seen as separate but constantly interacting and communicating is a valued activity. Use of this approach respects and values the speaker and their language and, rather than highlighting linguistic difference as deficiency, it recognises the strength of all languages and enriches the linguistic experiences of all children and adults (Kirsch et al., 2020). Being valued for who they are and for what they bring with them to the learning process facilitates children's engagement in their own learning. In a reflection on teaching successfully within a plurilingual primary school Kirwan (2017) makes the following points, which are as relevant to early childhood as to primary school:

children learn most effectively if they are encouraged to use all the languages at their disposal autonomously – whenever and however they want to.

even very young children can be trusted to know how to use their home language autonomously as a tool of learning.

development of oral proficiency, literacy and language awareness is a complex process in which reading and writing support listening and speaking and *vice versa*.

take the lead from the child, their knowledge and experience is the starting point for new learning.

Studies have found that while early childhood educators and primary teachers understand the importance of the home language to children, its importance to their sense of identity and the challenges it presents children in achieving their full potential they feel ill-equipped to respond effectively. As a result a number of studies have looked to intervention programmes focusing on children and professional development supporting educators. In a study by Dockrell et al. (2010) the authors found success in developing oral language skills in well-structured small group activities where each child had time and opportunity to speak. Another strategy was where educators modelled the relevant language needed to support children's activities, this was particularly important for activities which promote discussion, acting out, interactive games and the use of visual resources (Murphy et al., 2017). Although the studies reported tend to be small scale the evidence suggests that professional development programmes need a minimum length to be effective and benefit from associated workshops, tutorials and onsite coaching across time.

Early years settings can offer supportive and secure contexts within which children can develop their sense of personal identity and provide an inclusive atmosphere within which children's sense of belonging can be enhanced. Educators contribute to these developments through proactive practice, which encourages children and families to participate in the life of the setting. For this to be successful the educators themselves needs to actively promote inclusion and partnerships and create opportunities that take account of the needs of parents and family members. Simply inviting participation without considering what form it might take or how it might be sustained will disempower parents. Such general invitations fail to recognise and acknowledge that families, who are 'experts of experience' in relation to their children, can contribute valuable insights and knowledge about their children when clear about their role and setting expectations.

We know that even very young children have some sense of the factors that contribute to their well-being and happiness and give them a sense of belonging and being valued. In supporting well-being, identity and belonging in early years settings across the range of age groups we find research confirming the importance of relationships, time and authentic engagement. Every day provides opportunities for supporting children across these dimensions, moments that arise when individual children are concentrating on a task or in a group playing a game, solving a problem or 'messing about'. What seems to be important is the quality of practice, the level and depth of listening and communicating and the provision of opportunities from within the day-to-day experiences which requires educators to be attuned and sensitive to the possibilities that arise in the most ordinary of events. Most of all, thoughtfully supporting children's well-being, identity and belonging can be seen in the democratic nature of excellent early years practice, a practice that respects all children, that celebrates difference, that listens to children and hears them, that engages children in conversations, facilitates conversations between children and provides a context where they develop a strong sense of well-being in keeping with their own lives and the world in which we all live.

5 Communicating, exploring and thinking

Introduction

As in the previous chapter this chapter examines three themes, communicating, exploring and thinking. They are interlinked and focus on active learning and what might be called the early academic development of young children. We communicate in many different ways and the theme of communicating is examined to incorporate a wide range of methods and includes communication with parents and other professionals. Drawing on the thinking behind the influential book *The Hundred Languages of Children* (Edwards et al., 2012) it takes a close look at the many different ways in which children communicate from the infants crying and cooing to the body language and linguistic skills of young children. The themes of exploring and thinking provide the basis for examining how children develop their understanding of the world through activity and meaning-making and how this can inform high quality, effective early childhood pedagogy. It looks closely at the learning environment and how educators can design and utilise playful spaces that encourage the development of children's thinking towards the higher order thinking and executive function which form the basis of positive learning.

Communicating

Human beings are born with the desire and the ability to communicate in many different ways about ideas, feeling, opinions and facts. Communication is a two-way process of giving and receiving information. Children communicate from birth and do so both verbally and nonverbally. They communicate their feelings, their wants, their ideas, their fears and hopes and they do so through their body language, particularly when very young and later through sounds, talking, crying, laughing. They also communicate through expression, dance, music, drama, gesture, digital technologies and in some cases through Braille or sign language. By providing a balanced approach to allow for learning in and through play activity and the arts educators can create opportunities to transform symbols and meanings that allow children make sense of previous knowledge and experiences. It is through these multiple communication

DOI: 10.4324/9781003353164-5

mechanisms that children learn and share new knowledge and expand their representational, expressive and social skills. The many ways children use for communicating is captured evocatively in the title of a book written about the preschool practices of Reggio Emilia – *The Hundred Languages of Children* (Edwards et al., 2012).

Communication is central to the creation of a learning community where adults and children both recognise themselves as learners. But it is not only communication that matters, it is the act of communicating. The act of communicating has three elements – giving, receiving and interpreting or making sense of the information. The ability and facility to communicate is essential to learning and development and careful communication helps children to manage their emotion and think about themselves, others and the materials in the world around them. To learn how to communicate through language children need to develop in a social context with other language users. We know from studies of children brought up in the wild [feral children] that, in the absence of human language as a source, they do not acquire appropriate language skills, even though they do find ways to communicate. The adults in the lives of young children are a particularly important source of guidance on how, what, when and where to communicate. Where children are growing up in bilingual or multilingual environments, they do so successfully in all the available languages as long as they have good models in each language. We saw in the last chapter the crucial role of the early childhood educator in providing opportunities for quality communication where children do not speak the dominant language and the importance of this in facilitating a secure identity for a child. As well as environmental factors children's own abilities influence the development of their communicating skills. For early years educators it is important to understand the unfolding of communication skills in children so that you can adjust your own communicating style to meet the individual needs of a particular child or group of children. This also assists in identifying any early signs of language difficulties or delays. It is however important to bear in mind that children's developmental paths can vary a great deal in early childhood and so not all children will be at the same level of development on all dimensions. Where you do suspect a difficulty or a delay, particularly if you are considering outside help for the child it is useful to collect clear evidence to support your concern, identify specifically where you suspect some difficulty and discuss your views with a colleague before deciding on a final course of action.

Communication has both an important interpersonal dimension and a content dimension. At the interpersonal level the adult models the behaviour appropriate to communication such as eye contact, active listening and attentive responses. At the content level the early years educators can guide the level of detail, the choice of words, the type of information and the extent of new vocabulary to introduce and should base this on knowledge about the child or children. In early childhood the learning environments that children inhabit the adults, objects, materials and space therein provide the source of these interpersonal and content dimensions. Effective early years practice requires that educators build up the content from within the context. It is their role to work with and help children to make meaning from the children's own experiences and the environment around them and to provide opportunities for conversation, questioning and dialogue. This will provide children with the time, space and opportunity to reflect, infer, hypothesise and understand. The style, as well as the content of the language used by the adult is important. Rather than saying 'oh, that's lovely' in response to some activity or process you will be showing more engaging communication with the child if you say, '*You* did this, tell me about it . . .'. This more conversational style can be used with children of all ages and shows an interest in the child and their activity and further supports the sense of belonging in a child. It can also help develop a child's vocabulary and draw attention to more advanced grammatical structures. It is through maintaining an environment rich in oral language opportunities that children become comfortable and confident communicators.

Good educators recognise the important role they play in supporting young children in the development of their communication skills. Through timely responsiveness to the gestures of a baby they are helping the child learn the basis for communication. The baby learns that certain gestures or vocalisations yield a response, and that the response may be either positive or negative. Picking up a child who reaches out to you, looking directly at her, smiling and chatting as you do so all convey a positive reaction and send a clear message to the child that she is heard, she is cherished, she is important and that she belongs. Older children want to talk, to share their ideas, their discoveries and their queries and to do so they need time. Educators who find the time, who make eye contact are helping the child to recognise active listening and are signalling to the child that they, and their opinions, ideas or questions matter. Conversations can be extended by careful open-ended questions and vocabulary can be extended when you provide new or additional words to help a story flow.

It is also important to understand the power and potential of nonverbal communication and children may need help in recognising and reading such signals from others. An attentive adult will find opportunities to explain body language so that children become more attuned to the breadth and meaning of communications. For this to be effective both the language and the content of the communication must be clear. When communicating with young children, including with babies, educators can take opportunities to help children name their feeling. A crying baby can be consoled in a soft voice, which explains to them that 'you are hungry' or 'you are tired'. Older children can use the names you put on their feelings – 'you're sad . . .' 'you're happy . . .' or 'you're angry . . .' to help them develop their own understanding of emotions and learn to manage them more effectively. Extending communication skills can also occur where adults act as good role models and make conscious attempts to narrate or talk through routine activities such as 'I am preparing the table . . .' or 'I'm tidying up' or 'you are counting the plates . . .'.

Through providing opportunities for play, particularly pretend or role-play, both indoor and outdoor, you also help the development of communication as children often find a voice with other children in the safety of their play. It is through the process of their play that children are making sense of their social and cultural worlds and educators can provide varied learning environments, materials and playful opportunities to amplify this. Through careful observations of such play activities, it is possible to learn a great deal about how skilled children are in communicating. Finally, educators must be clear and distinct when requesting children to carry out some task or activity. Be sure to catch the child's attention through touch or eye contact and then make the request in simple sentences to assist their understanding.

How we communication with children influences their experiences and the quality of their learning. For instance, the quality of communication in joint attention to an activity can enhance the experience for both adult and child. Joint activity of this sort, where adult and child share a common focus of attention, is recognised as a valuable site for learning in the early years. As noted in Chapter 2 Siraj-Blatchford and her colleagues, in studying what constitutes quality joint activity between early years educator and children, identified 'sustained, shared thinking' [SST] as having a particularly powerful impact on children's development and learning. The term 'sustained shared thinking' captures the idea of time [evident in the word sustained] as being central to the process, time being given to engage meaningfully in the joint activity. It is characterised as 'an effective pedagogic interaction where two or more individuals "work together" in an intellectual way to solve a problem, clarify a concept, evaluate activities or extend a narrative' (Siraj-Blatchford & Manni, 2007, p. 7). Effective sustained, shared thinking requires educators to tune into the child with genuine interest and show this interest so that the child is aware of their attention. In addition, children's decisions and choices must be respected and time given to them to elaborate and explain. The communication that takes place to facilitate sustained shared thinking, the questioning, the adapting, the negotiation all contributes to enhancing the development of children's language and higher order skills, important to the development of the executive functions, which form the basis for positive learning, enhancing the dispositions to learn. Clear and attuned communication that is respectful in both directions offers a fertile space for such developments.

In a presentation on sustained shared thinking Siraj-Blatchford (2005) drew a useful distinction between sustained shared thinking and sustained shared conversations. It is often through sustained shared conversations that educators can expand into sustained shared thinking, not unlike the extended purposive conversations described by French (2014). Engaging meaningfully and intelligently with young children in extra talk provides a powerful context for developing their thinking and the metacognitive skills that strengthen their executive function. It can function to equip children, even very young children, with the language and thinking skills that are important to later personal learning style. Much of the adult talk that is observed in early childhood settings has been found to be of a fairly low level, largely managerial or organisational in style such as 'that's lovely' or 'put on your coat' or 'pick it up' or 'do this' or 'tidy up time'. While such demands can be an important part of the organisation of a setting, they are very limited as models of conversation for children and they do nothing to extend their learning or their thinking. Siraj-Blatchford argues that to really enhance children's development educators have to work together with children in an intellectual way to solve problems, clarify ideas or extend narrative. She offered the following strategies for engaging in effective sustained shared conversations:

Tuning in: listening carefully to the child, to what is being said, observing body language and what the child is doing

Showing genuine interest: giving your full attention to the child, maintaining eye contact, affirming, nodding and smiling

Respecting children's own decisions and choices by inviting children to elaborate, saying things like 'I really want to know more about this' and listening to and engaging with the response

Re-capping: 'so you think . . .'

Offering your own experience: 'I like to listen to music when I make supper at home'

Clarifying ideas: 'Right Darren, so you think that this stone will melt if I boil it in water?'

Suggesting: 'You might like to try doing it this way'

Reminding: 'Don't forget that you said that this stone will melt if I boil it'

Using encouragement to further thinking: 'You have really thought hard about where to put this door in the castle . . . where will you put the window?'

Offering an alternative viewpoint: 'Maybe Goldilocks wasn't bold when she ate the porridge?'

Speculating: 'Do you think the three bears would have liked Goldilocks to come and live with them as a friend?'

Reciprocating: 'Thank goodness that you were wearing Wellingtons when you jumped through those puddles Kwame. Look at my feet, they are soaking wet!'

Asking open questions: 'How did you . . .?'; 'Why does this . . .?'; 'What happens next?'; 'What do you think?'; 'I wonder what would happen if . . .?'

Modelling thinking: 'I have to think hard about what to do this evening. I need to take my cat to the vet because he has a sore foot, take my books back to the library and buy some food for dinner tonight. But I just won't have time to do all these things.'

She also provided a list of useful *positive phrases and questions* that can be used to extend thinking:

'I don't know, what do you think?'
'That's an interesting idea'
'I like what you have done there'
'Have you seen what X has done . . . why, do you think?'
'I wonder why you had . . .?'
'I've never thought of that before'
'You've really made me think'
'What would happen if we . . .?'
'I imagine . . .'

Finally, she offered some suggestions on *styles of practice:*

Repeat and use children's own words – restate
Be active about introducing new and interesting words to children
Limit questioning – sometimes it can seem like interrogating
Encourage children to describe their efforts, their ideas, their products
Use encouragement rather than praise – too much praise can be insidious as it can make children dependent on it
When you use praise be specific – focus on the children's actions and what they are doing rather than on whether it pleases the adult. Rather than saying 'that's a lovely painting' try something like 'I wonder how you made all those layers of colour?'

These strategies for practice illustrate how powerful the educator can be to the quality of children's early experiences and they provide a guide that is useful for when you reflect back on your practice, whether alone or with the team.

Children communicate in many different, or multimodal, ways. In their book on the many different languages of children Edwards et al. (2012) point to some of the forms of communicating to look out for, particularly important to those working with babies and young children. These include words, phrases, pictures, music, a look, an expression, body language, gesture, sounds and movements. Through careful attention and alertness to these many different ways of communicating educators can create rich and collaborative learning environments in responsive and inclusive ways. In an increasing multilingual world sensitive, attuned attention to children can unlock access to their interests, their thinking and their strengths, all of which adds to our understanding and can inform practice.

Within the early years setting educators have a dual role: the direct impact on the individual child in the setting from day-to-day and the indirect impact on the child through engaging with parents in understanding their children's development. This latter role is one that allows educators and parent realise their shared interest in a child and create a sense of partnership in informing and guiding their early learning experiences. The evidence suggests that parents are, generally speaking, more inclined to be relaxed and receptive to conversations and 'catch-ups' with early childhood educators than with primary teachers or social workers. This may be because, as parents of young children, they are simply curious to know how their child is settling into the early years setting, how they are progressing or they themselves may feel the need for support and guidance as they become more familiar with their young child. A quality learning environment for children is enriched where there is a good relationship between the home and the setting as this provides a reasonably stable context within which children can strengthen their learning and development across multiple environments. It also assists children develop and broaden their sense of identity and competence and overall sense of belonging. Communicating to parents about why quality early years experiences are so important to their children's development and learning and helping parents recognise what such experiences look like in early childhood is an important task for educators. This is particularly important as many parents are unaware of the unique features of early childhood education and care; in their anxiety to see their children acquire the skills traditionally associated with learning, reading, writing and arithmetic, they may not recognise the significance of nurturing relationships, conversation, story, exploration, play and discovery to children's overall development and learning.

We know from the work of Bronfenbrenner and others that the most central influence on the child is that of their immediate environment, the microsystem, which is any individual setting, for example the home or the early years setting. The people in these settings have the most immediate effect on the child, and if the relationships within and across these immediate settings break down it can cause the child difficulty. The relational network with others, consisting of linkages between any of the various settings in which the child spends time, is particularly important, and can exert an influence over the child in subtle ways, for example if early years educators and parents have differences of opinion on the education of the child. Consistency and continuity between the two settings is in the best interest of the child and requires that both work in partnership with the interests of the child at the forefront of their minds. The visible inclusion of their family in the early years setting and positive interactions between educators and parents create of a sense of inclusion as well as of belonging; it strengthens the link to activities that could be followed through in the home; it improves two-way access to information and encourages shared ambitions for the child.

In addition to linking settings explicitly with children's home learning environments early educators are well placed to link in with new places and centres and people in the wider community. Such connections can expand children's horizons and create opportunities to explore new places and meet new people. This could include visiting places such as the local shops or library or visiting people in their workplace such as the fire brigade. At a deeper and more considered level a number of intergenerational projects, linking young children with older people, have begun to be reported internationally. One such is the Together Old and Young [TOY] project (Gallagher & Fitzpatrick, 2018) which brought together young children and older people across both early childhood settings and settings for older people. The intention was to reduce the separation between generations, counteract negative stereotypes and enrich knowledge and relationships through spending time in each other's company doing simple activities, talking and having fun. The study found benefits for all ages in having the opportunity to meet and interact with groups previously unfamiliar to them. Details of the TOY project and how to set one up can be found at www.toyproject.net.

Early experiences support a vast array of children's communication skills including their awareness of verbal and nonverbal communication; their knowledge of sound, pattern, rhythm and repetition; their awareness of symbols such as print, pictures and digital; the opportunities that they have to become familiar with and enjoy print in a meaningful way; and the opportunities that they have to use mark-making materials. These broad communication skills, in turn, play a key role in the development of their literacy skills. In terms of mathematical literacy children's growing vocabulary and understanding of materials, shape, space, orientation, pattern and difference, classifying, matching, comparing and ordering are all important for the development of numeracy. The knowledge, skills, attitudes and dispositions developed in these early years impact significantly upon children's later learning experiences in science, technology, engineering and mathematics [what has come to be known as STEM].

The contemporary world has changed rapidly over the last decade and now comprises elements of the real world combined and influenced by the virtual or digital world. Children, even the very young, are familiar with digital communication which in turn contributes to their understanding of the digital world, one which informs the experiences they bring with them to the setting. Studies indicate that in social contexts digital games can be a very powerful pedagogical tool in developing new skills, expanding knowledge and acquiring the social skills necessary to successfully participate. Digital play can provide playful experiences where children can, among other things, create opportunities to communicate in new ways, to interact with diverse groups and collaborate with others in problem solving, can extend their literacy and numeracy skills through word and number games, introduce new worlds, new cultures and help them in their writing and drawing. In this way we can see the importance and potential of children's engagement with the digital world. The opportunity to support the growth and consolidation of the skills and knowledge underpinning literacy, numeracy and digital literacy emerges from children, their interests and their experience combined with the sensitivity of an informed educator. Research has found that adopting a balanced approach to learning through the various arts, of music, drama, dance, painting, drawing, educators can enhance the underlying skills that contribute to later literacy, numeracy and digital competence. Unlike in other levels of education the content of such arts based early education is not fixed and not easily prescribed and so it is can be challenging.

Studies have shown the importance of the quality of home and early years environments [socially and materially] to the development of children's learning dispositions and to their being actively literate, numerate and digitally competent. Where families and early childhood educators are involved in literacy-, numeracy- and digitally based activities children develop larger vocabularies, faster vocabulary growth and better cognitive abilities than children from homes with less engaged parents or from settings with less pedagogically aware educators. For children who come from disadvantaged or impoverished backgrounds the early childhood setting functions as a critical site for exposure to learning opportunities that include stimulating material from within the real and the digital world. In addition to impacting and enriching the early learning environment itself, the digital world can provide enhanced potential for linkage between the home and early years settings. However, we have limited information on how best to maximise the potential of this new form of communication so that it strengthens partnerships between educators and parents and works to the benefit of young children and their development. Some concerns have been raised about the issue of surveillance and the right to privacy for both educators and young children. This area of digital communication and its role, potential and challenges in early education and care is an exciting new field for exploration and research.

Improving literacy in its broadest is an urgent national priority in many countries. The current Irish strategy (DES, 2011) recognises the role of early educators in providing early literacy and numeracy experiences through the style and content of their communication and through play. The strategy identified the following six key areas for action among those working in the education sector:

- Enabling parents/communities to support literacy/numeracy development
- Improving teacher and early childhood education and care professional practice through in-service and pre-service training
- Building capacity of school leadership
- Getting content of literacy right at primary and secondary level
- Targeting resources to special areas of need
- Improving use of assessment processes

Following an interim review and consultation the DES (2017) is drafting a new strategy which will take account of, among other things the extensive reach of the digital world and will address

- Improving the curriculum and the learning experience
- Supporting learners with additional learning needs to achieve their potential
- Improving assessment and evaluation to support better learning in literacy, numeracy and digital literacy
- Digital literacy [https://www.gov.ie/en/consultation/14180-literacy-numeracy-and-digital-literacy-strategy-consultation/].

Literacy development usually occurs through hearing, listening, imitating and observing others. Reading and writing [being literate] can be encouraged through experiencing reasons to read and write. Early years educators have a critical role to play in children's early literacy and numeracy development both directly and indirectly; directly through the provision of literacy- and numeracy-rich environments with opportunities for extensive engagement with materials; using materials to extend literacy, numeracy and digital vocabulary, encouraging conversation and modelling active listening and making all literacy types visible through carefully considered pedagogical documentation. Educators also have an indirect influence on children through their work with families such as sharing pedagogical documentation; offering book lending schemes; sharing particular interests of individual children; being sensitive to literacy needs of parents, particularly those for whom English is a second language. Early years educators contribute to improved general literacy by ensuring that their practice in settings facilitates the development of the underlying skills necessary to later literacy, numeracy and digital competence; by fostering the enjoyment of story and narrative through storytelling, conversation, dialogues, reading stories and listening actively; creating awareness of the language of number and its everydayness; by promoting interest and enjoyment of literacy, numeracy and digital literacy activities to promote an improved attitude to reading, writing and numbers and by working with parents and other professionals to raise public awareness of the importance of oral language and listening skills to later literacy. Engagement with parents constitutes a core part of a quality literacy, numeracy and digital literacy plan in early years settings. Settings that are welcoming and accessible for parents and make meaningful provision for their involvement in the setting and beyond in activities that support the development of better literacy, numeracy and digital literacy skills will benefit children. Parents influence their children's literacy development and parents with literacy difficulties will need the particular support that early educators can offer, whether this support is directly within the setting or through links to external support.

Facilitating the emergent literacies can happen in the everyday activities of the setting, there is no need for formal activities such as workbooks or structured tabletop exercises. The evidence suggests that it is more effective to locate the facilitation and promotion of literacy, numeracy and digital literacy skills within the familiar and the meaningful for the young child. Our current understanding of literacy and numeracy development recognises that literacy skills [as opposed to skills of reading and writing] develop from birth, there is a strong link between language development and literacy skills and early literacy experiences in the home learning environment [HLE] and the early years setting can influence children's lifelong attitude or disposition to reading.

Improving early years outcomes for young children through improving oral language competence, developing the language of maths and supporting digital competence in early years settings takes time, careful planning and a keen awareness in the educator of the capabilities of individual children. There are many different suggestions available on how to foster enriching literacy, numeracy and digital environments for children and the key factors centre around the educator style, approach, knowledge and professional confidence. The content of particular situations will derive from the children and the adults and will be unique to each opportunity that presents. When considering how to carry through these suggestions you will be greatly assisted by applying your own knowledge, experience and understanding of child development, relevant research and the processes that assist learning and development most appropriately for individual children. Calls for a focus on developing early literacy, numeracy and school readiness in early childhood should not diminish educator attention to, and investment of time and energy in the development of individual children's capacities such as initiative, self-confidence, self-regulation, persistence, curiosity, love of learning, cooperativeness, conflict management and resolution. Attention to the support of these skills and dispositions in a pedagogically rich early learning environment, which values play and encourages exploration and communication, will contribute to later developmental progress on issues of more relevance to later schooling.

Exploring and thinking

Children are actively making sense of their world and their place in it; through their activities and their relationships they are learning about themselves, what they can do, where they need help. They are also learning how to manage feelings, how to respond to difficult situations, how to respond to others. Through their engagement with the world and the people, objects and material they find there they are learning new facts, new words, new ways of doing things; they learn how to wait, how to plan, how to negotiate and how to participate in groups. Exploring and thinking are just two of the important processes that assist children in their meaning-making. *Aistear* links these themes as one and has characterised exploring and thinking as 'active learning' which involves children using their senses to 'explore and work with objects and materials around them and they interact enthusiastically with the adults and other children' (NCCA, 2009a, p. 10). It is through this dynamic process that 'children develop the dispositions, skills, attitudes and values that will help them to grow as confident and competent learners' (p. 10).

While presented as a theme in itself exploring and thinking are processes that are also relevant across the previous themes. For instance, in relation to the theme of Communicating we find the observation that '[B]y capturing children's interest and curiosity and challenging them to *explore* and to share their adventures and discoveries with each other, this environment can fuel their *thinking*, imagination and creativity, thereby enriching communication' (NCCA, 2009a, p. 34). Hutt (1990) has drawn a distinction between exploration and play where exploration is that action that seeks to understand 'what is this? What does it do?' Play on the other hand asks, 'what can I do with this?' Exploration gives space for children to use their initiative to identify and seek solutions to problems and to develop negotiation skills with both children and teachers. Hedegaard (2020) argues that it is through exploration both within the home and early childhood settings but also further afield that children can expand their understanding and develop what they already know. By exploring, children are given opportunities to examine new ideas, to symbolise and use objects in new ways that are relevant to them in that moment. Placing the word exploration with thinking, as *Aistear* (NCCA, 2009a) does, links the two aspects of 'finding out', of getting to know more and understanding this knowing. Exploration, both physically and in the imagination, forms the basis of scientific enquiry and, as such, should be encouraged and supported. However, despite the fact that we know children are curious and enjoy exploring and problem solving, studies suggest that science-related activities are rarely built on or expanded in early childhood settings. This may be because educators feel unsure about how best to elaborate and deepen the activity in a scientifically meaningful way.

We see here the importance of early years educators creating an environment that invites children to explore and communicate about their experiences, which will enhance the development and refining of their thinking. It is through their active participation and engagement with adults, other children and their environment that children come to understand the world, the social and cultural norms and where they can play, investigate, question and test out and refine their ideas. The active participation of the child is central to the vision for this theme whether that participation refers to an individual child or a child within a group of children. Doing, pointing, asking questions, seeking solutions, setting up theories, making links with previous understandings, interacting with others, with objects, playing with words, laughing, crying, teasing, chortling, exploring and thinking all represent examples of how children learn through their active engagement with their environment in a playful and enriching way. Not only do they increase their knowledge and vocabulary, but they also learn new skills, strengthen dispositions and refine their communication and cooperation strategies. Children, even very young children, are using their senses to learn more about their world, explore and think about it and make sense of their place in it. In contemporary research there is increasing attention to the potential of early childhood education and care as a context within which to support children's awareness of and contribution to the challenges of climate change and sustainability. In our interconnected world it is important that we help children appreciate the importance of nurturing and caring for the environment and for people. Indeed UNICEF (2020) calls on educators at all levels to help children develop empathy and respect. While it is important for early childhood educators to be sensitive to these global challenges and to model and support empathy and care in a respectful and inclusive environment it is also important that we do not overburden young children with worries and concerns about the sustainability of the environment over which they have very limited control.

Creating and sustaining a learning environment to provide opportunities that encourages wide ranging exploration and meaningful thinking for children takes effort, thought and reflection. We know from research that the most effective early learning settings, those where children are engaged and interested and where they show positive indicators for development, learning and well-being, are those where educators intentionally plan for learning. In an extensive review of early childhood pedagogy Barblett et al. (2021) note that a responsive and intentional pedagogy has been found to be present in those settings considered to be of high quality. The concept of an intentional pedagogy has not gone unchallenged as it appears to be in opposition to the more traditional emphasis on a play-based pedagogy. The perception that there is a tension between an intentional and a play-base pedagogy is to misunderstand both. The evidence suggests that for play to have a pedagogical benefit to children educators must be skilled at balancing their roles and being flexible and nimble in their engagement with different children. Such a pedagogy can function in a playful environment where children's play and exploration are facilitated and are leveraged by educators to extend children's content knowledge, vocabulary, skills and dispositions. They create learning environments that encourage communication, they strike a balance of attention to assisting children in the development of their knowledge and understanding of the world and they maintain a language- and literacy-rich environment. In less effective early years settings, on the other hand, educators spend considerable time and effort focusing on children's physical development and creative endeavours (Siraj-Blatchford et al., 2002). Creative development is important, but it is most effective where the early years educator moves beyond simply providing the materials and the time so that, through attentive dialogue with the children within the context of creative activities, their own narrative abilities and conceptual skills can be extended. It seems therefore that the broad academic outcomes for children anticipated by policymakers and some parents, while not explicitly visible in the intentional pedagogy of the early childhood setting, are enhanced and become evident in later school settings. This is the case when educators themselves take an active and intentional role in creating and sustaining the learning environment, engage directly and meaningfully with children and know when it is best to stand back and observe, to listen or to question young children.

Early years setting should be attractive to children so that they can explore and play, be creative and take risks, question their ideas and their understandings and arrive at new problems for solving. In the main children are curious about their surroundings, they enjoy exploring, playing and getting to know how and why things work as they do. Challenges are good for children, but it is important to ensure that those provided take account of the individual child's capabilities and dispositions. When considering the act of thinking in young children it is likely that we expect it to include questioning, making connections, reasoning, evaluating, problem-solving and creative thinking. In the literature about thinking it is often described as either higher order [critical thinking] or lower order thinking. Lower order thinking refers to learning and remembering factual and procedural knowledge and the main responsibility of the early childhood educator here is to be clear in transmitting knowledge and procedural routines. Higher order thinking, on the other hand, refers to the metacognitive skills or 'thinking about thinking', the manipulation of ideas, evaluating and analysing information and includes the skills of problem-solving, predicting, questioning and justifying. These skills support the development of the executive functions mentioned earlier and here the role of the educator is more complex and sophisticated. It involves careful attention to designing a learning environment with activities and materials that inspire and motivate children in ways that enhance the development of the higher-level cognitive skills used to manage and control the actions and behaviour of daily life. Contemporary society is fast, complex and intertwined with information overload and multiple distractions. For positive early learning and development young children need calm and predictable early experiences which give them the encouragement and the time to develop the necessary functions and skills for later success in the more frantic world. The term 'executive function' is used to refer to these executive or management skills. Early childhood seems to be an especially sensitive period for the development executive function and research has shown the associated skills can be cultivated in children over 3 years of age (Blair, 2016).

A key contribution of quality early years practice to these developments is the provision of unhurried learning environments where educators themselves are calm and understand and respect the central developmental features of early childhood that need to be developed and refined during this first period of education. In her book *Mind in the Making: The Seven Essential Life Skills Every Child Needs* (2010) Ellen Galinsky elaborates on the skills of executive function in young children. The seven skills she identifies are (i) Focus and Self Control, (ii) Perspective Taking, (iii) Communicating, (iv) Making Connections, (v) Critical Thinking, (vi) Taking on Challenges and (vii) Self-Directed Engaged Learning.

She makes a strong case for giving very careful attention to the role of early childhood experience in the development of the skills she identifies and she points out that these skills are often referred to as 'soft skills', a term which is often used to describe the less measurable skills developed in early childhood. She fears that the term 'soft skills' undermines the value of the skills making the point that there is a strong cognitive dimension to them. She argues that these skills require intellect and are cognitive skills as much as they are social and emotional skills. They are important in their own right and not just as precursors to the development of other skills such as literacy or numeracy skills. They can be considered the essential cognitive 'how' skills to the more traditional cognitive 'what' skills. The importance of these skills was recognised and articulated by the United Nations when they wrote that the aims of education:

> not only include literacy and numeracy but also life skills such as the ability to make balanced decisions, to resolve conflicts in a non-violent manner and to develop a healthy lifestyle, good social relationships and

responsibility, critical thinking, creative talents and other abilities which give children the tools needed to pursue their options in life.

(2001, para. 9)

You can see the potential contribution that quality, intelligent early years practice makes to children's development of these skills and how it is uniquely placed to assist in the development of these particularly valuable foundational aspects of learning. Whether referred to as soft skills or life skills they are learned, developed and refined during early childhood and they act as the basis for later learning and development. They are critical dimensions to children's learning and they need time and appropriate early years experiences to strengthen and consolidate them. Armed with such a well-formed and supported tools, young children are better placed to gain more from other educational contexts and later life than children who have not had those opportunities. The opportunities can be missed in situations where children's early learning experiences are overly managed, too prescriptive, too academic or chaotic. It is a responsibility of the early childhood educator to understand, and explain where necessary, how these skills develop and to defend the need to attend to their development over and above the focusing on the more traditional learning skills we think of such as reading, writing and arithmetic. We now know from research that these latter, more formal school skills develop best when children feel confident about their own learning skills and interested in learning for its own sake, dispositions that are established in their early years.

Let us consider Galinsky's seven skills in more detail. *Focus and self-control* is a central executive function, which Galinsky further breaks down into component parts of (i) focus, (ii) cognitive flexibility, (iii) working memory and (iv) inhibitory control. We can see this focus and self-control in action when we look at how closely young children, even very young babies, attending to an activity they want to master. Think of the 14-month-old trying to get food onto a spoon in order to eat it; with encouragement they will try, try and try again. In addition to focus and self-control we also see, in the older child, concentration, often evident in facial expressions or actions such as biting the lower lip as if to hold on until the task is successfully completed. Cognitive flexibility refers to the ability to switch attention or change perspective from one thing to the next as necessary. It is important in that it assists children in functioning well in social situations as well as challenging cognitive activities. Working memory allows you to hold information in your head while you work with it or apply it. This capacity is central to, for instance, remembering stories told or read. It is to enhance the working memory that early years educators tell and retell stories and that children so enjoy hearing them again and again. Introducing 'mistakes' once the story is familiar and enjoyed can provide children with the opportunity to call on their memory and 'correct' the mistake. Inhibitory control refers to the ability to delay an action until it is appropriate, to manage impulses or feelings so that you can maintain attention on a particular task. Considered in its positive manifestation it is what we call self-control.

Perspective taking develops over time and involves the ability to step into another's shoes, working out what others may be feeling. It is through perspective taking that children make judgements about what adults mean and so it is important in early years practice that adults are attuned to a child's level of understanding and clear in the demands made. For instance, it is difficult for a 3-year-old to know exactly what you mean when you ask them to 'be good'. Being good depends on the context and can mean different things at different times. It is unhelpful to children to make such general demands. To encourage a child to behave in a particular way you should attract their attention and be specific about what you want – 'can you stay in your seat until . . .' or 'James, will you listen to Priya first and then . . .'. Galinsky points out that perspective taking uses a variety of executive functions such as inhibitory control, cognitive flexibility, reflection where you consider one person's view of things alongside your own. Where disputes or arguments happen, it can often come down to the fact that one person cannot or will not shift their perspective. We know from recent brain research and longitudinal studies into later school success that assisting children develop perspective taking skills, through providing a rich variety of different opportunities and allowing them the space to learn, is an important aspect of early childhood pedagogy across the age range from birth through to six years.

Communicating happens all the time both verbally and nonverbally and we have seen that it is recognised as a key element in children's development in the early years. Sensitive and attuned adults consciously strive to communicate clearly and to pick up on communication signals from children. This can be observed in babies at, for instance, changing time when a turn-taking, cooing session develop. The baby becomes animated, observant, participating in the game but is also learning important things about communication such as the role of tone of voice, the importance of eye contact and the rhythm of turn-taking which is a precursor to the rhythm of conversation. As well as the familiar aspects of language communication, understanding, speaking, reading and writing, communication also requires the development of understanding and selecting what is to be communicated or what aspect of a communication is important. These latter skills take time and are important forerunners to early literacy for instance. Evidence points to the importance of early education as a critical period for developing the foundations for later literacy and numeracy learning. For the development of these foundations, it is more important that educators focus attention on oral language development to support young children in becoming confident communicators, comprehending and speaking, during their early years experiences than on developing the skills associated with the act of reading or writing.

Making connections is a lot of what learning is all about. At a very basic level learning is about working out what is the same and what is different. Creativity comes about when unusual connections are made and we can see many examples of that in young children's play when, for instance they use materials in the 'wrong' way, when they explore and experiment. In observing how children play, how in pretend play they can make objects represent different things we are also observing how they are working things out, imagining new possibilities, making connections which ultimately inform their understanding of the world. While initially making connections may be simply about working out what is the same and different, it also includes finding out how things relate to each other. As they grow older and into later preschool age children can make multiple connections across objects, ideas and behaviours calling on executive functions such as working memory, self-regulation and cognitive flexibility. Early childhood educators contribute to these developments by allowing children the freedom and time to try out different connections and, through their leadership, facilitating the development of confident, engaged, creative learners.

Critical thinking is essential in seeking out knowledge and understanding and is a skill that can be strengthened and refined. It is that behaviour which poses questions such as 'what if?' 'why not?' or starts activities with 'suppose I do this . . .'. It involves testing ideas, challenging answers, developing ideas about what causes this and not that to happen. It is a skill that facilitates the scientific method, an ordered way of seeking to understand the world which is as important in day-to-day life as it is for scientists. Children need to be given the opportunities to engage in critical thinking; if they simply take unquestioned that which they are told then they become mere performers, behaving in the absence of understanding rather than learning. Opportunities to engage in critical thinking guide children in their learning and they grow to recognise the importance of questioning, of striving towards full understanding. In practice providing such rich learning opportunities for children to explore demands a transformation in educators from the traditional approaches in early years practice, where routines and activities are planned in advance for the children to 'do'. Based on our current understanding of child development and early learning we now recognise that quality practice is that which shares the learning experiences with children, and which is led more by the possibilities of the learning environment and the child's developing curiosity to explore and learn than by the transmission of facts or the training of specific skills. It is practice which recognises the greater understanding of the adult, but which also recognises that we are all learning. Taking the time to follow the child's lead in questioning, even where it may seem irrelevant, can often bring them to a richer learning experience than those we prescribe in advance. Such practice requires that we trust that children can and do learn without being told what to do or being overly guided in their actions.

Taking on challenges is an important life skill. Throughout our lives we will be challenged, some of us more than others, and it is in our earliest years that we learn how to respond to challenge. Challenge is often a good thing. For instance, Vygotsky (1978) encouraged adults to provide learning opportunities that lift children a little beyond what they can do easily when he introduced the concept of the Zone of Proximal Development [ZPD]. Challenging children in this way assists their progress along a developmental path. As adults we should not limit a child's opportunity to experience risk, to face physical and emotional challenges. Rather we should be alert to situations where some guidance may be necessary and provide assistance to children when they need it. In this way we can encourage the development of personal strategies for managing challenges and the coping skills necessary.

Finally, where education, at any level, is successful we observe children in *self-directed and engaged learning* which is as satisfying as it is useful. It is through this effective learning that we can all realise our potential, develop our individual talents and interests. This positive style of learning stays with us through life and can be called into action as each new situation and challenge arises. It is the type of behaviour we associate with educational success, but it also seems to be important to life success. It is professionally satisfying to observe children actively engaged in learning and, as they are busy playing, talking or thinking, we can take that time to observe them and to respond to them sensitively and effectively as necessary.

Positive executive functioning leads to more positive experiences and thence to more positive outcomes. On the other hand, poor executive functioning yields negative experiences and less positive outcomes. Two children can be similar in many ways, but one has poor executive function and the other has good executive function and, developmentally, they pull away from each other so that across a trajectory of time they are much farther apart behaviourally than they were initially. Differing executive functioning can be overcome with safe, secure and stimulating environments. So how might that manifest itself in practice? Well, a child with poor executive functioning is likely to be impulsive and by introducing a pause before a particular action or to get over some attention difficulty the child can learn to manage this impulsivity and the positive feedback from the environment [particularly the adults] will reinforce the value of pausing, managing impulsivity so that the overall effect is a sense of personal self-control. For children who are giddy or restless at times when you want their attention, for instance story-time, you can encourage them to attend and listen by actively including them in the process through, for instance naming them. As a general guide you can use a picture, perhaps of an ear, at the start of storytelling. The ear is associated with listening and so there is a concrete reminder for the child that it is listening time. Of course, for this to be effective there has to be something interesting and engaging in the listening activity. If it is forcing a child to be quiet and listen to something dull and/or boring it will be difficult to hold the attention of any children and there will be a general air of giddiness.

O'Reilly et al. (2022) present evidence that children from as early as 3 years old demonstrate early critical thinking and note that supporting the development of critical thinking is a key educational goal in many early childhood policy documents. Many researchers agree that critical thinking begins with students' engagement with a problem, no matter how small, where critical thinking is seen as the mental processes used to identify a problem, problem-solve, make decisions and learn new concepts. The skills of critical thinking are strengthened and meaningful when accompanied by thinking dispositions, such as the tendency to be open-minded, separating facts from assumptions, opinions or biases and being open to multiple viewpoints. With the extensive information available to children through various social media when compared to even ten years ago, it is crucial that children begin to learn how to filter this information through critical thinking. For this reason, supporting critical thinking as part of a child's digital literacy is important in early childhood.

The educator's role is to provide activities, objects, materials, space and time in learning environments that present opportunities for children to engage in higher order thinking. One of the ways to enhance critical thinking is through the use of storytelling and open-ended questioning of children to ascertain their views and help them to recognise that different children might hold different ideas. When early childhood educators take time and give attention to exploring the thinking behind children's communications and responses, they can identify the skills young children have developed and create further opportunities to strengthen them. It is important to understand that both lower and higher order thinking develop in parallel in the social context; we do not first acquire lower order thinking skills and then move on to higher order thinking. To assist children in realising their higher order thinking skills excellent educators provide challenge and should expect children, even very young children, to be capable, competent, thoughtful and reflective and assist them so that both types of thinking develop. Studies have found that where educators have high expectations of children, they are more successful at developing and refining thinking skills. Where expectations for children are lower adults are more likely to do things *for* rather than *with* children, to organise activities that direct children in their behaviour rather than providing opportunities for them to explore and discover new things for themselves. This may speed things up in a setting, but it does not allow children the time to bed down new skills and knowledge. While such environments may yield short-term performance in children, they are unlikely to facilitate children in becoming independent and confident learners. Achieving and sustaining early years practice that balances careful planning for the provision of opportunities for children's self-directed learning is challenging. It requires an understanding of child development, knowledge of individual children and their experiences so that the fine balance between child-initiated play and guided play can be achieved. It is, however, worthwhile as the evidence indicates that learner-centered practice, which invites children to explore and think about their world, yields the best outcomes for children.

A review of early years literature confirms that play is regarded as a critical element of early childhood education and care and considered a central process contributing to children's early learning and development. The word play is used to mean many things and is considered by some to be somewhat trivial and childish and relatively unimportant to the important task of growing up and succeeding 'at school'. For those of us who recognise the central role of play in the process of child development the perception of others that play is trivial and nonproductive poses a problem and a challenge. In an atmosphere where there is growing political attention to measurable academic outcomes and skill achievement for even very young children the value of play to children's learning is at risk of being lost. In such a climate there is a real danger that the foundational value of play may be missed in those areas of education, early childhood education and care setting, where it is most important.

The disappearance of play in childhood is not just a concern to those of us who see it as a fundamental process and driver of early development and learning (Gray, 2011). Article 31 of the UN Convention on Children's Rights articulates the child's right to rest, leisure and play. In its general comment on play (UN, 2013) the UN notes that 'play is one of the most distinctive features of early childhood through which children enjoy and challenge their current capacities' (2013, para. 34). This observation clearly locates the value of play in its immediate present, in the act, the process itself and not as a means towards instructing children in some particular skill or concept. In agreement with this observation the International Play Association note that 'there is a widespread lack of understanding of the value of play and it is often considered a trivial part of children's lives or dismissed as an unnecessary distraction from "more important" activities' [International Play Association, 2014, p. 2]. This lack of understanding on the critical role and value of play has presented challenges for early childhood educators who often find themselves having to defend their practice against the demands of parents and policymakers to achieve unrealistic, and often unhelpful, future-focused goals and outcomes. As the profession becomes more confident and the language of early childhood education and care becomes more polished and coherent there is a greater likelihood that the true worth of play will come to be recognised and the critical role of early childhood education and care in the developmental and educational life of children will be acknowledged and responded to.

Play is a central process in early childhood and is discussed in greater detail in Chapter 6. It is through play that children explore and develop their thinking and through it, children build resilience by developing such important aspects of development as self-regulation, emotional health and physical health. Within the relatively safe context of play emotions can find expression and management and children learn the complexities of interpersonal relationships (Lester & Russell, 2010). Through play children can follow their curiosity and their interests. There are a variety of essential features of play that have been identified by many authors including the view that play is a free and meaningful activity and carried out for its own sake – a safe place where children can overcome any sense helplessness they have where the experience itself, the process, is what matters. Play has an intrinsic value and facilitates the expression of feelings of joy, wonder, risk, anticipation, effort and intensity. Novelty can act as a motivation for exploration and play and can be the space within which educators can encourage thoughtful investigation, concentration and create opportunities for discussion and questioning. Playful exploratory learning requires risk-taking and this can challenge educators who are, rightly concerned with meeting basic standards of health and safety. However, a risk-free environment does not provide sufficiently for children's learning and developmental requirements with studies showing that children's overall well-being is supported in environments of safe risk and the benefits, the affordances, of risky play can be seen across a range of developmental dimensions. Our understanding of the value the outdoors and access to risky play has grown since the constraints of the COVID-19 pandemic. Within safe risky environments children can explore ideas and test their theories, they develop skills in planning and thinking ahead, they are challenged both physically and mentally. In planning learning environments where play is a meaningful activity and children are free to learn through their play successful educators exhibit positive attitudes to, and build in, safe risk opportunities and, through their engagement, observations and awareness they can avoid situations of dangerous risk and enrich and extend children's learning.

The science of learning confirms that children are active deciders rather than passive absorbers. The role of the educator includes creating environments that invite children to participate, that actively engage both children and adults to provoke their curiosity and exploration. Fostering the development of both the metacognitive and affective dimension to learning in early education can enable children to become ready, willing and able learners (Carr, 2001). Children are ready when they are motivated to use a particular skill or piece of knowledge to achieve something, they are willing when they can recognise where it is relevant to call on those skills or that knowledge and they are able when they know how to do something. The early years educator has an important role to play in motivating guiding and supporting children to become confident and capable learners who are ready, willing and able in most learning situations. Meta-cognitive and affective development is particularly important in young children as it facilitates the acquisition, comprehension, retention and application of what is learned, it assists with improving their learning efficiency, critical thinking and problem-solving and it gives children control or self-regulation over thinking and learning processes and products. Through the opportunities provided in early years settings children can, through their exploring and thinking develop and refine their learning and development.

In reflecting on how practice uses play to provide the learning opportunities for children early childhood educators can explain why they seek a balance between what adults do for and do with children. More experienced and well-informed educators not only understand the importance of a balance in their role in play but can also describe why it is good early childhood practice to integrate adult-guided with child-initiated activities and why play can, in and of itself, provide an excellent context for young children to develop and learn. This confidence comes from ongoing professional development, reflection and questioning in collaboration with colleagues. Reflection and questioning of practice can become a routine part of the daily practice in an early years' settings and contribute to creating and maintaining an atmosphere of learning which is both professionally satisfying and developmentally rewarding for children. To enrich and inform opportunities for reflection it is useful to take examples from your own day-to-day practice and reflect on them, alone or with colleagues, in the context of current literature and understandings of children's learning and taking account of guidance from curriculum frameworks. This can form the basis for regularly reviewing your own practice, questioning the ethos of practice in your setting and it can also provide a language within which you can consider the practice of others and explain your philosophy of practice as necessary. It should also present you with new questions and challenges, which in turn can enrich your practice, its effectiveness and your own professional satisfaction.

6 Play, pedagogy and pedagogical leadership

Introduction

Thus far this book has talked generally about aspects of relevance to early childhood education and care drawing on current issues related to how early childhood stands as a unique level of education, contemporary understandings of factors that influence and support children's early learning and development informed by what the research tells us about quality practice in early childhood settings. A number of interconnected themes were identified which, although drawn from the *Aistear* curriculum framework, can be seen in most international curriculum documents. The themes explored were well-being, identity and belonging, communicating, exploring and thinking. Evident throughout the chapters was the manner in which the early childhood educator can influence children's learning through their style of pedagogy and their important role in the preparation of environments that value play as a central process in guiding and extending early learning. This chapter is taking a closer look at what comprises quality early childhood practice, a practice that is both effective for children wherever they are in their developmental and educational life and also satisfying professionally for educators who, research tells us, are most effective when they are calm and stress free. The chapter will look at play as the process through which children explore, discover and learn and the play-based approach that most curriculum frameworks recommend as the most effective practice approach. The chapter also looks at the skill of responding to emergent content and discusses the science and art of early educational pedagogy and the role of pedagogical leadership.

In previous chapters we have mentioned play as an important process in children's lives and an important window into their development and learning. While play is recognised as a central feature of early childhood education its ubiquity in all our lives can render it commonplace and hardly worthy of notice. The expression 'just playing' suggests something trivial, unimportant and yet, in the lives of young children, play is their gateway into understanding and learning more about the world and their place in it. Despite all of the benefits of play, there is some evidence that play in early childhood is becoming used as a tool to achieve externally determined learning outcomes, rather than remaining at the core of childhood activity and a source of joy. Children's

DOI: 10.4324/9781003353164-6

early childhood experiences have changed significantly over the last two decades and they are spending extended periods away from the family unit, in family day-care or early childhood settings with children of 3 years of age being expected to devote more time on developing the skills of early literacy and numeracy skills than learning through their play and exploration, exercising their bodies and using their imaginations. Children impacted by poverty are often more at risk of missing out on the value of play and playful learning through the additional difficulty of limited access to play opportunities in neighbourhoods with fewer environments that are safe for children's play.

We know from studies into child development that, with careful support children can develop, through their play, from a simple understanding of their world towards more complex, abstract concepts. Research suggests that adult support for play allows children to develop new conceptual networks and knowledge that is valued in many early childhood curriculum documents. We also know that children learn best when they are actively engaged in meaningful and interesting tasks. Through sensitive and high quality early childhood practice educators can provide these meaningful learning opportunities in settings through drawing on the 'funds of knowledge' provided through the experience that children bring with them on a daily basis (Hedges et al., 2011). Children in early childhood settings play best in social surroundings where opportunities for interactions are available and the general atmosphere is one of content, compassion and joy. Providing such learning environments enrich and enhance children's development and learning.

Play is acknowledged as a critical part of a happy and a healthy childhood and looks different in different contexts. Because children's play takes many forms no single definition applies to all of them and agreeing a single definition is difficult. This absence of a clear and simple definition of play is reflected in the complexity of play we see in early childhood education and care. The critical features of play which contribute to young children's development and learning are hard to pin down, however, there are particular characteristics of play that are commonly used in discussions about play. For example Garvey (1990) provided a popular list of characteristics noting that play is pleasurable, with no extrinsic goals and is spontaneous and voluntary, involving engagement by the player, and is related to other cognitive and social purposes that exist outside of play. Bruce (2011) synthesised many different lists of play characteristics and proposed twelve features of play.

Features of play:

Children use first hand experiences from life.
Children make up rules as they play in order to keep control.
Children symbolically represent as they play, making and adapting play props.

Children choose to play, they cannot be made to play.

Children rehearse their future in their role play.

Children sometimes play alone.

Children pretend when they play.

Children play with adults and other children cooperatively in pairs or groups.

Children have a personal play agenda, which may or may not be shared.

Children are deeply involved and difficult to distract from their deep learning as they wallow in their play and learning.

Children try out their most recently acquired skills and competences, as if celebrating what they know.

Children coordinate ideas and feelings and make sense of relationships with their families, friends and cultures.

While these lists do not provide a definition of play they are a useful source of vocabulary that can help early childhood educators recognise and describe when children are playing. However, broad definitions of play have been criticised as too inexact and confusing. Zosh et al. (2018) suggest that rather than seeking out a specific list of types or features of play it is more productive and useful to think of play, not in terms of discrete types or linked to particular developmental outcomes, but rather as a continuum from free play through to guided play and games. From their research they propose 'a multidimensional definition of play that creates a spectrum of play opportunities' (p. 9).

Although play is recognised as a process through which children learn and is particularly relevant to learning in the early years, it is not the only way children learn. Many learning opportunities can arise in routine moments that arise throughout the day. Research by Edwards (2021), however, has found that such routine, basic activities are largely underutilised for learning even though they can provide predictability for children, act as safe periods where there are opportunities for conversation and can strengthen social skills. For instance, changing time with babies or meals times with small groups of children provide time for educators to strengthen children's oral language development and vocabulary. Preparing for different activities or health and hygiene routines also present educators with valuable learning opportunities.

To fully understand, and explain why play is so important in early childhood education and is, in fact, the key feature making early education a unique and distinct level of education, we need to look at what research tells us. Corsaro (2020), reflecting on his work with young children in early childhood settings, points out that play is often trivialised and its complexity and influence can be easily overlooked. It is, he argues, through their play that children display agency and creativity and provide educators with a window into their thinking and theories about the world and an insight into how to support their play. The evidence indicates that free play, child-led and with no particular goal, supports and strengthens children's social development, it is a space where children can safely discover the rules that apply and the strategies that serve them in building social networks. Guided play, where adults collaborate with children in a supportive way, has been found to promote and support the development of early academic skills and knowledge and foster learning dispositions. In sharing children's experiences within children's play educators can assist children in developing their vocabulary, their meaning-making and help them test out their ideas and theories. Such guided play differs from other types of play in that, while the child retains the power and agency to lead the play, the adult supports and structures the activity towards a learning goal, using the child's interest and capability as a learning opportunity to be extended and enriched. The adult does not direct the play nor plan the 'play' activity for the children, that would be what Zosh et al. (2018) call 'co-opted' play and, similar to direct instruction at this level of education, it is less effective across development than either free play or guided play.

Thinking about play as a spectrum enables us to retain the essence of play in our practice so that children continue to experience joy and have agency while we also recognise that play may take many different forms and serve many different functions. Free play, in which adults do not guide or scaffold, and in which there is no goal, is often what people think of when the think of young children playing. But this view is limiting and omits consideration, and understanding of the wider and more complex range of play experiences that are supported by adults but remain playful in essence. Research over the last few decades has repeatedly shown that learning is optimised when adults scaffold an environment or feedback toward a learning goal but the learning environment maintains a playful child-led atmosphere and encourages exploration and discovery. The evidence indicates that guided play, where adults support but children lead, impacts more positively on learning across many dimensions such as physical and motor, verbal and social skills, maths and science than either free play or direct instruction. There is some evidence that it is through a combination of free play in carefully created learning environments and supportive collaborative play with adults that children will develop what Golinkoff and Hirsh-Pasek (2016) have identified as the 6Cs – that is the six skills necessary for life success in the twenty-first century. The 6Cs are reminiscent of some of the features of development already mentioned and are: collaboration, communication, content, critical thinking, creative innovation and confidence. These skills appear as objectives or goals in many curricular frameworks and provide a useful list to consider when reflecting on and evaluating your practice.

Children have a right to play, a right that recognises that play supports child agency, allows children make choices, develop skills, succeed and fail, creates space for children to learn the social code, care for and respect others and their environment, all components of democratic society. However, a child's right to play is an abstract and somewhat vague concept and an insufficient reason for explaining why play is so important an element of early childhood practice or why committing to a play-based approach to pedagogy make such sense. To argue in support of play and play-based practice it is important to understand the theoretical basis for a play-based approach and provide evidence of its value relating to children's development across a variety of different developmental and educational domains.

Play and learning

There are also some myths about play that are best recognised and challenged. The most serious include the belief that:

If you do not teach children, they will not learn.

When children play they are not learning.

If children are playing, you are not teaching.

Children who are viewed as behind their peers academically do not have time to play.

Play is only for very young children, schoolchildren no longer need to play.

These myths are remarkably persistent and, in their contact with parents and other professionals, early childhood educators are well placed to counteract them. We know, for instance, that it is through their play and the safety of their play spaces, both physically and emotionally, that children process their feelings, strengthen their bodies and learn about the world around them and their place within it. In addition children's play is important as a source of information on how best to support children's development and learning through:

Giving adults insight into aspects of their inner world

Providing information about their language comprehension and cognitive capabilities

Helping adults understand how children to process and heal from stressful experiences

There is a complex relationship between play, learning, pedagogy, curriculum and outcomes (Brooker et al., 2014). Understanding this relationship requires both knowledge and experience. In terms of empirical, observed progression we know that children's play begins with solitary play and moves through parallel play towards social play as they begin to share and cooperate. Over time children actively collaborate in their play where we see the increased prevalence of pretend or imaginative play towards play with initially rudimentary rules towards more standard game play. We also know that these developments open up much wider opportunities for learning. However, children's play does not comprise discrete elements or stages that the child works through. Rather, the different types of play may interweave within one play episode and may serve different purposes. It is through observing children's progression across different levels of play that educators gather the information necessary to plan ahead for providing the environment and the opportunities that facilitate more complex play for children. Without this child-centred planning by educators, children's play may become repetitive, boring or fractious.

Bodrova and Leong (2007) in their influential writing on play point out that when thinking of the role of play in early childhood it can be regarded in terms of developmental learning, where the overall development of the child is the focus and includes both their socio-emotional and cognitive development. On the other hand the role of play can be characterised as focusing on academic learning where an emphasis is placed on the development of the skills and knowledge necessary to develop literacy, numeracy and other 'school' type capabilities. Studies have identified a tension between these different approaches to the role and use of play in early childhood. On the one hand the developmental role of play is emphasised whilst the other notes its role in academic learning. In turn, these two different views yield different pedagogical approaches with the former advocating the power of free play and a noninterventionist role for the educator, while a focus on academic learning supports the value of adult-directed play where the educator has a more active role in play. Given what we know about the way young children learn and the strong social dimension to it, research suggests that it would be most beneficial to move away from this binary distinction, as discussed in Chapter 3, towards an integration of both approaches as complementary rather than incompatible (Pyle et al., 2017).

One danger identified with the separation of focus to either an academic or a play-based practice is that early childhood pedagogy may become more teacher directed and 'schoolified' while guided play and free play would come to be regarded as trivial and unimportant, particularly for older 'preschool' children. Increasingly, research into quality and effective early years' practice is showing that a balance of all approaches is beneficial to young children with the balance changing in different contexts and across time. In relation to working with young children under school age current research advocates limited adult planned and directed practice and supports the value and effectiveness of a mutually directed pedagogy, where intentional teaching guides educator practice whilst children's play remains the context for learning. Research into sustained shared thinking and the pedagogical practices reported from Reggio Emilia support this integrated and collaborative approach where educator and child work together within the child's play space with the balance of influence fluctuating depending on the context (Siraj-Blatchford et al., 2002; Purdon, 2016). Figure 6.1 illustrates this integrated process.

A current dilemma experienced by early childhood educators, beyond the academic versus play-based debate, is the tension created between the traditional commitment to play as a central process in early development and the

Figure 6.1 Integrated play-based practice

external demands for a greater focus in practice on responding to new challenges such as climate change, sustainability and the influences of the digital world. While endeavouring to respond to these external demands, which crowd the curriculum space, early childhood educators continue to provide inclusive early learning environments for young children through providing play and learning opportunities that involve children in exploration, problem solving and social interactions. In addition, educators support children's learning more directly with their involvement in their play through collaborative practice where they share in conversation, meaning-making, questioning and discussion with children.

As our world becomes increasingly digital educators in early childhood settings are also integrating digital technologies into their settings, both as means of engaging with parents and also more explicitly into children's play and pedagogical practice. Children are in contact with and using many different digital devices, even from an early age and are experiencing the power of the digital world in their daily lives from their home environments through to different context within their communities. Research into early experiences with technology highlights the breath of its influence and the competence of young children as users. Even the youngest babies show skills of swiping and navigating mobile phones, home pods and tablets. Nonetheless, studies also show that there is anxiety and fear about the influence of technology on children's worlds and limited certainty about how best to avail of the digital power while at the same time ensuring the beneficial effects to the early education for young children. A review of research into practices with and attitudes to digital technology in early childhood has shown the multiple ways in which digital technology can open up new possibilities for children while also highlighting concerns regarding the suitability of digital technology for young children. Observation studies have found that young children's contemporary play practices include a mixture of 'real' and digital play practices, in which non-digital and digital toys and tools are combined in various ways in their play. Edwards et al. (2020) have characterised this play as 'converged' play and see it as providing many opportunities for learning across the span of early childhood.

Research from the Conceptual Playlab (Fleer, 2021), which investigates how young children form concepts about science, engineering and technology continues to provide evidence of young children's playful competence in a technologically supported world. Details of the research can be accessed at: https://www.monash.edu/education/research/projects/conceptual-playlab. There has been an extensive body of research into the impact of digital technology in early childhood settings and, in her review of this research, Undheim (2022) concludes with a call for:

> a play-based and child-centred practice where the teachers have knowledge of and acknowledge the children's varying experiences with digital technology but, at the same time, provide proximal support and guidance when children explore, create, play and learn with the technology.
>
> (p. 484)

She goes on to call for policy-makers and educators to define digital technology in a sufficiently broad way that acknowledges children's varying experiences with digital technology and notes that educators need time and opportunities to reflect on and discuss how they can implement and embed digital technology into their pedagogical practice and also how they can use it to support their own professional development.

Curriculum and pedagogy intertwined

The relationship between curriculum and pedagogy has an impact on the quality and effectiveness of practice in early childhood education and care. Edwards (2021) identifies two different ways of considering this relationship. In the first instance she suggests that the curriculum outlines guidance on the content, resources and practices that children are offered and experience in an early childhood setting. The term curriculum, derives from the Latin '*currere*' and has come to mean 'a course of study'. The word is used to define the content and/or goals of early childhood practice and, in early childhood education, it is generally presented in the form of a framework of guidance rather than a prescriptive content. In the second approach to considering the relationship, pedagogy is given prime position and represents the different types of practice that educators can use to animate the curricular guidance to support children's learning and development. The word pedagogy refers to that set of instructional techniques and strategies which enable learning to take place and provide learning opportunities for the acquisition of knowledge, skills, attitudes and dispositions within a particular context. Pedagogy is distinct from and complementary to the curriculum, where curriculum is understood to denote the knowledge, skills and values that children are meant to learn in educational settings and pedagogy is the action which requires an understanding of how the learning process unfolds, coupled with an awareness of the theory that supports that understanding. It is often referred to as the art or science of practice/teaching. Where curriculum values and peda-gogical guidance align educators have a secure basis from which to progress and against which to evaluate and reflect on their practice options. Successful learning environments are those that provide an 'enriched curriculum' realised by a pedagogy that both follows and leads children's interests and responds to individual differences.

In the early years definitions of practice must be sufficiently broad to cap-ture the unique nature of early childhood education and learning, allow for the educative value of exploration and play and provide space within it to include the caring dimension of the educator's role. The evidence tells us that too strong a focus on direct teaching and instruction should be avoided in the early years. While effective early childhood practice must, to some degree, be 'instructive' Siraj-Blatchford and Manni (2008) argue that where young chil-dren have freely chosen to play in a learning environment where the educator values intentional practice in collaboration with children in play, educators may be especially effective. They point out, however, that in their research, these collaborative interactions were rarely seen in early childhood practice.

Both the curriculum and pedagogy of early childhood are markedly differ-ent from that of older children in primary and secondary education, primar-ily due to the very young ages of the children involved, from birth through to school starting age. To smooth children's experiences of transitions from the apparently informal early childhood setting to the more formal primary school, policy documents often refer to the importance of curricular and peda-gogical continuity. I say 'apparently' informal early childhood setting because, to those unfamiliar with the process, the curriculum [the content] and peda-gogy [the how] children experience can be difficult to identify and articu-late. The content can be dismissed as mere play and the interactive and fluid way in which educators interact with children, individually or in groups, can seem content free and aimless. This is an unjustifiable misunderstanding of the unique and complex nature of early childhood learning environments and pedagogy.

Unlike primary school curriculum documents the early childhood frame-works do not detail any subject areas or content for educators to follow. Recognising the integrated way in which young children learn they provide guidance with the expectation that early childhood educators will have the professional skills and knowledge to design and plan practice that will achieve the goals or outcomes expected. This can be challenging for educators as the guidance on content is often vague and general and framed by references to play, active learning, and an emergent curriculum rather than to the specific content guidance one finds in school curriculum documents. Reviews of vari-ous frameworks have found consistent references to the importance of rela-tionships, interactions, children's active involvement in learning, daily routines, inclusive practice, assessment of and for learning and partnership with parents. References to play are ubiquitous throughout early childhood frameworks and many documents call for a play-based approach to curriculum and pedagogy, without elaborating on what exactly that means. This broad focus on play with the expectation that everyone knows what 'play' means, coupled with a generalised reliance on professional knowledge to achieve the expected outcomes, has left many educators unclear on how best to facilitate children's development and learning through play. In their comprehensive literature review of various curriculum frameworks Barblett et al. (2021) found that there was no consensus on a definition of play amongst educators, with different educators interpreting their role in play differently across different setting types. While play is broadly understood as a process through which children learn there is less evidence from research that educators understand the idea of play as a pedagogical approach or that play can be used in different ways to promote higher order thinking, connecting to content knowledge and building children's learning and social dispositions.

Play-based practice

In many contemporary western societies the current demands on early childhood educators to meet externally defined learning goals and outcomes has seen the traditional commitment to play as a central process in early development diminish. This has focused attention on exploring how to reconcile these apparently conflicting positions and develop an early childhood practice that can meet the demands for measurable achievements while continuing to support a play-based pedagogy. Research in the early childhood sector has established that simply providing play material and space for playing is insufficient for supporting children's acquisition of skills or content knowledge. To be developmentally effective the educator has to have a more active, collaborative role in the overall play process to facilitate children's learning. The interactive unit of the child, educator and environment is powerful and places the educator in a central role as architect of the environment and guide in the learning process. Edwards (2017) draws attention to the role of educators in providing a 'rich reality' for children, an enhanced learning environment through the provision of materials for exploration and experimentation in open-ended play and opportunities for discussion and problem-solving that can amplify the link between existing and new knowledge. The creation of an inclusive and calm environment that stimulates wonder, curiosity, discovery and joy can, in combination with motivated attuned and supportive educators, guide children as they learn new skills and travel the journey from not knowing to knowing.

The requirement to introduce more outcome-led practices has created anxiety among some educators who are committed to the traditional developmental play approach. Studies suggest that they are unsure and confused as to how best they can balance a child-centred and adult-directed pedagogy while maintaining a commitment to a play-based pedagogy where they have more freedom to make choices about the curriculum and pedagogy used and children are free to develop and learn at their own pace. Studies have found concerns among educators that the term 'intentional teaching', mentioned earlier and often referred to in curriculum guidance, can in itself lead to practice where structured play, templates and didactic teaching techniques are used, a practice more appropriate to primary education than early childhood education. There is a perception that the term 'intentional' means that educators are in control, know what children have to learn and should plan activities to lead rather than guide children towards specific learning goals. Such an understanding is at odds with the highly regarded early childhood practices found in many play-based settings and misunderstands the powerful relevance of purposive, intentional practice where the emphasis is on relationships, interactions, uncertainty and the power of novelty and surprise, where children and adults collaborate in learning and meaning-making. Externally determined curriculum demands can seem incompatible with playful environments resulting in classrooms favouring direct instruction but they need not be. The pull between supporting play and achieving nominated learning outcomes has led some early childhood educators to report that they feel uncertain about how to deliver learning through play and this tension and confusion is added to by perceived pressure from parents. There is evidence that while parents may agree in theory on the value of child-led, play-based learning but are sceptical that a play-based curriculum is not 'real' education.

A shift in practice focus to a blended approach, which includes intentional practice in collaboration with children, can appear challenging and difficult to enact and curriculum documents are not overly clear in their guidance, relying on the professional knowledge of educators for interpretation on what such a practice might look like. Thoughtful intentional teaching, or intentional practice, requires a level of systematic planning, but planning at a holistic rather than a day-to-day level. It is characterised by careful attention to providing a rich and exciting learning environment, indoors and out of doors, and is responsive to learning opportunities and teaching moments emerging from children's play, utilising the possibilities of guided play in balance with child-led activities. Guided play differs from free play in two ways: the educator helps to structure the activity and it is guided towards a specific learning goal. Critically, however, the child must still retain agency to direct the activity. Where a child initiates a context for play and then the educator intervenes to direct the play in a particular direction it is no longer guided play and has shifted away from a play-based approach towards an adult-directed activity.

While play-based programmes are not designed explicitly to achieve academically oriented outcomes such as literacy and numeracy, research has repeatedly shown that guided play, within an enriching learning environment, results in positive learning experiences for children on both the socio-emotional and academic dimensions. This is particularly likely where the environment has been carefully planned to provide opportunities for exploration, play and discovery. In balancing guided play with children playing independently educators are exemplifying a play-based pedagogy as opposed to those educators who merely make different types of play available within a setting.

Striking a balance between following a play-based approach while also meeting the nominated goals and outcomes demanded in curriculum documents is difficult and realising play-based pedagogy in practice is complicated. In discussion with educators research has found that educators can identify the challenge they face as a tension between choosing practice that focuses on academic content and school-readiness through direct instruction or following the evidence on how children learn best and allowing them the time and opportunity to engage in child-led play. A number of studies identified a number of common difficulties including that educators, although they recognise that play is important, experience difficulty integrating play and learning explicitly into their practice. Educators stated beliefs about play and learning are not always evident in the practice observed and practical problems, such as the power of parental expectations of what quality early childhood looks like, can influence less confident educators away from a play-based practice. One study found that a perceived inability to plan for children's play led educators to question the integration of play-based pedagogy, 'not because they did not value play but because they struggled to negotiate a balance between the child-directed play they felt was essential and the mandated academic standards' (Pyle & Daniels, 2017, p. 287). Recognising a mismatch between the concept of play-based practice and achieving certain learning outcomes for babies and young children, educators have called for enhanced initial teacher education and continuing professional development to improve their skills and knowledge base so they can support young children, confident that their practice has a sound theoretical and practical base.

Restricting views on play and learning to direct instruction versus free play, with a type of adult-guided play emphasised as child led somewhere in the middle, is too restrictive to encompass the multiple play-based strategies used by educators. The purpose of play-based learning is inherent in its name: to learn while at play. It does not need to be exclusively child-led but allows for intentional practice, in both planning and through guided play, where the child is positioned as an intentional learner. Child-directed play, collaboratively created play, and guided play all present important opportunities for personal, social, and academic growth. Recognising the challenges and anxious to remain true to the principles of early childhood pedagogy, while meeting external demands, early childhood educators themselves are calling for more professional development to build up the 'sophisticated planning responses' needed in order sustain strong play-based approach in practice (Kirkby et al., 2018, p. 677).

Pedagogical leadership

Visionary and dynamic leadership is regarded as a key element for improving and sustaining quality in early childhood settings and enhancing the effectiveness of early childhood education and leadership (Rudd, 2012). Within the field of education studies in general the specific level of early childhood education is a relatively new field of study. As such there has been somewhat of an absence of early childhood education and care voices influencing key national policy initiatives and, as the profession matures, there is a need for pedagogical leadership to influence and shape early childhood policy agendas (Barnes et al., 2019). This is critical because, although there is a great deal of information available about leadership and different styles of leadership, simply importing ideas from other professions into early childhood is problematic. The unique relational nature of early childhood education and care requires a very particular type of leadership, one that is collaborative, reflective, respectful and confident in realising and supporting the entire learning community within settings and beyond. Research has shown that successful, valuable practice with young children has been more frequently observed within settings where strong pedagogical leadership is evident and where leaders and educators share a clear vision of the setting's practices (Ang, 2014).

The many different models and approaches to early educational practice present many types of practice options and emphasise different dimensions of pedagogy as relevant to their particularly philosophy. It has been suggested (Siraj-Blatchford et al., 2002) that there is no one 'effective' early childhood pedagogy. Instead, in high quality settings effective educators apply practices that are sensitive to the curriculum focus of the moment and congruent with the balance of the child-initiated or adult-guided practice. Indeed, in the literature you will find reference to many different types of pedagogy which draw attention to specific aspects of practice deemed crucial including relational pedagogy and a pedagogy of listening. As noted earlier in this book I believe there is a strong underlying pedagogy of early childhood education and care, a nurturing pedagogy, that is sufficiently embracing to incorporate within it the different pedagogical elements that are specific to different approaches to practice while also maintaining those fundamental elements of quality practice that have been identified through both developmental and educational research. Nurturing pedagogy is a style of practice that is explicit in engaging with children, respecting them and integrating the learning opportunities provided across the care and education dimensions. It is derived from the belief that the close interactions between children and between children and adults drive development and learning. These close interactions have been called 'proximal processes' and are considered the engines of development (Bronfenbrenner & Morris, 2006). The key tools in early childhood education are the people in the process and the learning opportunities provided by the encounters. The extent to which practice is responsive to learning opportunities of even the most mundane activity, such as nappy changing, transition from one space to the next or tidy-up time, will influence the quality of that experience for the child.

A challenge of early childhood pedagogy is the 'messy' dynamic and interactive nature of development that requires educators to be attuned, responsive and reflective throughout their engagement with children. The term 'nurturing pedagogy' (Hayes, 2007) is a concept that was developed to capture the complexity of such a pedagogy and is informed by a belief in the active nature of child development and includes the child as a partner in development. In choosing to link the term 'nurture' with the word pedagogy attention is drawn to the unique nature of pedagogical practice within early childhood education and care with the intention of:

Reconceptualising care as nurture
Foregrounding the educative nature of care
Placing as central the critical and active role of the adult in effective, engaging and quality early education
Allowing for a more appropriate 'nurturing pedagogy' to emerge in early education learning environments.

A nurturing pedagogy foregrounds the educative role of care as nurture within the context of responsive relationships and playful interaction which support young children in exploration, dialogue and collaborative learning. Central to the concept is the idea that pedagogy provides a unique integration space for care and education which functions as a guide to an emergent and responsive early childhood curriculum and a form of assessment for and of learning where the role of the educator is one of low intervention and high response. In embracing the integrated nature of care and education, emphasising the role of relationships and valuing play as the central process in early learning, a nurturing pedagogy provides a framework within which pedagogical leadership can be framed towards supporting high-quality early childhood practice.

In Ireland, as elsewhere the quality of management and leadership for learning is one of the areas which is considered critical to the achievement of sustainable and quality early childhood services and the demands regarding quality made in policy documents anticipate highly qualified and skilled leaders. When considering leadership in early childhood two roles emerge as important, on the one hand management leadership and, on the other pedagogical leadership. The former is concerned with structural and organisational running of a service and the latter is more concerned with the ethos and philosophy of setting and the day-to-day practice. Expectations of pedagogical leaders might include documenting children's learning, reflecting on and evaluating practice, modelling and providing ongoing pedagogical guidance and support within settings and advocating for early childhood education and care with families and across the wider community. Where an early childhood service is small, such as in family day-care or childminding, the educator may fill both those roles but, for the purposes of this chapter the focus is on pedagogical leadership specifically.

In their study on effective leadership in early childhood Siraj-Blatchford and Manni (2007) discussed how 'leadership for learning' connects with effective communication, collaboration and the development of young children's learning. They identified a number of features common to the leadership styles observed in high quality settings including:

Identifying and articulating a collective vision, especially with regard to pedagogy and curriculum

Ensuring shared understandings, meanings and goals: building common purposes

Effective communication, providing a level of transparency in regard to expectations, practices and processes

Encouraging reflection which acts as an impetus for change and the motivation for ongoing learning and development

Commitment to ongoing, professional development, supporting staff to become more critically reflective in their practice

Monitoring and assessing practice through collaborative dialogue and action research

Building a learning community and team culture, establishing a community of learners

Encouraging and facilitating parent and community partnerships, promoting achievement for all young children

The skills required to achieve these various dimensions of pedagogical leadership require training, ongoing support and time and the evidence suggests that there is insufficient support and opportunity for educators to address this important ambition. Research has found that some educators have difficulty articulating what marks out leadership from regular practice while others report a lack of external understanding of the time required for providing visionary and transformative leadership in early childhood pedagogy, particularly the sensitive issue of capacity building among colleagues. In a review of the challenges and opportunities surrounding pedagogical leadership Heikka and Waniganayake (2011) draw attention to the collaborative and cooperative functions involved and identify the importance of communication and role clarity whilst also recognising the importance of connections and shared pedagogical vision among all educators.

Pedagogical leadership comprises a number of roles that include guiding and supporting children's learning directly through practice and indirectly through modelling good practice, capacity building within the early childhood profession both locally and beyond and raising the awareness of the wider community to the values and beliefs underpinning quality early childhood education and care. Those who take on a pedagogical leadership role also take on responsibility for the cultivating and sustaining a shared understanding of theoretical context and knowledge base informing pedagogy with young children. Through their research Siraj-Blatchford and Manni (2007) make a valuable distinction between supporting pedagogical interaction, that is the day-to-day practices within settings, and pedagogical framing – that is the more holistic planning that informs selection of materials, arrangement of spaces and routines. Through creating an atmosphere of discussion and reflection within settings educators can collectively work towards providing a nurturing pedagogy that honours young children's learning styles. A broad and deep understanding of how to leverage learning opportunities and unlock the content knowledge from within an emergent curriculum is an essential part of quality early childhood practice. Research has found however, that even in effective settings, there is a limited understanding of those curriculum areas relevant to the early years. Strengthening this aspect of practice, encouraging exploration of how best to support linguistic and conceptual development, enhance high order thinking and support creative skills is a crucial role for pedagogical leadership.

Providing early childhood education and care has become standard practice in contemporary society, with many countries offering access to free preschool for children aged 3–5 years for either one or two years. This creates a situation where children are spending long periods of their early life in the care of early childhood educators. For pedagogical leaders this presents the challenge of guiding colleagues to provide rich and effective learning environments which consider and respond to children's differing interests and capabilities so that their play and learning opportunities are diverse and developmentally relevant as they progress through the years. Planning and meeting the requirements of a two year old is clearly different to meeting those of a 4-year-old, however, recognising the difference between what meets the developmental needs of 4-year-old when compared to those of a 3-year-old may be more difficult. Differentiating the curriculum for children from one year to the next, while at the same time maintaining a playful, responsive and challenging learning environment entails excellent observational, interpretive and planning skills. This is best achieved where educators know their children well, recognise their interests and think ahead in terms of providing stimulating materials and activities in learning environments that invite children's participation and exploration.

Beyond influencing practice in individual settings the role of a pedagogical leader also involves connecting settings and their practices to a wider community and advocating for the profession where possible. As a profession, early childhood education and care is relatively new and so developing networks with other pedagogical leaders can be both personally supportive and build up a reservoir of resources to share on how best to practice the leadership role to the benefit of children, families, local communities and pedagogical leaders themselves.

The following section draws on a number of recent studies to illustrate some of the ways in which early childhood pedagogy can be enriched under the guidance of a pedagogical leader.

1) *Unlocking children's voices*

Supporting the development of oral language should be a primary objective for early educational settings. It is the basis of communication and a key foundation for thinking, strategising and problem-solving skills. To encourage and sustain children's oral language expression and comprehension educators need to know how to be good listeners of both the spoken word and nonverbal communications from children. Clark (2005) identified the following five principles as central:

> Respect for all children
> Openness and collaboration in communication
> Honesty about the extent to which we can take on board and act on children's views
> Patience and timing, particularly with the very young
> Imagination in designing varied and enjoyable way to listen that are also sensitive.

Listening is not limited to one exchange between two individuals but a more complicated web of interactions that are further influenced by the social and physical contexts within which communication happens (Clark & Moss, 2011). In discussing a pedagogy of listening Rinaldi (2012) challenges educators to be responsive and receptive to the multiple ways in which children communicate and respect the different voices that children use. A particularly rich context where conversations can be encouraged is the routine around mealtimes where social chatting can be scaffolded by adults to facilitate more complex conversation and where the everyday can provide content for expanding children's language with new vocabulary and their thinking with open-ended questions. Facilitating the development of a rich oral language in children is often undervalued in early childhood environments and pedagogical leaders have a significant role in encouraging educators to be available to children, to listen to them actively, to expand their vocabulary, provide language-rich environments and allow time to promote conversation.

2) Making children's learning visible

Historically in education, documentation meant the collection of records to be referred back to if and when necessary. In early childhood settings however, we have seen how documentation has become a central part of quality practice and reference was made to the use of Learning Stories in Chapter 3. Documenting learning has become part of early childhood practice because it provides a suitable mechanism for the assessment of children's learning, a requirement and expectation of many regulatory systems. It also provides a very useful context from within which to assess 'for' children's learning in that it provides educators with an excellent access point into children's strengths and also into their current position on many different dimensions of learning. It is important to stress that assessment here does not mean testing, rather it is a form of checking in over time, portraying progress and identifying areas for pedagogical and curricular improvement. Furthermore it is a safe space for unlocking the cultural and emotional experiences that inform children's activities and guide practice. What changes traditional record keeping into pedagogical documentation is the movement beyond simple recording into interpretation, reflection and, in particular the sharing of the documentation with colleagues, parents and children themselves to broaden and deepen the scope of our understanding of young children. This latter point is particularly relevant to the advocacy role of pedagogical leadership.

Documentation gathered over time and collaboratively can inform educators, while making visible to children and parents, children's growth across a wide range of dimensions including socio-emotional, intellectual, physical and linguistic development. Documentation also provides a space within which to consider those early skills and knowledge that can contribute to later achievements in more mainstream educational areas such as reading, mathematics, science, digital competence and the various arts such as music, drawing, painting and drama. Documenting children's journeys of exploration, discovery and knowing across time is a powerful tool for informing practice and transforming learning for both adult and child.

3) Connecting with children

We have seen how valuable pedagogical documentation can be in early childhood settings. An important role for the pedagogical leader is to encourage colleagues to take the time necessary to collaborate meaningfully with children, this collaboration is a key dimension of effective pedagogical documentation. In their report on children's perspectives of quality Coleyshaw et al. (2010) investigated how educators access and respond to children's perspectives in their use of documentation. They identified three different levels of practice, some pedagogically more meaningful than others. At its most basic settings merely offered children choice in accessing materials and activities while more consultative approaches managed the context of choice carefully so that all children were afforded an opportunity to be included. In the most effective settings educators exhibited a more mature and respectful approach where they facilitated children in their participation and provided clear feedback to support children in their contributions to documenting their activities and learning. To be a useful tool in achieving and sustain quality practice documentation needs to be systematically gathered, comprising observations, notes, photographs and children's work which interact with each other across time to provide a rich portrayal of the learning journey of each child.

Documentation also has a role in helping educators make the most of what is observed and recorded in collaboration with children. There is very little value in jotting down a few notes, affixing a drawing or a photo and leaving it at that! There is a skill to accessing material from children on their ideas, their successes or their feelings and interpreting these messages through the multiple media that is available. The pedagogical leader can support the educator role to enquire into the meaning behind children's activities and communications, reflect on what it tells us about their feelings, learning, their thoughts and share the data in a way that communicates clearly what has been interpreted. Halpenny (2021) notes the potential for pedagogical documentation as a generative process or 'learning in action' with the potential to be transformative through transforming knowledge and thinking. Pedagogical leadership can maximise the benefits from documentation through modelling exemplary practice and creating space for colleagues to experience safe discussion and reflection.

4) Celebrating time

The practice style of pedagogical leaders will influence the style of colleagues. A serene leadership creates and encourages a tranquil early years environment. There is a trend in early educational literature to talk about 'slow pedagogy' and 'slow knowledge'. This move echoes the message behind the concept of the hurried child, first introduced by Elkind (1990/2007), in his book *The Hurried Child*. His concern was that children are living in a society of distraction and information overload and require early learning environments that are calm, where there is time given to them to play and learn at a pace that allows them to assimilate, refine and bed in new skills and knowledge. Clark (2022) reiterates his point and calls for early childhood educators to give time to listening, to slow down their practice and give children the opportunity to assimilate and explore new opportunities. Providing an unhurried environment where educators respect the central features of individual children's development and are themselves calm, favours supporting children over delivering particular goals or outcomes. Halpenny (2021) argues that setting aside time for pedagogical documentation can enable a slowing down of practice which can build up a strong relationships between educators and children allowing for careful observation and recording of children's interest, activities and opinions.

In atmospheres of calm this supports children's excitement, joy and wonder with attention to collaboration in the moment rather than focusing on the next thing to be done. This is particularly important with babies and toddlers where they are beginning to seek out their place in the world, distinguishing their own self from others and where their play is becoming more social and complex. Pedagogical leaders can support these developments by foregrounding the importance of time into their day and encouraging colleagues to allow less happen but in a more meaningful way, to recognise that such 'wasting time' can be invaluable. Dalli et al. (2011) have reported on the effectiveness of this type of practice in gaining an understanding of how babies and toddlers learn. The primary skills for educators identified in their study were emotional sensitivity and orientation which requires a level of organisation and planning so that there is a systematic approach to gathering the data to inform practice. Such organisation frames the context that allows time to be valued and celebrated.

5) Honouring story

Storytelling is a fundamental feature of early childhood practice and has the potential to be pedagogically meaningful. A systematic review of storytelling linked to the development of critical thinking in young children (O'Reilly et al., 2022) found that dialogue and questioning techniques, the use of thinking language by educators and story-based approaches were successful strategies for strengthening young children's critical thinking.

Results suggest that a range of interactions promote critical thinking. When educators are aware of the concept of critical thinking and enquiry-based activities and used dialogue or questioning techniques various critical thinking skills were promoted. O'Reilly et al. (2022) note that stories, storytelling and drama in early education are seen as a natural way to stimulate dialogue, investigation and problem-solving in children. The advantage of these story-based approaches over more direct instructional approaches is that children are drawn to stories and motivated to listen and participate. When considering story and storytelling in practice the role of the pedagogical leader is to explore and explain findings that can guide educator practice in storytelling to draw out emergent critical thinking skills and stimulate thinking.

6) Expanding pedagogy beyond the bounds of the early childhood setting

The concept of pedagogy can be extended to beyond educational settings into community and public settings. Such expansion creates opportunities for experiencing new places, meeting new people and learning new things across a range of dimensions. The majority of people simultaneously inhabit many different microsystems, and the intermingling of these spaces underlies learning, both formal and informal, across time (Jackson, 2011). Broadening the learning ecology for educators and young children can change the learning horizon making new skills and knowledge acquisition possible. It is in the richness of new learning that understandings of the world and our identity in it grows and is transformed. The content of a learning ecology comprises all the things that are within the learning space including the people within and around it, the linguistic and cultural dimension, the materials available, the technologies, new ideas and information that are used. Planning to find new learning environments and learning possibilities beyond the setting requires educators to reconsider the concept of educational space as fixed and open up a range of possibilities on what education and learning can include. Learning is more than the achievement of a set of prescribed learning goals outlined in a curriculum framework. Rather the framework can be used as a stepping off point to explore new opportunities. There are many examples of the impact of learning that happens in the home and community, evident even in the behaviour and activity of babies and young children and ordinary, everyday experiences can have a pivotal role in children's learning.

Learning in any setting comes, not only from experiences in that setting but from the full range of settings experienced by the person (O'Toole et al., 2019). Extending a focus to learning beyond educational settings has the potential to create educational spaces for young children that are more diverse and inclusive than the early childhood setting alone. An interesting example of how pedagogical leadership in early childhood settings led to facilitating connections to the community beyond the settings is provided in the context of intergenerational learning [IGL], mentioned in Chapter 5. IGL involves bringing together people from different generations where they can learn together and learn from and about each other (Gallagher & Fitzpatrick, 2018). IGL is presented as a new pedagogical strategy which links children, educators and families with the older generation. As part of the project young children visited old people in care homes. During the visits the young children played and chatted to the older people and, for their part, many of the older people shared stories from the past and demonstrated crafts that they learned as young children. An evaluation of the Together Old and Young, or TOY, project (www.toyproject.net) found that IGL offered a complex context for learning across the generations. For young children in particular the researchers found an expansion of language, the development of critical thinking and social skills and opportunities for reflection and recall. Also highlighted was the kindness and empathy of young children, the pleasure for parents (some of whom became involved) and for older people.

IGL is just one of many possible ways in which the role of educational settings can be extended to generate linkages between children, their families and other settings in the broader community. It takes time and planning to extend the reach of settings in a way that is beneficial to children and others. Pedagogical leadership within settings can create an ethos which supports efforts to extend the boundaries of the learning environment and utilise the many different learning spaces available.

6) Advocacy

Where educators need to defend their practice or advocate for support for play-based early learning environments as effective early educational practice they can call on the research literature and science for support. They can also find support through sharing their pedagogical documentation as a visual illustration of how and what children learn in such environments. In their work with Reggio Emilia the Project Zero research team (Kerchevsky et al., 2013) argue that making learning visible is important in raising awareness of quality practices at a time when external pressure may be more focused on standards and outcomes than the role of educators or the needs and rights of children. It also acts as a form of accountability and their research identified three specific forms of accountability that were enhanced by careful documentation gathered collaboratively over time with children. The first level of accountability was 'accountability to self' where the opportunity to review and reflect on documentation allowed for identification of the progression of learning and the quality of recording all of which goes to raising personal awareness of day-to-day curriculum and pedagogy. Secondly, 'accountability to each other' where the community of learners, which can extend to parents and families, support each other and build up a shared identity. Finally 'accountability to the wider community' as a means of awareness raising and advocacy which can strengthen the professional identity of early childhood educators among themselves, other professions and society. The role of pedagogical leadership is important in advocating for greater understanding and support for the type of quality early childhood services that benefits children and staff alike and, in this regard, making the learning of young children visible is a powerful tool.

7 Sustaining quality early years practice

Introduction

The intention behind presenting the material in this book was to introduce contemporary thinking and experiences of quality early childhood education and care practice. The evidence provides information that can inform practice and act as a prompt or provocation for reflection drawing on your own beliefs and your experiences of early years practice. This final chapter reflects on the previous chapters towards contributing an integrated reflection on early years practice to stimulate the conversation proposed so that we can all work towards achieving, supporting and sustaining high-quality early years practice that adds constructively to the lives of babies and young children. Chapter 1 begins with an introduction to the authors foundational beliefs about early childhood and its importance to the quality of lives of young children who, in the Western World [or Global North], are spending more time in such settings than ever before. It goes on to consider what is meant by early childhood education and care, its characteristics and the features that contribute to making it such a distinctive period of education. Drawing on research and policy literature it also touches on some of the opportunities, challenges and tensions facing early childhood educators. Chapter 2 looks more closely at why early childhood practice is important in children's learning and development. It reviews what the research tells us about optimising environments so that they are welcoming, inclusive and influential spaces for babies and young children, professionally satisfying for staff and meeting the needs of parents and requirements of regulation. This chapter also introduces the concept of a nurturing pedagogy, an early childhood practice which is returned to a number of times. Looking more deeply at research on practice Chapter 3 looks at enhancing quality early childhood practice and addresses some of the curricular debates and tensions about beliefs on what sort of curriculum should inform what children are learning in early childhood settings and if there is a particular pedagogy that is more effective than others. Chapters 4 and 5 introduce six selected themes for practice, themes commonly found across curriculum frameworks internationally. The themes, while treated separately, intertwine in both practice and effect; they are well-being, identity and

DOI: 10.4324/9781003353164-7

belonging addressing topics of importance to the socio-emotional, affective development of children and communicating, exploring and thinking referring to the activity of learning, the development of early academic skills and acquisition of knowledge. The aim of these chapters is to name and describe the reasons behind much of the current understanding of what makes for quality early childhood experiences, particularly those that enhance young children's quality of life in our complex, interconnected, fast-paced and multicultural world. Chapter 6 introduced three wide-ranging topics current in early childhood discourse and scholarship – play, play-based practice and pedagogical leadership. Throughout the chapters there have been references to the critical role of the early childhood educator interspersed with references to findings about 'best' practice uncovered by research.

This chapter presents an opportunity to review the theory and practice sections of the book, to reflect on the key aspects contributing to quality early years practice and to consider how best to utilise this knowledge in enhancing and sustaining it. The content of this book is based on the premise that the most effective early childhood practice is that which is always open to new knowledge, new ideas and which has a sound theoretical basis. Our own history and experiences of learning influence our practice in a way that can be less than useful. We carry knowledge and some of the myths from our past with us into our practice. And they can be hard to move on from, even where the evidence suggests they may be misguided or simply wrong. Our understanding of child development and learning is expanding all the time and some of our folk knowledge is out of date. Contemporary society is changing at an accelerated rate with families and communities becoming more diverse and interconnected. Children are bringing a wide range of different experiences to early childhood settings which can enrich them or create difficulties. In settings that celebrate these changes educators show willingness to welcome the new and challenge and explore personal assumptions and attitudes. In this way they can provide young children with the rich learning environments they need to experience in order to develop the skills dispositions and new knowledge essential to adapting to the changing world.

In addition to social changes in the lives and communities that young children are growing up in there are also changes in the broader environment. Our world is becoming increasingly connected and interconnected. Technological advances speed up the arrival of information and require the development of new skills on an almost daily basis. Social media allows families and educators to be in contact throughout the day and we have yet to explore and fully understand the impact of this level of surveillance and interaction on the lives of children but also on the parent/professional relationship. These social and technological changes are happening within a world that has become increasingly conscious of the fragility of the environment and our position within this. As we have seen in Chapter 4 this has led to increased attention to the role of early education, at the macro and micro level, to topics such as climate change, biodiversity and sustainable development raising awareness of the role of nature in our lives and its importance to the lives of babies and young children.

In Chapter 1 I presented six personally influencing beliefs about young children, which were then considered in more detail from the perspective of contemporary research knowledge. These beliefs have informed the choice of content in this book and bear repetition. They are (i) that children are central to quality practice; (ii) children are basically good; (iii) interactions are the key process through which we learn and develop; (iv) children have agency and contribute to the learning; (v) early year experiences are critical to the journey of learning and development; and (vi) adults play a crucial role in providing quality early years experiences.

No one of these beliefs can stand in isolation from the next and their interconnectedness provides an opportunity to identify some holistic assumptions which collectively act as a useful basis for reflecting on early childhood education and care and the curriculum and pedagogy that contributes to providing quality early learning environments for babies and young children. In the first instance we can see that *young children are active agents in their own learning*. This concept has emerged from the influence of both psychological understandings and the impact of the UN Convention on the Rights of Child (1989) recognising children's capabilities and rights to participate in matters affecting them. It is a key consideration for early childhood educators as it may present tensions between your structuring or planning for practice and the agency in children's lives. In exploring this dilemma, the importance of early educators applying a collaborative rather than a directive approach to practice has emerged as crucial. This connects with a second idea that foregrounds *the dynamic, social and interactive nature of early learning*. Whilst the child is located at the heart of practice, we acknowledge the interdependent nature of the relationship between the child and adult as they engage in joint learning and sustained shared thinking. Research confirms the social nature of development and the centrality of relationships in the lives of young children. It highlights the critical role of the positive interactions and relationships to brain development and the associated executive functions in the early years.

As described here, research into quality early childhood pedagogy highlights *the critical role of the adult* in supporting children's learning through designing enriching learning environments and well maintained, interesting materials that facilitate exploration and play. An understanding of play as a process is one that can be found in most curricular documents and it is the expected activity in early childhood settings. However, when considering the reality of providing a play-based approach, also frequently noted in guiding frameworks, research has found that, when asked educators indicated that they value play, but their observed practice does not always support this. Other studies found that educators may have difficulty in fully appreciating the balance in roles between themselves and the child in relation to play. This is particularly relevant when considering the relationship (or tension) between providing a play-based curriculum while also engaging in intentional practice when children's play and activity afford particular learning opportunities. It may help to think of intentional practice as an approach to guiding the child as an intentional learner in overcoming the implicit, but mistaken, expectation that intentional practice is a directive or teaching practice. The key finding from the research is that the effectiveness, for children, of early childhood education and care relies on the quality of the early childhood educator, skilled in the specific art of early childhood practice. In support of the critical nature of early years experiences the concept of *early childhood education and care practice* has been reconceptualised into many different forms of pedagogy including the pedagogy of listening, relational pedagogy, slow pedagogy, critical pedagogy and creative pedagogy. In considering these, and other pedagogies, I have suggested reflecting on early childhood pedagogy in a more holistic, overarching way which I have called a 'nurturing' pedagogy. Elaborated more fully in Chapters 2 and 6 the concept of a nurturing pedagogy recognises the entwined nature of care and education rather than separating them out as discrete concepts or privileging one over the other. The concept of nurture has a historical precedent in early childhood studies and was implicit in the practice proposed by many early childhood pioneers. One such was Margaret McMillan who established nursery schools in the UK and US and proposed that children 'be nurtured by women who understood child development socially, emotionally [and] academically' (Liebovich, 2016). This has a contemporary resonance in that it allows us view care as an educative process. It is reformulated here to emphasise the educative nature of care and to place the critical and active role of the adult as central in effective, engaging and quality early education (Hayes, 2007).

Another theme to emerge throughout the book was the importance of *content, language and risk-rich learning environments.* Children's interactions with the social and physical environments [indoor and outdoor] are the central location of development and the interactions should be challenging and rich in both language and content and afford quality opportunities for exploration, play, risk and thinking. The onus is on the educator to provide and support such enabling environments and be flexible in responding to the learning opportunities that arise in children's process of being. When working from a curriculum framework, such as *Aistear*, rather than a more prescribed curriculum, the challenge for educators is to translate the curricular guidance into content that supports disposition and skill development and knowledge acquisition. The curriculum informing practice emerges from the encounters between children and their environments and the adults and other children there. The skilled educator can draw out content and learning possibilities from a combination of educator knowledge, children's behaviour and environmental affordances. Another idea to emerge stresses the *importance of play and playfulness as a pathway to learning.* Play is not the only way children learn and in Chapter 6 we noted the value of the learning opportunities, frequently underused, provided in the routines of daily life. Nonetheless play is a primary process in young children's learning and it is this fact that separates early childhood education and care out from other levels of education. Play research has explored the many potentials of different types of play from the perspectives of both the child and the adult, recognising its importance to babies and young children, as well as its role as a window for the adult into the world of the sensing, active and playful child. We note in places the tensions that can exist between the desire to remain true to a play-based pedagogy while responding to external demands for early childhood to be a preparation space for children prior to attending primary school. The final idea we see threaded through the book concerns the *affective dimension of learning*. This dimension of learning focuses on what have been called the 'soft skills' of learning and are captured in the term socio-emotional learning, although they also have a cognitive aspect. The affective dimension of learning is less easy to measure than the more familiar cognitive/academic dimension. This may account for why we often assess success on outcome measures like literacy and numeracy skills rather than outcomes in well-being, happiness or self-regulation. In early childhood education and care the support of the affective is a central task of educators. It is here that children consolidate their dispositions and the executive functions that allow them to manage their behaviours. It is these aspects of learning that are essential to establishing the learner identity of children and supporting much of the learning that will occur across the lifespan. Regrettably, notwithstanding the research evidence to the contrary, they are often seen by parents and policymakers as less important than the traditional skills and knowledge associated with learning, the 3Rs [reading, writing and arithmetic]. This in turn raises one of the important roles for pedagogical leaders noted in the previous chapter, the importance of advocacy for early childhood education and care as a unique level of education and a nurturing pedagogy as the most effective practice. As the field matures a common professional language is emerging and a research base is consolidating all of which contributes to a sound professional identity. It is from within a confident professional space that educators can voice their professional position when challenging certain external demands and help parents, for instance, appreciate the pivotal role play has in early learning and explain that through play, in the 'apparently' informal environments of early childhood settings, children are developing the dispositions and skills they will use in later learning.

Celebrating play and play-based learning and practice

Those of us familiar with the factors that contribute to high quality early childhood education and care are aware that play is important and that the type of play children engage in and its purposes change over the course of childhood. Play is more than the activities we characterise as play, it is the very process through which children explore their world, imagine other worlds and establish a sense of themselves as an individual and part of a wider social group. While most parents and other adults recognise the value of play and playing to a child's physical and emotional development, they are less secure in their belief that it contributes to what they might consider real learning. For educators the challenge is to help them appreciate the way in which play, and a child directed play-based approach to practice, establish the foundations on which later, more traditionally recognised academic skills and knowledge can be built.

When you consider the skills that enrich and expand children's thinking, remembering, paying attention, you can see how play has a prime role. These skills, acquired and strengthened in play, allow children to solve problems, to imagine new possibilities or new solutions and to refine their conceptual understandings of shape, colour, counting, letters and numbers, all relevant to cognitive development and academic learning, early literacy and numeracy skills. It is in play that children experience the opportunities to explore language in their interactions, in sustained conversation with adults and other children, through story reading and storytelling. It is within these activities and experiences that their language, both their expressive language and their receptive language, is improved and extended. Play, in its broadest sense, provides the opportunities that help babies and young children learn the importance of listening and the rules underpinning dialogue and conversation. It is here also that, in multilingual environments the diversity of communication possibilities can be observed and built upon and the nature of languages explored. Story time is where children come to understand how narrative works in terms of plot, character, structure and through story reading they acquire the underlying skills of reading, in English, from left to right and top to bottom. It is also how children learn that sentences comprise words that are made up of letters. Coming to understand the symbolic nature that underpins reading and writing lays the foundation for how symbols are handled across a range of academic areas including maths, science, drama and music. Beyond this we saw that storytelling offers excellent opportunities for helping children develop higher order, critical thinking skills.

Play-based practice has been discussed at some length in Chapter 6. It is an approach to education that nurtures those skills, understandings and dispositions that are essential for a child's lifelong learning and well-being. It is a very different approach to educating children when compared to primary or post-primary education and it should be. It is suited to the unique nature of early learning where the content of children's skill and knowledge development is integrated across different domains. Play-based practice requires the educators to know their children well, have a sound underpinning knowledge base and intentionally prepare environments that will attract and challenge children to explore and play. Through their planning educators facilitate quality play opportunities that allow children the time and space to become deeply involved in activities, to concentrate and to construct knowledge. Within these learning environments the educator observes how children are interacting and playing and, when the time is right for a particular child or group of children, to join and intentionally guide conversation or actions or questioning that can strengthen learning. For instance in water play, through careful and regular observations, concepts of maths, science, oral language and drama can be identified. It is the skill of the early childhood educator to catch these emergent learning opportunities and intentionally expand and enhance them in collaboration with children so that they progress in their learning while working within the play process. One of the skills of the professional early childhood educator is to articulate to others the pedagogical nature of play-based practice and this can be done through thoughtful use of explanatory language and clear, well-constructed documenting of learning. In discussing play-based practice and intentional instruction we mentioned the idea of the intentional learner. Where children feel welcome in their early childhood setting, where their identity is secure and respected, where the environment is calm and responsive they are more likely to be interested in exploration, play and learning and so, the quality educator has a role in inspiring young children to be intentional in their learning and to respect that intentionality, the motivation, with a pedagogy that nurtures their potential.

Planning the environment is an important role. One of the first figures in early childhood to point to this was Maria Montessori whose work influenced the creation of environments that were fitted to the size of children and called attention to the need to consider children's visual viewpoint when designing and planning learning spaces. While her ideas continue to be influential contemporary contexts are very different now and we know more about the way children learn. As a consequence, many early childhood environments, while still planned around children, look very different to those Montessori would have worked in. Early years environments are now designed to encourage and support children in their interactions and their play. They are equipped with materials and spaces to stimulate exploration, conversation and rest and, in many settings, children are now encouraged to move freely between the indoor and outdoor areas. There has been a move away from structuring the early childhood day around a fixed timetable of activities to a more fluid approach which affords greater freedom for children to follow their interests and promotes their independence. Research has shown how important the quality of the environment is and recommends that more attention be given to making environments comfortable and attractive, to taking care that equipment, books, materials and spaces are pleasing on the eye and invite attention. Too much equipment and too many books of mixed quality can be off-putting for children and defeat the purpose of making them available in the first place. It is possible to see the way practice in Reggio Emilia has drawn attention to the learning environment, its aesthetic and the use of space, while the Scandinavian experience has informed the growth of interest in outdoor settings as sites of learning.

While recommending an approach that is free from timetabling activities, high-quality settings do have overarching routines that are predictable and this predictability is something that children benefit from. A loose routine allows time for activities but also offers a consistency that allows children to plan while also requiring a level of adaptation to certain requirements. Getting the balance between expecting children to sit or to attend to something versus the opportunity for them to lead their own play and activities is realised best when educators have given careful attention to planning the environment and know their children well.

Strengthening early childhood practice

Early childhood settings that are of high quality, beneficial to children and their families and professionally satisfying are those where adults are knowledgeable and up to date with contemporary understanding of how young children learn and develop and exhibit engaged and intelligent practice. This requires appropriate initial training and on-going professional development. Well-trained educators provide appropriate sensory input and stable responsive relationships for the babies and young children they work with and provide the strong foundations of learning, well-being and health across time. It is clear from research evidence that the interactions between children, adults and environments are key to development and it is here that the adult has a primary role. One cannot overstate the importance of relationships in the early years. We now know that brains are built over time. 'Decades of research tell us that mutually rewarding interactions are essential prerequisites for the development of healthy brain circuitry and increasingly complex skills' (NSCDC, 2007, p. 96). The brain architecture is constructed through a process that begins before birth and the process is enhanced by stable, secure and caring early life experiences. Engaged interactions, responsive to the child's natural tendency to interact reciprocally and attuned to the natural give and take that can be seen in infants as young as days old, have a profoundly positive effect on early development.

A balanced practice that integrates educator input with child-initiated activities provides a dynamic context for learning and development. The idea of integrated learning is not new, Dewey stressed the importance of interest as a motivating force for activity and reflection and saw the role of the adult in the process as that of guide or mentor. A respectful and democratic early years environment provides children with the opportunity to develop those skills essential to participation in a democratic society. Babies are now recognised as socially competent and active in their engagement with people, places and things comprising their learning environments. The evidence suggests that, even with babies, early childhood practice that emphasises the affective dimensions of learning and early cognitive skills can positively influences children's later academic cognitive development in terms of content knowledge, literacy and numeracy skills. This approach yields foundational short-term benefits and sustainable long-term benefits across social and educational dimensions. This highlights once again the crucial nature, the centrality, of relationships to learning and development. The child's interactions, whether with an adult, another child, an object, materials, an idea, the natural or the digital world, are the site of learning. The relational process around these interactions itself is a key part of the educational experience as, particularly in early childhood, it drives development and, as such deserves reflection and analysis in and of itself.

Recognising the importance of the social context to development supports the view that development is not an isolated, individualistic pursuit and that children's participation within a social context transforms their experiences. The research has found that learning environments where educators facilitate more involvement with, and attention to activities by children result in their learning more skills and concepts, including the kind of knowledge that gets tested on achievement measures. In addition, children from such settings show more cognitive advance and variety in their verbal and social skills. This may arise because attending longer or more intently to interesting activities gives children practice in paying close attention, a skill highly valued by early childhood educators or because making decisions and having some responsibility for their own learning and actions may help children internalise control or strengthen the positive dispositions that enable children to succeed in life. Perhaps the explanation lies in the fact that children may just be happier, and so better motivated, and may, in turn, be responded to more positively by educators. One way or another, contemporary studies in early childhood move beyond a focus on the individual to consider the broader, interactive, integrated nature of learning and development, the role of the individual [child and adult] and the environment as actors each with the potential to transform the other. Early childhood educators who are knowledgeable, skilled and well trained have an important role to play in creating positive early learning environments, facilitating healthy interactions and, where relevant, the early identification of, and response to difficulties or problems. A review of research suggests that the following strategies are pivotal:

Listening to children across the ages to observe and understand the learning strategies children themselves bring to a problem or an activity, the strengths they have and the opportunities that allow more knowledgeable other [peers or educators] to help.

Establishing common knowledge through using the learning opportunities presented by situations where children are playing or gathered together in groups provides examples of common experiences and therefore common ground for expanding children's thinking.

Opportunities: Ensuring that young children have many situations in which to speak and listen so that their communication experiences are broadened.

Finding ways to look beyond the obvious or the familiar and to reflect in words to babies and young children what they are doing in action. This helps them to clarify processes and ideas and acts as a form of scaffolding.

Encouraging children to recall experiences associated with a shared task to assist children build learning continuity and establish new or enriched concepts and understandings.

Using positive modelling is a powerful way to assist children to extend their meta-cognitive strategies to regulate task achievement. For instance, using 'thinking language' can provide children with the words to express their thoughts [what is the problem I am working on; what is my plan; how will I proceed; what has worked to solve this problem; how do I know?].

Asking children to build theories that can explain events in which they show interest is thought to keep children interested and active in particular tasks. In such situations it is helpful for educators to use open-ended questions to allow children expand their thinking and imagination and strengthen their skills of communication.

Focusing through recall and restatement. This requires careful questioning, clear responses and explanations linked through to events or activities. It is important in gathering pedagogical documentation including children's learning stories.

Spending time in observation either through standing aside from or joining in children's play activities, with sensitivity. Gathering observation records as a basis for reflection or a source of planning enriches practice.

Listening to and coordinating with parents and family members to establish children's strengths and interests, their dispositions and how the child's development and learning is mediated through the home. Close contact between early educators and the home learning environment is beneficial as it allows sharing with parents and educators share their understandings of an individual child's development.

Celebrating diversity through expanding children's knowledge and understanding of diverse cultures, languages, music, stories, images and rituals. The context and content for this can come from the children themselves and from their families.

The evidence suggests that quality early childhood practice depends on attuned, motivated and calm staff who are informed by a combination of personal experience, a secure knowledge base and an understandings of early child development. A central element of a quality, nurturing pedagogy is the quality of communication and interaction with babies and young children and, as societies become more diverse, creating opportunities for connections between settings and the child's home learning environment is also regarded as beneficial.

Assessment and pedagogical documentation in quality practice

We saw in Chapter 3 how assessment can be used in early years practice as either assessment for learning or assessment of learning and noted that the former, assessment for learning, has a powerful contribution to play in informing practice and planning. Here we consider assessment in greater detail to illustrate how assessment can be used in the daily routine of an early years setting. Dynamic assessment is an interactive form of assessment; it is neither an assessment instrument nor a method of assessing. Rather it is a framework for considering practice and assessment as an integrated activity useful in understanding young children's abilities while supporting their development, it is assessment in practice. It draws on Vygotsky's (1978) concept of the Zone of Proximal Development, which highlights the developmental importance of providing supports to learners that encourage them stretch beyond their own independent performance. Effective dynamic assessment represents a unification of theory and practice where the theory offers a basis to guide practice but at the same time practice functions to refine and extend theory as learning opportunities arise for children.

A key element in assessment for learning is the expectations that educators have of the children they are working with. Research has shown that adult expectations have a profound effect on the direction and style of children's learning. There is evidence to suggest that those working directly with children and families from disadvantaged backgrounds may presume that, simply because children come from limited or impoverished environments, the children themselves may be somewhat limited. This is problematic as most children, even those who come from severely disadvantaged or chaotic backgrounds can be motivated and enthused for learning if they meet with an engaged adult who trusts their capabilities and provides doable activities in a safe and secure environment where the child has a sense of belonging, of being an active and respected member of the early years setting. The research tells us that the impact of early childhood education and care on all children, but particularly those who start life with disadvantages, can be profound and life enhancing. Where educators are engaged and attuned to young children and have high expectations for them, they create rich and challenging learning opportunities where children are more likely to develop positive learning dispositions.

Planning, as has been mentioned throughout the book, is important to effective practice, however it can be constraining if too directive, rigid or over-prescriptive. Effective planning is often not explicitly evident in settings but is a well-established habit of mind within educators themselves and supported by the ethos of the setting. How can we reconcile the tension between responding to the expectation of others that there is 'a plan' or a timetable of activities while ensuring that our practice is meaningful and effective in the moment for the child who is living and learning in the moment? In considering this tension the following example from my own experience may be helpful in understanding how important and valuable it is to plan and that careful planning allows for rich, spontaneous practice in the day-to-day practice of early years settings.

When I am invited to present a lecture or a presentation to a seminar of students or an audience of educators I approach it in the same way. I find a focus and title for the topic, I draw on my experience and reading to draft an outline for the presentation. Once this is done I reflect on the topic and may develop, for instance, a powerpoint presentation. Over time I run through the issues and points I want to raise to ensure they fit within the timespan I have been allotted. On the day I then use the powerpoint as a frame within which to present my seminar or lecture. I am well prepared and so am free to engage in a type of conversation with the audience, add anecdotes that spring to mind in the moment and generally personalise the content to the context and the audience. Thus, when it works, planning presents a framework within which I am free to draw on my experience and knowledge to present key ideas and points to the particular audience in a way that, at its best, is responsive to the moment, natural, flowing and engaging and ultimately satisfying for both myself, and the audience.

Translating from this example to planning for responsive practice in the early years requires a slightly different approach which comprises three elements: (i) the structure needs to take account of the characteristics of the learning environment and the profile and age of the children, (ii) the content can be informed by experience, knowledge, research or guidance from curriculum and quality frameworks and (iii) the time available is guided by the routine and the flexibility you have as an adult within that. Thus, the planning and the content ideas exist in advance, but the practice is guided by the moment, is responsive to the group and engaging for both the adult and child. In addition, confident educators are ready to be surprised and challenged by children who can ask profound questions which may not be readily answered. Acknowledging our own knowledge gaps and modelling ways to fill them is an important skill and provides a strategy for discovery which children can repeat.

Planning is greatly enhanced where the educator is familiar with the children and families attending the setting. Such familiarity is acquired through good communication and careful collection and management of documentation. In general, there are two types of documentation of use to early years settings – administrative and pedagogical. The former is essential for meeting the legal and regulatory requirements for providing early years services and for maintaining accurate and up-to-date data on children. For the purposes of this book however it is pedagogical documentation that is of more interest. Pedagogical documentation is a means towards observing learning in action, studying and enriching ones understanding of the whole child. It was mentioned in Chapter 3 where using Learning Stories as a form of assessment was discussed. It has a long history going back the Child Study Movement in early twentieth century Europe and the US (Hayes, 2012). Observation, where data is recorded and reviewed, is a tool for understanding, for observing how the whole child in context is developing and learning, for unpacking what observed behaviour can tell us through reflection and discussion, rather than deciding what the behaviour represents on the basis of our immediate reaction to it. There is a tension between the need to understand how children learn and develop and allowing us to let the child show us their learning and development in action which can often yield explanations and understandings that are both particular to the child or group and also offer a path for practice that is relevant and meaningful. In early years practice observation for understanding the developing child in the day-to-day midst of life in early years settings is central. Pedagogical documentation is far more than simply recording or interpreting isolated dimensions of development of the child such as physical or language development, it allows educators the opportunity to know the whole child in context, recognise diversity and acknowledge, value and learn from different perspectives and interpretations.

In her influential paper on the use of pedagogical documentation Alcock (2000) lists a number of elements of documentation that are necessary for it to become an effective element of practice. In the first instance she discussed the tools which can be used. These include cameras, audios, videos, computers, photocopiers, pen, paper and voice, all of which can be augmented with the extensive array of digital technologies now available. The type of content that can be included in documentation includes children's work; photographs; plans; drafts of work in progress; audio/video clips of children and adults in action; written transcripts of children spontaneous articulations and recordings of language; comments and interviews with children and adults; illustrations, which can be accompanied by child commentary and standard child observations.

A critical dimension to using certain pedagogical documentation constructively is how it is displayed and this takes thought, time and regular revisiting. It requires clear walls with no unnecessary clutter and this, in turn, involves careful team consideration of what exactly constitutes clutter. Careful attention needs to be given in terms of what to display and why; material may lose its meaning and value if it is dis-embedded from its context when displayed and hold little or no meaning for the children even where it might appear meaningful to adults. Visual material marking events in particular can lose its relevance very quickly and nothing suggests lax practice than festive posters weeks after the occasion has passed. While displaying art work and project-based material is important Alcock notes that '[W]ithout an analytical explanation or explicit link to learning goals or outcomes these colourful products can create a sense of chaotic clutter rather than inspiring pedagogical reflection' (Alcock, 2000, p. 2). Carefully managed documentation can unlock a rich seam of learning opportunities; it can stimulate memories; conversations and reflections on plans met, ideas forgotten, successes, failures and new ideas emerging.

Pedagogical documentation is documentation that documents learning in action. It requires a change from more traditional practices, a change which research suggests alters rather than adds to the time in practice. It is not about multiple individual reports for each child on a daily basis or an additional element of practice to add to the daily routine; rather it is a change in practice, a revision of routine through a collective dialogue around pedagogical documentation – creating it, displaying it, reflecting on it, making it part and parcel of your daily practice. Simply gathering material and putting it on display is not what we mean when we talk about pedagogical documentation. The name itself suggests it is recording learning as it happens and reflecting on it. Pedagogical documentation links ideas, events and behaviours, it bridges across time and content, it allows for discussion among children themselves or with an adult, sometimes a parent or grandparent. It is enriching and informing for those involved and yields positive change in children visible in their behaviour, their engagement and the overall learning environment. In addition to impacting on adults and children in the early years setting pedagogical documentation also facilitates the home links and bridges the daily transitions that children make. It also acts as the basis for the larger transition bridge through to the infant classes in the primary school and, in some cases, a personal learning portfolio may be developed for and with the child as part of this.

Documentation, whether for learning, assessment or planning, is most effective when approached collaboratively rather than through isolated individual activity. While individual observations of individual children have a key role to play in aspects of early years practice, such as gathering specific developmental or social information, the more general day-to-day documentation in practice is a social activity and its value rests in that fact. When we talk about collaboration in these contexts it often includes the active participation of the children themselves. Realising this in practice with very young children is challenging but there are many resources to assist. We have mentioned the work of Carr and her colleagues (Carr & Lee, 2019) on the use of visual documentation such as drawings, photos and video clips which has proved more powerful than the traditional written documentation. The visual impact of a photo, for instance facilitates the inclusion of children who can see themselves belonging and who recognise themselves in their past and can reflect on and discuss it in the present. Such practice is democracy in action and facilitates a context where learning becomes more reciprocal, where children learn in an engaged way with adults and other children who respect each other. This reciprocal practice makes visible for children their place in the setting and enhances their sense of belonging and self-worth.

Contemporary digital technology has widened the possibilities of peda-gogical documentation. Video recordings provides a useful temporal or time dimension to pedagogical documentation in a way that other materials fail to. However, it needs to be used in a specific way, it is not entertainment and the content needs to be well understood by the adult to exploit its potential in understanding the children and understanding their stories. To overcome the view that photography and videoing children is an invasion of their privacy it is important to respect and include children and their families. When you understand and recognise the value of this form of pedagogical documenta-tion you will be in a position to share this with parents and engage them in the process as interested and important participants. Over time this becomes a normal part of the settings practice and routine. In certain situations, parents may also wish to share video material from the home learning environment with the early years setting.

Educators may also gather less public pedagogical documentation in the form of their own personal professional learning portfolios. Critical to the effectiveness of such documentation as a pedagogical tool is the way in which it is discussed, reflected on either individually, collectively in the team or with a critical friend. This type of self-evaluation is both personally satisfying in giv-ing a language and focus to daily practice and also effective as a form of Pro-fessional Development [PD] to improve practice and so increase supportive environments for children. It offers a space for connecting theory to practice. Studies have found that early years educators are more likely to be effective when they enjoy and seek out the challenge of practice. The impact of adults who are disengaged or disaffected can be damaging. While everyone may have days where they are not all that 'on task' it is crucial that those adults charged with the responsibility for the education and care of young children love what they are doing and recognise both the value and the limitations of their role so that they find satisfaction through their daily practice and are less likely to become bored or suffer burn out.

Establishing a professional identity

As is evident from the material presented, working with children under 6 years of age requires educators with a very particular skill set. Common features noted in commentary and research include a genuine interest in young chil-dren and curiosity about, and respect for, their learning and development. Relationships are central to effective practice and outstanding early childhood educators are good communicators, flexible and responsive to children's play and many different ways of communicating and caring and compassionate. The research also points out that, while experience is valuable those educators who are most effective hold relevant qualifications.

In general a profession is understood to be an occupation that requires specialised education, knowledge, training and a code of ethics. In the con-text of early childhood education and care as a profession we can see that, broadly speaking, it meets these criteria. However, as attention to the field has increased at both a policy and scholarly level one finds 'competing and contradictory discourse of professional identity' (Woodrow, 2008). Professional identity is a contentious and problematic concept and it is certainly one that generates significantly different views accompanied by different expected outcomes for early childhood education (Moloney, 2010). Research has found that, while in some countries early childhood educators have a secure professional identity, in general there is a desire among many early childhood educators for greater certainty and for a status reflecting the complexity and importance of their work. A secure professional identity gives visibility to a profession and a sense of satisfaction and self-worth to the professional. In terms of professional identity this book proposes that the profession of those working with young children from birth to 6 in a range of settings from family day-care/childminding through crèche/preschool to early primary be recognised as Early Childhood Education and Care. Internationally, this has been the accepted title for the profession since 2001 (Neuman, 2019). Although it has proven complicated to name and frame the profession, with job titles as diverse as childcare worker, teacher, practitioner and educator, this book has opted for the title early childhood educator. This reflects the belief that the work is more than a vocation, involves complex and challenging practice to be successful and is increasingly moving towards a graduate workforce with an internationally strong academic presence establishing across a range of colleges and universities.

Although here is not the time to discuss the topic of professionalism and professional identity in any depth one can judge the problem from research findings going back over the years. Studies show that maintaining the professional standards and remaining true to the ethos of early childhood practice is difficult for early childhood educators and internationally many are grappling with low status, poor working conditions (Mooney Simmie & Murphy, 2021; OECD, 2019) and increased regulatory and administrative demands. Despite such difficult and demanding work situations there continues to be significant external demands made of early childhood educators which can make the day-to-day situation very disheartening. The professionalisation of the early childhood system in Ireland, as elsewhere has been considered key to ensuring the provision of quality early childhood services with new standards, regulations and qualifications being introduced and promises of professional status and rewards. This policy attention is often accompanied by unrealistic expectations about how such a quality early childhood system can address child poverty, inclusion, school readiness, digital literacy, climate change and the work-life balance for parents! These unrealistic expectations of a, generally, poorly resourced system add to the pressure on educators. The process of professionalisation has been much debated and contested amidst concerns that a techno-rationalist professionalism imposed from above is at odds with an autonomous, agentic professionalism from within (Osgood, 2010; Campbell-Barr, 2018). A study in Ireland (O'Regan et al., 2019) found that while participants favoured the model of autonomous agentic professionalism from within, the external regulatory processes were very powerful. Working in such a demanding environment, individual educators need strong professional support from within the profession itself to challenge the status quo. From within the profession itself they can draw on the expertise of practice and give visibility to the professional nature of their work. To achieve this requires a strong commitment to change and support through professional development programmes. A review of three studies on effective professional development approaches (Peeters & Sharmahd, 2014) found that educators participating in a change process aimed at developing a new pedagogical approach to working with children and parents found that pedagogical support as a form of professional development, sustained over long periods of time and developed by specialised staff (such as pedagogical coaches), was regarded as a successful way to develop reflective thinking on practice and to construct new knowledge and practices when working with families and children. Such a proactive approach, established through a supportive network of professional development and pedagogical leadership, can lead to changes in the way in which the profession of early childhood education and care is understood and consolidate the unique professional identity of early childhood educator.

Reflective practice

The power of collective reflective thinking has been noted throughout this book. A challenge to reflective thinking is that the 'knowledge' we routinely use, and rarely reflect on or question, comforts us with a familiar structure but may lead us to replicate what has always been done with the danger of repeating mistakes or failed approaches to practice. This in turn restricts the space within which to challenge ourselves and develop our professionalism. This folk knowledge is rarely articulated, discussed or made visible, it is just the way things are. Reflection and reflective thinking can bring it to our attention and provides the basis for the evaluation of practice on an ongoing basis. The term reflection within the current literature is often used to describe a variety of practices, from simply thinking of one's own plans to considering the social, ethical, and even political implication this thinking has on actual practice. The word reflection carries with it the idea of looking back which can lead one to consider that reflection is something that happens after the event. We plan an activity and carry it out and we review and reflect on it later. However, reflective practice is richer when it is considered in the context of being present in the moment, an inclination towards careful consideration of what exactly is happening in the moment, a reflection in process. This is a deep level of reflection, which requires an awareness and engagement with the moment rather than wondering how this moment will impact on some distant outcome. It suggests an interest in the potential of this moment for you and those children you are working with. Such practice emerges from a well-established understanding of what early years practice is about and it depends on careful planning that allows you to unlock the possibilities of practice in the present.

There are many levels and types of reflections in the growth of reflective practice. Some definitions of reflective practice focus on the connection between particular practice to identify learning goals and outcomes, through for instance, reviewing and analysing one's own actions, decisions or choice of materials. Other definitions characterise reflective practice as a lifelong attempt involving a longer and more lasting commitment to the ongoing learning and continuous improvement of the quality of one's professional practice (York-Barr et al., 2006). Still other definitions consider reflective practice as requiring one to move beyond a focus on isolated events to consider the broader context including the personal, pedagogical, societal as well as ethical contexts associated with professional work. There is general agreement that reflection can be considered as functioning on the following three levels:

> The *surface level* is the level that focuses on the practice skills, actions and roles, generally looking at each teaching episode as an isolated event. The focus is often on the educator reflecting on approaches and techniques used to reach particular goals.
>
> The *pedagogical level* is a more advanced level where the educator considers the theory and rational for current practice. At this level the educator is expected to be working towards understanding the theory behind a particular practice and applying these theories to their practice.
>
> The *critical level* represents the higher order where educators examine the social, ethical and political consequences of their educational processes and practices. At this level, they also inspect both their professional and personal convictions and how they impact directly, and indirectly, on children.

Larrivee (2005) recognises that new early childhood educators and students in training may be at a pre-reflective stage, requiring guidance in developing the skill of reflective practice. He notes that those who are truly self-reflective examine how expectations and assumptions, family influences and cultural conditioning impact on them. They also recognise that there are tensions between theory, policy and practice, which they need to reconcile. This level of critical reflection moves educators to look not only at their own practices but also at the social implications of these practices.

In many documents addressing curriculum and practice for quality early childhood practice the educators are urged to be reflective with little elaboration on what this might mean in a busy early childhood setting. Some authors have argued that the term 'reflective practice' has become so prevalent as to be almost meaningless and its potential, particularly through collective critical reflection, to question dominant understandings of young children and early childhood education may be lost. In a study exploring the development of skills for reflective practice in early childhood Lemon and Garvis (2014) used a template drawn from the work of Anderson and Krathwohl (2001). The template comprised a reflective process of six stages:

Remembering relevant practice related knowledge drawn from observation
Understanding through interpreting, comparing and explaining
Applying knowledge to, for instance, the requirements of practice in a curriculum framework
Analysing determining how different elements relate to each other to inform practice
Evaluating and making judgements through checking and critiquing
Creating further questions from evaluating new constructions of practice.

The research found that using this systematic approach on a professional development programme aimed at assisting the quality of reflective thinking contributed to enhancing the development of reflective practice in the early childhood educators and the development of skills essential for the profession. This underpinning strategy can, over time, become habitual and central to informing the process of practice on an ongoing basis. A reflective early childhood educator is one who regularly reviews their practice, asking 'why am I doing this, of what value is it to the child, the group, my colleagues, parents, community?' Such reflection shows an understanding that part of working professionally in the early years is to be willing to recognise that there is always something more to learn about child development, learning environments, practice in general. As noted in Chapter 2 the word 'why' should be a key word in quality early years practice. It acknowledges the need for constant reflection on the quality of the environment, both indoors and outdoors, and the impact on young children. Furthermore, when answered, it can give confidence and a professional identity to educators who, when called upon, can defend the value of early childhood educators as professionals to policymakers, other professionals and parents.

This book has been designed to contribute to the ongoing professional development of early years educators. It is, as outlined in Chapter 1, intended to be the start of a conversation. It presents research evidence to explain why quality early years practice is important and what such practice looks like. Central to the effectiveness of early years practice is the well-informed and knowledgeable early years educator: one who knows why certain approaches are best and who is present and engaged in early learning environments which are not only rich in objects and materials but also in opportunities, which are language, content and risk rich and where relationships are nurturing, and pedagogy maintains and sustains children's learning and development. To raise the status of early childhood education and care, to achieve recognition for the unique education period it is and to access the support necessary to sustain high quality, there needs to be a confident and consistent professional language of early years practice. This can enrich our descriptions of what we do in early childhood settings and, more importantly, explain why educators do what they do and what makes early childhood education and care a unique period of education. Curriculum and quality frameworks can contribute to the emergence of a common, shared language of practice with a view to participating in the development of a cohesive professional identity for educators across the variety of early years settings. Within this context of reflection, conversation, discussion and continued learning we can provide quality early childhood learning environments which are satisfying to educators and of benefit to the young children who spend time there confident that we are getting it right from the start.

Advanced reading list

This list is made up of references to articles, reports and books that provide an introduction to research in early childhood education and care and guidance for further reading on a variety of practice related topics covered in the book. They are a personal selection which I hope you find useful.

*Barblett, L., Carmel, J., Hadley, F., Harrison, L., Irvine, S., Bobongie-Harris, F. & Lavina, L. (2021). *National Quality Framework Approved Learning Frameworks Update Literature Review*. Australian Children's Education and Care Quality Authority (ACECQA). https://www.acecqa.gov.au/sites/default/files/2021-09/2021NQF-ALF-UpdateLiteratureReview.PDF

*Bodrova, E. & Leong, D. J. (2007). *Tools of the Mind: The Vygotskian Approach to Early Childhood Education*. 2nd ed. Columbus, OH: Merrill/Prentice Hall.

*Bronfenbrenner, U. & Morris, P. A. (2006). The bioecological model of human development. In R. M. Lerner & W. E. Damon (Eds.) *Handbook of Child Psychology: Vol 1: Theoretical Models of Human Development*. 6th ed. Chichester: Wiley & Sons, pp. 793–828.

*Brooker, L., Blaise, M. & Edwards, S. (Eds.) (2014). *The Sage Handbook of Play and Learning in Early Childhood*. London: Sage Publications.

*Clark, A. (2017). *Listening to Young Children: A Guide to Understanding and Using the Mosaic Approach*. Jessica Kingsley.

*Clark, A. (2022). *Slow Knowledge and the Unhurried Child: Time for Slow Pedagogies in Early Childhood Education*. London: Routledge.

*Dalli, C., White, E. J., Rockel, J. & Duhn, I., with Buchanan, E., Davidson, S., Ganly, S., Kus, L. & Wang, B. (2011). *Quality Early Childhood Education for Under-Two Year Olds: What Should it Look Like? A Literature Review*. Report to the Ministry of Education. Wellington, NZ: Jessie Hetherington Centre for Educational Research, Institute for Early Childhood Studies, Victoria University of Wellington.

*Department of Education and Skills (2019). *Wellbeing Policy Statement and Framework for Practice*. Dublin: DES.

*Derman-Sparks, L. & Olson Edwards, J. (2019). *Anti-Bias Education for Young Children and Ourselves*. 2nd ed. Washington: National Association for the Education of Young Children.

*Edwards, C., Gandini, L. & Forman, G. (Eds.) (2012). *The Hundred Languages of Children*. 3rd ed. Santa Barbara, CA: Praeger.

*Edwards, S., Mantilla, A., Grieshaber, S., Nuttall, J. & Wood, E. (2020). Converged play characteristics for early childhood education: Multi-modal, global-local, and traditional-digital. *Oxford Review of Education*, 46(5), 637–660. https://doi.org/10.1080/03054985.2020.1750358

*Erwin, E. J., Valentine, M. & Toumazou, M. (2022). The study of belonging in early childhood education: Complexities and possibilities. *International Journal of Early Years Education*. https://doi.org/10.1080/09669760.2022.2128307

*European Commission (2018). *Monitoring the Quality of Early Childhood Education and Care: Complementing the 2014 ECEC Quality Framework Proposal with Indicators: Recommendations from ECEC Experts.* https://data.europa.eu/doi/10.2766/99057

*Fleer, M. (2021). How conceptual PlayWorlds in preschool settings create new conditions for children's development during group time. *Learning, Culture and Social Interaction*, 28. https://doi.org/10.1016/j.lcsi.2020.100438

*French, G. & McKenna, G. (2022). *Literature Review to Support the Updating of Aistear, the Early Childhood Curriculum Framework.* Dublin: NCCA.

*Golinkoff, R. & Hirsh-Pasek, K. (2016). *Becoming Brilliant: What Science Tells Us About Raising Successful Children.* New York, NY. American Psychological Association. https://doi.org/10.1037/14917-000

*Government of Ireland (2018). *A Whole of Government Strategy for Babies, Young Children and Their Families 2019–2028.* Dublin: The Stationery Office.

*Hayes, N., O'Toole, L. & Halpenny, A. M. (2023). *Introducing Bronfenbrenner: A Guide for Practitioners and Students in Early Years Education.* 2nd ed. London: Routledge.

*Hedegaard, M. (2020). Children's exploration as a key in children's play and learning activity in social and cultural formation. In M. Hedegaard & E. E. Ødegaard (Eds.) *Children's Exploration and Cultural Formation.* Springer Open, pp. 11–27.

*Johansson, E. & Puroila, A.-M. (2021). Research perspectives on the politics of belonging in early years education. *International Journal of Early Childhood*, 53(1), 1–8. https://doi.org/10.1007/s13158-021-00288-6

*Kernan, M. (2014). Opportunities and affordances in outdoor play. In L. Brooker, M. Blaise & S. Edwards (Eds.) *The Sage Handbook of Play and Learning in Early Childhood.* London: Sage Publications, pp. 391–402.

*Lester, S. & Russell, W. (2010). *Children's Right to Play: An Examination of the Importance of Play in the Lives of Children Worldwide.* Working Paper 57. The Hague: Bernard van Leer Foundation.

*Moss, P. (2019). 'To aspire towards ECEC systems that support broad learning, participation and democracy': Reflections on John Bennett's final words on *Starting Strong*. In N. Hayes & M. Urban (Eds.) *In Search of Social Justice: John Bennett's Lifetime Contribution to Early Childhood Policy and Practice.* London: Routledge, pp. 26–38.

*National Council for Curriculum and Assessment (2018). *Education for Sustainable Development: A Study of Opportunities and Linkages in the Early Childhood, Primary and Post-Primary Curriculum.* Dublin: NCCA.

*National Scientific Council on the Developing Child (NSCDC) (USA) (2020). *A Science-Based Framework for Early Childhood Policy: Using Evidence to Improve Outcomes in Learning, Behavior, and Health for Vulnerable Children.* Harvard University, Center on the Developing Child.

*Organisation for Economic Co-operation and Development (2019). *Starting Strong Teaching and Learning International Survey 2018 Conceptual Framework*. Paris: OECD. https://one.oecd.org/document/EDU/WKP(2019)5/en/pdf

*Pascal, C., Bertram, T. & Rouse, L. (2019). *Getting It Right in the Early Years Foundation Stage: A Review of the Evidence*. Centre for Research in Early Childhood. https://shop.earlyeducation.org.uk/sites/default/files/EYFS%20Coalition%20Chris%2 0Pascal% 20slides%20for%20sharing.pdf

*Pramling Samuelsson, I. & Kaga, Y. (2008). *The Contribution of Early Childhood Education to a Sustainable Society*. Paris: UNESCO.

*Pyle, A. & Danniels, E. (2017). A continuum of play-based learning: The role of the teacher in play-based pedagogy and the fear of hijacking play. *Early Education and Development*, 23, 274–289. https://doi.org/10.1080/10409289.2016.1220771

Reese, E., Gunn, A., Bateman, A. & Carr, M. (2021). Teacher-child talk about learning stories in New Zealand: A strategy for eliciting children's complex language. *Early Years*, 41(5), 506–521. https://doi.org/10.1080/09575146.2019.1621804

*Sezgin, E. & Ulus, L. (2020). An examination of self-regulation and higher-order cognitive skills as predictors of preschool children's early academic skills. *International Education Studies*, 13(7), 65–87.

Shonkoff, J. P. (2017, May). What science tells us about supporting early childhood development. *Young Children*, 72(2), 8–16.

Siraj-Blatchford, I. (2009). Conceptualising progression in the pedagogy of play and sustained shared thinking in early childhood education: A Vygotskian perspective. *Educational and Child Psychology*, 26(2), 77–89.

*Siraj-Blatchford, I. & Manni, L. (2007). *Effective Leadership in the Early Years Sector: The ELEYS Study*. London, UK: Institute of Education.

Tomlinson, M. M. (2013). Literacy and music in early childhood: Multimodal learning and design. *SAGE Open*, 1–10. https://doi.org/10.1177/2158244013502498 sgo.sagepub.com

*Tonge, K., Jones, R. & Okely, A. (2020). Environmental influences on children's physical activity in early childhood education and care. *Journal of Physical Activity and Health*, 17(4), 423–428.

*United Nations (2015). *Transforming our World: The 2030 Agenda for Sustainable Development*. Geneva: UN.

*United Nations Children's Fund (UNICEF) (2020). *Worlds of Influence: Understanding What Shapes Child Well-Being in Rich Countries* (No. 16; Innocenti Report Card). UNICEF Innocenti Research Centre. https://www.unicef-irc.org/child-well-being-report-card-16

*United Nations Children's Fund (UNICEF) (2021). *Understanding Child Subjective Well-Being, A Call for More Research and Data Policy Making Targeting Children*. UNICEF.

Wood, E., Nuttall, J., Edwards, S. & Grieshaber, S. (2019). *Young Children's Digital Play in Early Childhood Settings*. London: Routledge.

*Zosh, J. M., Hopkins, E. J., Jensen, H., Liu, C., Neale, D. Hirsh-Pasek, K., Solis, S. L. & Whitebread, D. (2018). *Learning Through Play: A Review of the Evidence*. The LEGO Foundation. https://www.legofoundation.com/media/1063/learning-through-play_web.pdf

References

Alcock, S. (2000). *Pedagogical Documentation: Beyond Observation. Occasional Report.* Institute for Early Childhood Studies. Wellington, NZ: Victoria University of Wellington.

Alexander, R. (2004). Still no pedagogy: Principles, pragmatism and compliance in primary education. *Cambridge Journal of Education,* 34(1), 7–33.

Anderson, L. W. & Krathwohl, D. R. (Eds.) (2001). *A Taxonomy for Learning, Teaching, and Assessing: A Revision of Bloom's Taxonomy of Educational Objectives.* New York: Longman.

Ang, L. (2014). Preschool or prep school? Rethinking the role of early years education. *Contemporary Issues in Early Childhood,* 15(2), 185–199.

*Barblett, L., Carmel, J., Hadley, F., Harrison, L., Irvine, S., Bobongie-Harris, F. & Lavina, L. (2021). *National Quality Framework Approved Learning Frameworks Update Literature Review.* Australian Children's Education and Care Quality Authority (ACECQA). https://www.acecqa.gov.au/sites/default/files/2021-09/2021NQF-ALF-UpdateLiteratureReview.PDF

Barnes, K., Hadley, F. & Cheeseman, S. (2019). Preschool educational leaders: Who are they and what are they doing? *Australasian Journal of Early Childhood,* 44(4), 351–364.

Blair, C. (2016). Developmental science and executive function. *Current Direction in Psychological Science,* 25(1). https://doi.org/10.1177/0963721415622634

Blakemore, S. J. & Frith, U. (2000). *The Implications of Recent Developments in Neuroscience for Research on Teaching and Learning.* London: Institute of Cognitive Neuroscience.

*Bodrova, E. & Leong, D. J. (2007). *Tools of the Mind: The Vygotskian Approach to Early Childhood Education.* 2nd ed. Columbus, OH: Merrill/Prentice Hall.

Bronfenbrenner, U. (1989). *Who Cares for Children?* Paris: UNESCO.

Bronfenbrenner, U. (Ed.) (2005). *Making Human Beings Human: Bioecological Perspectives on Human Development.* London: Sage Publications.

*Bronfenbrenner, U. & Morris, P. A. (2006). The bioecological model of human development. In R. M. Lerner & W. E. Damon (Eds.) *Handbook of Child Psychology: Vol 1: Theoretical Models of Human Development.* 6th ed. Chichester: Wiley & Sons, pp. 793–828.

*Brooker, L., Blaise, M. & Edwards, S. (Eds.) (2014). *The Sage Handbook of Play and Learning in Early Childhood.* London: Sage Publications.

Brooks, D. (2011). *The Social Animal: The Hidden Sources of Love, Character and Achievement.* New York: Random House.

Bruce, T. (2011). *Learning Through Play: Babies, Toddlers and Young Children*. 2nd ed. London: Hodder Education.

Bruner, J. (1996). *The Culture of Education*. Cambridge, MA: Harvard University Press.

Cagliari, P., Castagnetti, M., Giudici, C., Rinaldi, C., Vecchi, V. & Moss, P. (Eds.) (2016). *Loris Malaguzzi and the Schools of Reggio Emilia: A Selection of his Writings and Speeches, 1945–1993*. London: Routledge.

Campbell-Barr, V. (2018). The silencing of the knowledge-base in early childhood education and care professionalism. *International Journal of Early Years Education*, 26(1), 75–89.

Carr, M. (1998). A project for assessing children's experiences in early childhood settings. *Paper Presented to the 8th European Early Childhood Education Research Association (EECERA) Conference*, Santiago de Compostela, Spain.

Carr, M. (2001). Ready, willing and able: Learning dispositions for early childhood? *Paper Presented at Cultures of Learning: Risk, Uncertainty and Education Conference*, University of Bristol, 19–22 April.

Carr, M. (2012). Kei tua o te pae: Tracing learning journeys beyond the horizon. *Paper Presented to the 22nd European Early Childhood Education Research Association (EECERA) Conference*, Oporto, Portugal, 29 August–1 September.

Carr, M. & Lee, W. (2019). *Learning Stories in Practice*. London: Sage Publications.

Centre for Early Childhood Development and Education (CECDE) (2006). *Síolta: The National Quality Framework for Early Childhood Education*. Dublin: CECDE.

Clark, A. (2005). Listening to and involving young children: A review of research and practice. *Early Child Development and Care*, 175(6), 489–505.

*Clark, A. (2017). *Listening to Young Children: A Guide to Understanding and Using the Mosaic Approach*. London: Jessica Kingsley.

*Clark, A. (2022). *Slow Knowledge and the Unhurried Child: Time for Slow Pedagogies in Early Childhood Education*. London: Routledge.

Clark, A. & Moss, P. (2011). *Listening to Young Children: The Mosaic Approach*. 2nd ed. London: National Children's Bureau.

Coleyshaw, L., Whitmarsh, J., Jopling, M. & Hadfield, M. (2010). *Listening to Children's Perspectives: Improving the Quality of Provision in Early Years Settings: Research Report*. London: Department of Education.

Corsaro, W. A. (2020). Big ideas from little people: What research with children contributes to social psychology. *Social Psychology Quarter*, 83(1), 5–25.

*Dalli, C., White, E. J., Rockel, J. & Duhn, I., with Buchanan, E., Davidson, S., Ganly, S., Kus, L. & Wang, B. (2011). *Quality Early Childhood Education for Under-Two Year Olds: What Should it Look Like? A Literature Review*. Report to the Ministry of Education. Wellington, NZ: Jessie Hetherington Centre for Educational Research, Institute for Early Childhood Studies, Victoria University of Wellington.

Daly, M. & Forster, A. (2012). Aistear: The early childhood curriculum framework. In M. Mhic Mhathúna & M. Taylor (Eds.) *Early Childhood Education and Care: An Introduction for Students in Ireland*. Dublin: Gill & Macmillan, pp. 93–106.

Delors, J. (1996). *Learning: The Treasure Within*. Report to UNESCO of the International Commission of Education for the 21st Century. Geneva: UNESCO.

*Department of Children and Youth Affairs [DCYA] (2016). *Diversity, Equality and Inclusion Charter and Guidelines for Early Childhood Care and Education*. Dublin: DCYA.

Department of Children, Equality, Disability, Integration and Youth (2021a). *Partnership for the Public Good: A New Funding Model for Early learning and Care*. Dublin: DCEDIY.

Department of Children, Equality, Disability, Integration and Youth (2021b). *Nurturing Skills: The Workforce Plan for Early Learning and Care and School Age Childcare 2022–2028*. Dublin: DCEDIY.

Department of Education and Skills (2011). *Literacy and Numeracy for Learning and Life: The National Strategy to Improve Literacy and Numeracy among Children and Young People 2011–2020*. Dublin: DES.

Department of Education and Skills (2017). *National Strategy: Literacy and Numeracy for Learning and Life: 2011–2020: Interim Review*. Dublin: DES.

*Department of Education and Skills (2019). *Wellbeing Policy Statement and Framework for Practice*. Dublin: DES.

*Derman-Sparks, L. & Olson Edwards, J. (2019). *Anti-Bias Education for Young Children and Ourselves*. 2nd ed. Washington: National Association for the Education of Young Children.

Dockrell, J., Stuart, M. & King, D. (2010). Supporting early oral language skills for English language learners in inner city preschool provision. *British Journal of Educational Psychology*, 80(4), 497–515.

Duignan, M. & McDonnell, F. (2022). An overview of the development of government regulation and inspection in the early childhood education and care sector in Ireland, 1921–2021. In N. Hayes & T. Walsh (Eds.) *Early Childhood Education and Care in Ireland: Charting a Century of Development (1921–2021)*. London: Peter Lang, pp. 203–229.

Dweck, C. (2016). The remarkable reach of growth mindsets. *Scientific American Mind*, 27(1), 36–41.

*Edwards, C., Gandini, L. & Forman, G. (Eds.) (2012). *The Hundred Languages of Children*. 3rd ed. Santa Barbara, CA: Praeger.

Edwards, S. (2017). Play-based learning and intentional teaching: Forever different? *Australasian Journal of Early Childhood*, 42(2), 4–11. https://doi.org/10.23965/AJEC.42.2.01

Edwards, S. (2021). *Process Quality, Curriculum and Pedagogy in Early Childhood Education and Care OECD Education Working Paper No. 47*. Paris: OECD.

*Edwards, S., Mantilla, A., Grieshaber, S., Nuttall, J. & Wood, E. (2020). Converged play characteristics for early childhood education: Multi-modal, global-local, and traditional-digital. *Oxford Review of Education*, 46(5), 637–660. https://doi.org/10.1080/03054985.2020.1750358

Egan, D., Egan, S. M. & Brophy, T. (2022). The growth of forest school: A review of the evidence base. *An Leanbh Og – Irish Journal of Early Childhood Studies*, 15.

Elkind, D. (1990/2007). *The Hurried Child: Growing Up Too Fast, Too Soon*. 3rd ed. Cambridge, MA: De Capo Press.

*Erwin, E. J., Valentine, M. & Toumazou, M. (2022). The study of belonging in early childhood education: Complexities and possibilities. *International Journal of Early Years Education*. https://doi.org/10.1080/09669760.2022.2128307

*European Commission (2018). *Monitoring the Quality of Early Childhood Education and Care: Complementing the 2014 ECEC Quality Framework Proposal with Indicators: Recommendations from ECEC Experts*. https://data.europa.eu/doi/10.2766/99057

European Commission (2020). *Early Childhood Education and Care: How to Recruit, Train and Motivate Well-Qualified Staff*. https://op.europa.eu/en/publication-detail/-/publication/47ba3c3a-6789–11eb-aeb5–01aa75ed71a1

Fitzpatrick, A. & Halpenny, A. M. (2022). Intergenerational learning as a pedagogical strategy in early childhood education services: Perspectives from an Irish study. *European Early Childhood Education Research Journal*. https://doi.org/10.1080/1350293X.2022.2153259

Fleer, M. (2003). Early childhood education as an evolving 'community of practice' or as lived 'social reproduction': Researching the 'taken-for-granted'. *Contemporary Issues in Early Childhood*, 4(1), 64–79.

*Fleer, M. (2021). How conceptual PlayWorlds in preschool settings create new conditions for children's development during group time. *Learning, Culture and Social Interaction*, 28. https://doi.org/10.1016/j.lcsi.2020.100438

French, G. (2014). *Let Them Talk: Evaluation of the Language Enrichment Programme of the Ballyfermot Early Years Language and Learning Initiative*. Dublin: Ballyfermot/Chapelizod Partnership.

French, G. (2019). Key elements of good practice to support the learning and development of children from birth to three. *Research Paper Commissioned by the National Council for Curriculum and Assessment*, National Council for Curriculum and Assessment.

French, G. (2021). Slow relational pedagogy with babies and toddlers. *An Leanbh Óg – The OMEP Ireland Journal of Early Childhood Studies*, 14(1), 134–246.

*French, G. & McKenna, G. (2022). *Literature Review to Support the Updating of Aistear, the Early Childhood Curriculum Framework*. Dublin: NCCA.

Gaffney, M. (2011). *Flourishing*. Dublin: Penguin Ireland.

Galinsky, E. (2010). *Mind in the Making: The Seven Essential Life Skills Every Child Needs*. New York: Harper Collins.

Gallagher, C. & Fitzpatrick, A. (2018). 'It's a win-win situation' – intergenerational learning in preschool and elder care settings: An Irish perspective. *Journal of Intergenerational Relationships*, 16(1–2), 26–44.

Garrity, S., Moran, L., McGregor, C. & Devaney, C. (2017). An informed pedagogy of community, care, and respect for diversity: Evidence from a qualitative evaluation of early years services in the West of Ireland. *Child Care in Practice*, 23(3), 305–321. https://doi.org/10.1080/13575279.2017.1329707

Garvey, C. (1990). *Play*. 2nd ed. Cambridge, MA: Harvard University Press.

*Golinkoff, R. & Hirsh-Pasek, K. (2016). *Becoming Brilliant: What Science Tells Us About Raising Successful Children*. New York, NY: American Psychological Association. https://doi.org/10.1037/14917-000

Government of Ireland (1937). *Bunreacht na hEireann [Constitution of Ireland]*. Dublin: Stationery Office.

Government of Ireland (2000). *Our Children – Their Lives: National Children's Strategy*. Dublin: The Stationery Office.

*Government of Ireland (2018). *A Whole of Government Strategy for Babies, Young Children and Their Families 2019–2028*. Dublin: The Stationery Office.

Gray, P. (2011). The decline of play and the rise of psychopathology in children and adolescents. *American Journal of Play*, 3(4), 443–463.

*Halpenny, A. M. (2021). *Capturing Children's Meanings in ECE Research and Practice: A Practical Guide*. Abingdon, Oxon: Routledge.

Hayes, N. (2007). *Perspectives on the Relationship between Education and Care in Early Childhood*. Background Paper Prepared for the National Council for Curriculum and Assessment. Dublin: NCCA.

Hayes, N. (2010). *Early Childhood: An Introductory Text*. 4th ed. Dublin: Gill & Macmillan.

Hayes, N. (2012). Children at the centre of practice. In M. Mhic Mhathúna & M. Taylor (Eds.) *Early Childhood Education and Care: An Introduction for Students in Ireland*. Dublin: Gill & Macmillan.

Hayes, N. (2013). *Early Years Practice: Getting It Right from the Start*. Dublin: Gill and Macmillan.

Hayes, N. & Filipović, K. (2017). Nurturing the 'buds of development': Changing the narrative from learning outcomes to learning opportunities in early childhood pedagogy. *International Journal of Early Years Education*. https://doi.org/10.1080/09669760.2017.1341303

Hayes, N., Maguire, J., Corcoran, L. & O'Sullivan, C. (2017). An arts education research project in early childhood settings. *Irish Educational Studies*, 36(2), 203–219. https://doi.org/10.1080/03323315.2017.1324804

*Hayes, N., O'Toole, L. & Halpenny, A. M. (2023). *Introducing Bronfenbrenner: A Guide for Practitioners and Students in Early Years Education*. 2nd ed. London: Routledge.

Hayes, N. & Walsh, T. (Eds.) (2022). *Early Childhood Education and Care in Ireland: Charting a Century of Developments (1921–2021)*. London: Peter Lang.

Hedefalk, M., Almqvist, J. & Östman, L. (2015). Education for sustainable development in early childhood education: A review of the research literature. *Environmental Education Research*, 21(7), 975–990. https://doi.org/10.1080/13504622.2014.971716

*Hedegaard, M. (2020). Children's exploration as a key in children's play and learning activity in social and cultural formation. In M. Hedegaard & E. E. Ødegaard (Eds.) *Children's Exploration and Cultural Formation*. London: Springer Open, pp. 11–27.

Hedges, H. & Cullen, J. (2005). Subject knowledge in early childhood curriculum and pedagogy: Beliefs and practices. *Contemporary Issues in Early Childhood*, 6(1). https://doi.org/ 10.2304/ciec.2005.6.1.10

Hedges, H., Cullen, J. & Jordan, B. (2011). Early years curriculum: Funds of knowledge as a conceptual framework for children's interests. *Journal of Curriculum Studies*, 43(2), 185–205.

Heikka, J. & Waniganayake, M. (2011). Pedagogical leadership from a distributed perspective within the context of early childhood education. *International Journal of Leadership in Education*, 14(4), 499–512. https://doi.org/10.1080/13603124.2011.577909

Hohman, M. & Weikart, D. (2002). *Educating Young Children: Active Learning Practices for Preschool and Childcare Programs*. 2nd ed. Ypsilanti, MI: HighScope Press.

Horgan, D., Forde, C., Martin, S. & Parkes, A. (2016). Children's participation: Moving from the performative to the social. *Children's Geographies*, 15(3), 274–288. https://doi.org/10.1080/14733285.2016.1219022

Huizinga, J. (1938/2016). *Homo Ludens [Playing Man]*. Boston, MA: Beacon Press.

Hutt, C. (1990). *Play, Exploration and Learning: A Natural History of the Pre-school*. London: Routledge.

International Play Association (2014). *Declaration on the Importance of Play*. IPA. http://ipaworld.org

Jackson, N. (Ed.) (2011). *Learning for a Complex World: A Life-Wide Concept of Learning, Education Personal Development*. Bloomington, IN: AuthorHouse.

*Johansson, E. & Puroila, A.-M. (2021). Research perspectives on the politics of belonging in early years education. *International Journal of Early Childhood*, 53(1), 1–8. https://doi.org/10.1007/s13158-021-00288-6

Katz, L. (1993). Dispositions: Definitions and implications for early childhood practices. *Perspectives from ERIC/ECCE: A Monograph Series No. 4.*

Katz, L. (1995). The distinction between self-esteem and narcissism: Implications for practice. In L. Katz (Ed.) *Talks with Teachers of Young Children: A Collection*. Norwood, NJ: Ablex.

*Kernan, M. (2014). Opportunities and affordances in outdoor play. In L. Brooker, M. Blaise & S. Edwards (Eds.) *The Sage Handbook of Play and Learning in Early Childhood*. London: Sage Publications, pp. 391–402.

Kernan, M. & Singer, E. (2010). *Peer Relationships in Early Childhood Education and Care*. London: Routledge.

Kickbusch, L. (2012). *Learning for Well-Being: A Policy Priority for Children and Youth in Europe: A Process for Change*. Brussels: Universal Education Foundation.

Kirkby, J., Keary, A. & Walsh, L. (2018). The impact of Australian policy shifts on early childhood teachers' understandings of intentional teaching. *European Early Childhood Education Research Journal*, 26(5), 674–687. https://doi.org/10.1080/135 0293X.2018.1522920

Kirsch, C., Aleksić, A., Mortini, S. & Andersen, K. (2020). Developing multilingual practices in early childhood education through professional development in Luxembourg. *International Multilingual Research Journal*, 14(4), 319–337. https://doi.org/10.1080/19313152.2020.1730023

Kirwan, D. (2017). Multilingual environments: Benefits for early language learning. *TEANGA*, (10), 38–57.

Konrad, C., Hillmann, M., Rispler, J., Niehaus, L., Neuhoff, L. & Barr, R. (2021). Quality of mother-child interaction before, during, and after smartphone use. *Frontiers in Psychology*. https://doi.org/10.3389/fpsyg.2021.616656

Krechevsky, M., Mardell, B., Rivrd, M. & Wilson, D. (2013). *Visible Learners: Promoting Reggio-Inspired Approaches in All Schools*. Hoboken, NJ: Jossey-Bass.

Lally, J. R. & Mangione, P. (2017). Caring relationships: The heart of early brain development. *Young Children*, 72(2), 17–24.

Larrivee, B. (2005). *Authentic Classroom Management: Creating a Learning Community and Building Reflective Practice*. Boston, MA: Allyn and Bacon.

Lemon, N. & Garvis, S. (2014). Encouraging reflective practice with future early childhood teachers to support the national standards: An Australian case study. *Australasian Journal of Early Childhood*, 39(4). 89–94.

*Lester, S. & Russell, W. (2010). *Children's Right to Play: An Examination of the Importance of Play in the Lives of Children Worldwide*. Working Paper 57. The Hague: Bernard van Leer Foundation.

Lewis, A. (2019). Examining the concept of well-being and early childhood: Adopting multi-disciplinary perspectives. *Journal of Early Childhood Research*, 17(4), 294–308.

Liebovich, B. (2016, May). Our proud heritage: Abigail Eliot and Margaret McMillan – bringing the nursery school to the United States. *Young Children*, 1–6.

Lockhart, S. (2010). Play: An important tool in cognitive development. *Extensions, HighScope Curriculum Newsletter*, 24(3).

Maslow, A. H. (1987). *Motivation and Personality*. 2nd ed. New York: Harper and Row.

McCabe, U. & Flannery, M. (2022). Well-being and the arts in Irish primary teacher education: Aligned or apart? A policy and self-study perspective. *European Journal of Teacher Education.* https://doi.org/10.1080/02619768.2022.2040478

Mitchell, L. & Cubey, P. (2003). *Characteristics of Effective Professional Development Linked to Enhanced Pedagogy and Children's Learning in Early Childhood Settings: A Best Evidence Synthesis.* Wellington, NZ: Ministry of Education. www. education-counts.govt.nz/publications/ece/36086/36087.

Moffitt, T. E., Arseneault, L., Belsky, D., Dikson, N., Hancox, R. J., Harrington, H., Houts, R., Poulton, R., Roberts, B. W., Ross, S., Sears, M. R., Thomas, W. M. & Caspi, A. (2011). A gradient of childhood self-control predicts health, wealth and public safety. *Proceedings of the National Academy of Science,* 108(7), 2693–2698.

Moloney, M. (2010). Professional identity in early childhood care and education: Perspectives of pre-school and infant teachers. *Irish Educational Studies,* 29(2), 167–187.

Mooney Simmie, G. & Murphy, D. (2021). Professionalisation of early childhood education and care practitioners: Working conditions in Ireland. *Contemporary Issues in Early Childhood,* 1–15.

*Moss, P. (2019). 'To aspire towards ECEC systems that support broad learning, participation and democracy': Reflections on John Bennett's final words on *Starting Strong.* In N. Hayes & M. Urban (Eds.) *In Search of Social Justice: John Bennett's Lifetime Contribution to Early Childhood Policy and Practice.* London: Routledge, pp. 26–38.

Moyles, J., Adams, S. & Musgrove, A. (2002). *SPEEL Study of Pedagogical Effectiveness in Early Learning.* DfES Research Report 363. London: Department for Education and Skills.

Murphy, V. A., Karemaker, J., Sylva, K., Kanji, G. & Jelley, F. (2017). Effective intervention to support oral language skills in English as an additional language in the early years. *TEANGA,* (10), 1–18.

Murray, C. (2017). Conscious noticing: Anti-bias from policy to practice. *International Critical Childhood Policy Studies,* 6(1), 22–37.

National Council for Curriculum and Assessment (2004). *Towards a Framework for Early Learning: A Consultative Document.* Dublin: NCCA.

National Council for Curriculum and Assessment (2009a). *Aistear: The Early Childhood Curriculum Framework.* Dublin: NCCA.

National Council for Curriculum and Assessment (2009b). *Aistear: The Early Childhood Curriculum Framework and Síolta: The National Quality Framework for Early Childhood Education: Audit of Similarities and Differences.* Dublin: NCCA.

National Council for Curriculum and Assessment (2009c). *Aistear: The Early Childhood Curriculum Framework: Guidelines for Good Practice.* Dublin: NCCA.

*National Council for Curriculum and Assessment (2018). *Education for Sustainable Development: A Study of Opportunities and Linkages in the Early Childhood, Primary and Post-Primary Curriculum.* Dublin: NCCA.

National Council for Curriculum and Assessment (2021). *Updating Aistear: Rationale and Process.* Dublin: NCCA.

National Scientific Council on the Developing Child (NSCDC) (USA) (2007). *The Science of Early Childhood Development: Closing the Gap Between What We Know and What We Do.* Cambridge, MA: Harvard University, Center on the Developing Child.

*National Scientific Council on the Developing Child (NSCDC) (USA) (2020). *A Science-Based Framework for Early Childhood Policy: Using Evidence to Improve*

Outcomes in Learning, Behavior, and Health for Vulnerable Children. Cambridge, MA: Harvard University, Center on the Developing Child.

Neuman, M. (2019). Improving policies for young children through comparison and peer review. In N. Hayes & M. Urban (Eds.) *In Search of Social Justice: John Bennett's Lifetime Contribution to Early Childhood Policy and Practice.* London: Routledge, pp. 10–23.

New Zealand (1996/2017). *Te Whariki: Early Childhood Curriculum.* Wellington, NZ: Learning Media Ltd.

Nic Gabhainn, S. & Sixsmith, J. (2005). *Children's Understandings of Well-Being.* Dublin: National Children's Office.

O'Regan, M., Halpenny, A. M. & Hayes, N. (2019). Childminding in Ireland: Attitudes towards professionalisation. *European Early Childhood Education Research Journal*, 27, 757–775.

O'Reilly, C., Devitt, A. & Hayes, N. (2022). Critical thinking in the preschool classroom – A systematic literature review. *Thinking Skills and Creativity*, 46, 101110. https://doi.org/10.1016/j.tsc.2022.101110

O'Toole, L., Hayes, N. & Halpenny, A. M. (2019). Animating systems: The ecological value of considering Bronfenbrenner's bio-ecological model of development. In R. Barnett & N. Jackson (Eds.) *Ecologies for Learning: Emerging Ideas, Sightings, and Possibilities.* London: Routledge.

O'Toole, L., Walsh, G. & Kerins, L. (2023). *A Consultation with Babies, Toddlers and Young Children to Inform the Updating of Aistear, the Early Childhood Curriculum Framework (NCCA, 2009).* Dublin: NCCA.

Organisation for Economic Co-operation and Development (OECD) (2001). *Starting Strong I: Early Childhood Education and Care.* Paris: OECD.

Organisation for Economic Co-operation and Development (OECD) (2006). *Starting Strong II: Early Childhood Education and Care.* Paris: OECD.

Organisation for Economic Co-operation and Development (OECD) (2015). *Early Childhood Education and Care – Pedagogy Review [England].* Paris: OECD.

Organisation for Economic Co-operation and Development (OECD) (2018). *Early learning Matters.* Paris: OECD.

*Organisation for Economic Co-operation and Development (OECD) (2019). *Starting Strong Teaching and Learning International Survey 2018 Conceptual Framework.* Paris: OECD. https://one.oecd.org/document/EDU/WKP(2019)5/en/pdf

Osgood, J. (2010). Professional identities in the nursery: Contested terrain. In M. Robb and R. Thomson (Eds.) *Critical Practice with Children and Young People.* Milton Keynes: Open University Press, pp. 233–248.

*Pascal, C., Bertram, T. & Rouse, L. (2019). *Getting It Right in the Early Years Foundation Stage: A Review of the Evidence.* Centre for Research in Early Childhood. https://shop.earlyeducation.org.uk/sites/default/files/EYFS%20Coalition%20Chris%2 0Pascal% 20slides%20for%20sharing.pdf

Peeters, J. & Sharmahd, N. (2014). Professional development for ECEC practitioners with responsibilities for children at risk: Which competences and in-service training are needed? *European Early Childhood Education Research Journal*, 22(3), 412–424. https://doi.org/10.1080/1350293X.2014.912903

Penn, H. (2009). Early childhood education and care: Key lessons from research for policy makers. *An Independent Report Submitted to the European Commission by the Network of Experts in Social Science of Education and training (NESSE)*, Brussels, European Commission.

*Pramling Samuelsson, I. & Kaga, Y. (2008). *The Contribution of Early Childhood Education to a Sustainable Society.* Paris: UNESCO.

Purdon, A. (2016). Sustained shared thinking in an early childhood setting: An exploration of practitioners' perspectives. *Education 3 – 13. International Journal of Primary, Elementary and Early Years Education,* 44(3).

*Pyle, A. & Danniels, E. (2017). A continuum of play-based learning: The role of the teacher in play-based pedagogy and the fear of hijacking play. *Early Education and Development,* 23, 274–289. https://doi.org/10.1080/10409289.2016.1220771

Pyle, A., DeLuca, C. & Danniels, E. (2017). A scoping review of research on play-based pedagogies in kindergarten education. *Review of Education (Oxford),* 5(3), 311–351. https://doi.org/10.1002/rev3.3097

Rinaldi, C. (2012). The emergent curriculum and social constructivism, an interview with Lella Gandini. In C. Edwards, L. Gandini & G. Forman (Eds.) *The Hundred Languages of Children: The Reggio Emilia Approach to Early Childhood Education.* Norwood, NJ: Ablex, pp. 101–111.

Rosenow, N. (2012). *Heart-Centred Teaching Inspired by Nature.* Lincoln, NE: Dimensions Educational Research Foundation.

Rudd, J. (2012). *Leadership in Early Childhood.* 4th ed. London: Routledge.

*Sezgin, E. & Ulus, L. (2020). An examination of self-regulation and higher-order cognitive skills as predictors of preschool children's early academic skills. *International Education Studies,* 13(7), 65–87.

Sheridan, S. (2011). Characteristics of preschools as learning environments and conditions for children's learning in Ministry of Education and Research (Norway). In *Nordic Early Childhood Education and Care – Effects and Challenges: Research, Practice and Policy Making.* Oslo: Ministry of Education and Research, pp. 19–23.

Siraj-Blatchford, I. (2005). Birth to eight matters! Seeking seamlessness-continuity? Integration? Creativity? *Presentation to the Association for the Professional Development of Early years Educators,* Cardiff, 22–24 November.

*Siraj-Blatchford, I. & Manni, L. (2007). *Effective Leadership in the Early Years Sector: The ELEYS Study.* London, UK: Institute of Education.

Siraj-Blatchford, I. & Manni, L. (2008). Would you like to tidy up now? An analysis of adult questioning in the English foundation stage. *Early Years: An International Journal of Research and Development,* 28(1), 5–22.

Siraj-Blatchford, I., Sylva, K., Muttock, S., Gilden, R., Melhuish, E. & Bell, D. (2002). *Researching Effective pedagogy in the Early Years.* London: Department of Education and Skills.

Siraj-Blatchford, I., Taggart, B., Sylva, K., Sammons, P. & Melhuish, E. (2008). Towards the transformation of early childhood practice. *Cambridge Journal of Education,* 38(1), 23–36.

Slot, P. L., Mulder, H., Verhagen, J. & Leseman, P. (2017). Preschoolers' cognitive and emotional self-regulation in pretend play: Relations with executive functions and quality of play. *Infant and Child Development,* 26(6), e2038, Hoboken, NJ.

Smiley, P. A. & Dweck, C. S. (1994). Individual differences in achievement goals among young children. *Child Development,* 65, 1723–1743.

Start Strong (2011). *If I had a Magic Wand: Young Children's Visions and Ideas for Early Care and Education Services.* Dublin: Start Strong. www.startstrong.ie/contents/213

Stephen, C. (2010). Pedagogy: The silent partner in early years learning. *Early Years,* 30(3), 15–28.

Sumsion, J. & Wong, S. (2011). Interrogating 'belonging' in belonging, being and becoming: The early years learning framework for Australia. *Contemporary Issues in Early Childhood*, 12(1), 28–45. https://doi.org/10.2304/ciec.2011.12.1.28

Svinth, L. (2018). Being touched – the transformative potential of nurturing touch practices in relation to toddlers' learning and emotional well-being. *Early Child Development and Care*, 188(7), 924–936. https://doi.org/10.1080/03004430.2018.1446428

Sylva, K., Melhuish, E., Sammons, P., Siraj-Blatchford, I. & Taggart, B. (2011). Pre-school quality and educational outcomes at age 11: Low quality has little benefit. *Journal of Early Childhood Research*, 9(2), 109–124.

Thompson, R. A., Meltzoff, A. N. & Gilliam, W. S. (2021). Race, equity, bias, and early childhood: Examining the research. *Zero to Three Journal*, 42(1), 5–16.

Thulin, S. (2008). Sustainable development – Language and a sense of belonging. In I. Pramling Samuelsson & Y. Kaga (Eds.) *The Contribution of Early Childhood Education to a Sustainable Society*. Paris: UNESCO, pp. 128–133.

Tillett, V. & Wong, S. (2018). An investigative case study into early childhood educators' understanding about 'belonging'. *European Early Childhood Education Research Journal*, 26(1), 37–49. https://doi.org/10.1080/1350293X.2018.1412016

*Tonge, K., Jones, R. & Okely, A. (2020). Environmental influences on children's physical activity in early childhood education and care. *Journal of Physical Activity and Health*, 17(4), 423–428.

Toth, K., Sammons, P., Sylva, K., Melhuish, E., Siraj, I. & Taggart, B. (2020). Home learning environment across time: The role of early years HLE and background in predicting HLE at later ages. *School Effectiveness and School Improvement: International Journal of Research, Policy and Practice*, 31(1).

*Undheim, M. (2022). Children and teachers engaging together with digital technology in early childhood education and care institutions: A literature review. *European Early Childhood Education Research Journal*, 30(3), 472–489. https://doi.org/10.1080/1350293X.2021.1971730

United Nations (UN) (1989). *United Nations Convention on the Rights of the Child*, adopted by the UN General Assembly 20 November 1989.

United Nations (UN) (2001). *Committee on the Rights of the Child, General Comment 1: Aims of Education*. Geneva: UN.

*United Nations (UN) (2015). *Transforming our World: The 2030 Agenda for Sustainable Development*. Geneva: UN.

United Nations Children's Fund (UNICEF) (2007). *An Overview of Child Well-Being in Rich Countries: A Comprehensive Assessment of the Lives and Well-Being of Children and Adolescents in the Economically Advantaged Nations*. Florence: UNICEF Innocenti Research Centre.

*United Nations Children's Fund (UNICEF) (2020). *Worlds of Influence: Understanding what Shapes Child Well-Being in Rich Countries* (No. 16; Innocenti Report Card). UNICEF Innocenti Research Centre. https://www.unicef-irc.org/child-well-being-report-card-16

*United Nations Children's Fund (UNICEF) (2021). *Understanding Child Subjective Well-Being, A Call for More Research and Data Policy Making Targeting Children*. Geneva: UNICEF.

United Nations Committee on the Rights of the Child (2005). *General Comment No. 7 on Implementing Child Rights in Early Childhood*. Geneva: UN. http://www2.ohchr.org/english/bodies/crc/docs/AdvanceVersions/GeneralComment7Rev1.pdf

United Nations Committee on the Rights of the Child (2013). *United Nations Convention on the Rights of the Child – General Comment No. 17 (2013) on Article 31.* http://www.ohchr.org/EN/HRBodies/CRC/Pages/CRCIndex.aspx

Vygotsky, L. (1978). *Mind in Society: The Development of Higher Psychological Processes.* Cambridge: Cambridge University Press.

Wagner, P. (2008). 'Categorisations and young children's social constructions of belonging' in 'enhancing a sense of belonging in the early years'. *Early Childhood Matters*, 111, 20–24.

Wolfe, C. D. & Bell, M. A. (2007). Sources of variability in working memory in early childhood: A consideration of age, temperament, language, and brain electrical activity. *Cognitive Development*, 22(4), 431–455.

Woodhead, M. & Brooker, L. (2008). 'A sense of belonging' in 'enhancing a sense of belonging in the early years'. *Early Childhood Matters*, 111, 3–7.

Woodrow, C. (2008). Discourses of professional identity in early childhood: Movements in Australia. *European Early Childhood Education Research Journal*, 16(2). 269–280.

York-Barr, J., Sommers, W. A., Ghere, G. S. & Montie, J. K. (2006). *Reflective Practice to Improve Schools: An Action Guide for Educators.* 2nd ed. Thousand Oaks, CA: Corwin.

Zanatta, F. & Long, S. (2021). Rights to the front: Child rights-based pedagogies in early childhood degrees. *Journal of Early Childhood Education Research*, 10(1), 139–165.

*Zosh, J. M., Hopkins, E. J., Jensen, H., Liu, C., Neale, D., Hirsh-Pasek, K., Solis, S. L. & Whitebread, D. (2018). *Learning through Play: A Review of the Evidence.* The LEGO Foundation. https://www.legofoundation.com/media/1063/learning-through-play_web.pdf

Referenced websites

Access and Inclusion Model [AIM]: https://aim.gov.ie

Aistear Siolta Practice Guide: https://www.aistearsiolta.ie/en/introduction/

Conceptual Playlab: https://www.monash.edu/education/research/projects/conceptual-playlab

DES Literacy Strategy Consultation: https://www.gov.ie/en/consultation/14180-literacy-numeracy-and-digital-literacy-strategy-consultation/

Developing Child Project: https://developingchild.harvard.edu

HighScope Project: https://highscope.org

Mother Tongue Resources: https://mothertongues.ie

National Council for Curriculum and Assessment: www.ncca.ie.

OECD Starting Strong Reports: https://www.oecd.org/education/school/starting-strong.htm

Reggio Emilia Approach: https://www.reggiochildren.it/en/reggio-emilia-approach/

Start Strong 'If I had a Magic Wand': https://issuu.com/startstrongireland/docs/if_i_had_a_magic_wand

TOY Project: www.toyproject.net

UN Committee of the Rights of the Child: https://www.ohchr.org/en/treaty-bodies/crc/general-comments

Index

Printed in Great Britain
by Amazon

38381660R00097